"The magic begins in you. Feel your own energy, and realize that similar energy exists within the Earth, stones, plants, water, wind, fire, colors, and animals."

—Scott Cunningham

Scott Cunningham authored more than fifty books in his lifetime, fifteen of which lay the foundation for the non-institutional growth of modern Wicca. In addition, Scott also opened up a new understanding of positive, nature-based magics such as herb, gem, and elemental magic. Scott simultaneously demystified magic and brought through its power in vivid words that inspired many to perform their first acts of magic.

In his personal life, as in his books, Scott Cunningham was a catalyst for many people to find and understand their own inner natures and to live happier, more productive lives. Here at last is the autobiography begun by this pioneer of modern-day nature religion—completed and expanded by two of his friends and colleagues who were given access to his personal files and records. David Harrington was co-author with Scott of *The Magical Household* and *Spell Crafts*, deTraci Regula was the producer for Scott's *Herb Magic* video and is the author of *The Mysteries of Isis*.

Whispers of the Moon traces Scott Cunningham's life and growth as a writer as well as a philosopher-magician who helped to revolutionize modern Paganism.

A revealing look at the man behind the magic, *Whispers of the Moon* includes rare photographs, previously unpublished poetry, portions of letters, exposition of his personal philosophy and religion, and the complete text of his self-published pamphlet from 1982: *A Formula Book of Magical Incenses & Oils.*

Whispers of the Moon is an essential resource including a complete list of Scott's published works, his birth-data and horoscope—not available previously, and remembrances of many people who were touched by his gentle magic. *Whispers of the Moon* is a unique blend of magical lore, personal anecdotes, and rare insights into the forces that molded Scott Cunningham's life.

About the Authors

David Harrington is a folklorist and student of the magical arts who collaborated with Scott Cunningham on two books, *The Magical Household* and *Spell Crafts*. When not writing, David collects tales of ancient folklore and pursues his interests in Mesoamerican archeology and paranormal phenomena. He lives on the West Coast with his menagerie of rescued animals.

deTraci Regula is a Priestess of Isis and author of *The Mysteries of Isis*, recently published by Llewellyn Publications. In addition to work in the animation industry on such secular productions as the animated version of *Attack of the Killer Tomatoes*, deTraci also produced and directed the Llewellyn video programs *Herb Magic* with Scott Cunningham and *Witchcraft: Yesterday and Today* with Raymond Buckland. When not writing, deTraci practices Taoist painting, guides tours of ancient Goddess sites, and collects miniature books.

To Write to the Authors

If you wish to contact the authors or would like more information about this book, please write to the authors in care of Llewellyn Worldwide, and we will forward your request. Both the authors and publisher appreciate hearing from you and learning of your enjoyment of this book and how it has helped you. Llewellyn Worldwide cannot guarantee that every letter written to the authors can be answered, but all will be forwarded. Please write to them at:

Llewellyn's New Worlds of Mind and Spirit
P.O. Box 64383, Dept. K559-2, St. Paul, MN 55164-0383, U.S.A.
Please enclose a self-addressed, stamped envelope for reply, or $1.00 to cover costs. If outside U.S.A., enclose international postal reply coupon.

Whispers

of the

Moon

The Life and Work
of
Scott
Cunningham

Philosopher–Magician, Modern–Day Pagan

David Harrington
deTraci Regula

1997
Llewellyn Publications
St. Paul, Minnesota, U.S.A. 55164-0383

FIRST EDITION
Second Printing, 1997

Cover design: Tom Grewe
Cover photo: Linda Mace Pirkle Photography
Book editing and layout: Connie Hill, Marilyn Matheny and Kathy Thill
Book design: Susan Van Sant

Library of Congress Cataloging-in-Publication Data

Harrington, David
    Whispers of the moon: the life and work of Scott Cunningham; philosopher,
  magician, modern-day pagan / David Harrington and deTraci Regula. — 1st ed.
      p.   cm.
    Includes bibliographic references and index.
    ISBN # 1-56718-559-2
     1. Cunningham, Scott, 1956-1993.   2. Occultists—United States—Biography.
  3. Witches—United States—Biography.   4. Prophets—United States—Biography.
  5. Witchcraft.   6. Reincarnation.   7. Magic.   8. Incense—Miscellanea.
  9. Perfumes—Miscellanea.   10. Essences and essential oils—Miscellanea.
  I. Regula, deTraci, 1960-   .   II. Title.

BF1408.2.C85H37   1996
133.4'3'092—dc20   95-47504
[B]   CIP

Printed in the United States of America

Llewellyn Publications
A Division of Llewellyn Worldwide, Ltd.
P.O. 64383, St. Paul, MN 55164-0383

Dedication

To all whose lives have been touched
by the works of Scott Cunningham.

Other Books by the Authors

By David Harrington and Scott Cunningham
  Magical Household, 1987
  Spell Crafts, 1993

By deTraci Regula
  The Mysteries of Isis, 1996

Scott Cunningham
1956 – 1993

Acknowledgements

To Chet and Rosie Cunningham, Scott's parents, for all of their assistance in the preparation of this book and for permission to use family photographs, and to Chet for originally proposing the idea for this biography to Llewellyn.

Christine Cunningham Ashworth, for sharing memories of her childhood as "Scott's little sister."

Carl and Sandra Weschcke for sharing details of their long association with Scott, and for making this book possible.

Nancy Mostad, for her wise comments on early drafts of this work, and for sharing her personal memories of Scott.

Marilee Bigelow, for her generous support of *Whispers of the Moon,* clarification of various facts and dates, and her personal insights into Scott's early years in magic, though, of course, she is not responsible for our perspective on Scott's life.

Mark Benitez, a special *mahalo* for bringing back many memories of Scott and for donating his skills as a photographer in Hawai'i and on the mainland.

Charles Salinas, for his support, encouragement, and facilitation of this work.

Lorna McGaw, for "Casa Isis" and for willingly tolerating the authors during the writing of this book.

Morgan MacGregor for her evocative sense of humor, and to her husband Ralph Weill, for revitalizing a reluctant computer.

And finally, to the many friends of Scott Cunningham who shared comments and memories about him, including Jeffrey Boshart, Don Kraig, Ray and Tara Buckland, Lucy Brown, John Saltzgiver, Jeff Bohannon, Vinnie Gaglione, Judith Wise-Rhoads and Scot Rhoads, Dorothy Jones-Nevelow, John and Elaine Burchard, and the many readers who responded to our request for memories of Scott.

Table of Contents

PART VI: ROOT AND GROWTH — 187
1993 and beyond

Introduction

SCOTT CUNNINGHAM EMERGED ONTO THE METAPHYSICAL BOOK world with *Magical Herbalism—The Secret Craft of the Wise* in 1982. The first rosy clouds of the dawn of "The New Age" were just appearing. Many books on magic and witchcraft were stuffed with nasty spells excavated from ancient texts by authors with doubtful intentions. There were more positive books on witchcraft—few heard the word "Wicca" in those days—but most of these emphasized the need to join a coven, learn a new liturgy of rules, regulations, expectations, and rites, and acquire enough magical equipment, books, furniture, and costuming to fill a room to the ceiling.

But Scott's writing was different. Gentle in tone, he opened the world of positive magic to everyone who chose to wander among the clearly written, poetic pages of his books. From a tiny printing of only five thousand copies, *Magical Herbalism* swiftly sold out by word of mouth. A second printing evaporated from the bookshelves. As the New Age movement brightened and found its footing, more bookstores replaced the somber "Occult" section title with the hopeful "New Age" label. Magical teachers from many traditions recognized this book's worth and began to recommend this small book whose author, in his introduction, simply asked that the work be used with love.

In the next eleven years, Scott produced fifteen magical books, and with every volume the number of his readers increased. For tens of thousands of new Wiccans, their first magic circle, their first rite of magic, was cast using his words of power.

Scott was not just admired and trusted. He was beloved. His brush with life-threatening illness in 1990 shook the pagan and magical community to its roots and readers rushed to donate money to pay his medical expenses.

In 1992, Scott began work on a biographical book titled *A Ritual Autobiography*. Aware that his wide readership was filled with curiosity about him, Scott wanted to provide a document that would give some insight into his magical life. Unfortunately, obligations for already contracted books prevented him from completing this work. We all regretted that this book was one that went unfinished.

At the urging of Scott's father, the author Chet Cunningham, and some of Scott's associates at Llewellyn Publications, we (David Harrington and deTraci Regula) agreed to attempt the biography that Scott intended to write, working from interviews, letters, our own memories of our friendship with Scott, and Scott's own notes for his autobiography. Information which originated from these sources will appear throughout this book set off in italics.

The result you hold in your hands. It is our hope that this book will give Scott's readers some sense of the wonderful experience it was to know Scott Cunningham, and to understand the life forces that molded him. While no one is without flaws, Scott's benevolent spirit, spiked with a fierce loyalty to his convictions and, often, righteous impatience with anything or anyone failing to strive to meet the highest standards possible, had a powerful effect on everyone who came in contact with him. In his personal life, as in his books, Scott was a catalyst for many people to find and understand their own inner natures and to live happier, more productive lives.

Because this book is essentially a completion of the biography Scott himself began to write, it is not an exposé. Scott was fiercely private about some aspects of his life, and we have tried to respect the curtains he drew. He also kept his magical vows of secrecy, though he was adamant that magical secrecy was unnecessary and even harmful. Still, he kept his word. We have not knowingly revealed anything that he was bound to keep private.

We've attempted to be objective, to present facts and reminisce about Scott without distorting him. (This, along with the pain of reliving so many of the happy and sorrowful moments, has been the hardest part of writing this book.) We loved Scott. We are not objective. We feel blessed to have known him, and we hope that we have shared this joy of knowing Scott with you, his readers.

Bright blessings,
David Harrington and deTraci Regula

Who will listen to silvery whispers of the moon?
—from a notebook entry of Scott Cunningham

Tall and lean, a lone figure stands at the edge of the dark cone of Cowles' Mountain. He turns toward the east, where the first glow of the rising moon to come triumphs over the scattered lights. No clutching robes hamper his figure; he wears nothing that would distinguish him from another late hiker. He breathes deeply, smelling the soft tang of the mugwort growing wild on the mountain. Now the creamy golden orb begins to crest the far mountains. Magnified by the horizon, the full moon slowly emerges before his gaze. Once more blessed by the appearance of the lunar light, he speaks a chant memorized so long ago that the words tumble from his lips as he feels the power and awe gather in his heart.

> *"O Moon that rid'st the night to wake,*
> *Before the dawn is pale,*
> *the hamadryad in the brake*
> *The Satyr in the Vale,*
> *Caught in thy net of shadows,*
> *what dreams has thou to show*
> *who treads the silent meadows*
> *to worship Thee below . . ."*[1]

---

1. The complete version of this chant was presented by Gerald Gardner in his *The Meaning of Witchcraft*. It was probably written by Doreen Valiente, at that time a member of Gardner's group. Scott memorized it and would say it whenever the full moon rising caught his eye.

Part I

Seed and Sprout

1956—1971

Chapter One

A Birth at Royal Oak

Gather your rose on the 27th of June . . .

—from an old love spell

WHEN DR. JESSE KETCHUM DELIVERED THE WAILING BABY BOY IN the delivery room of the John Beaumont Hospital in Royal Oak, Michigan, he had no idea that he was participating in an event that one day would give Witches cause to dance for joy. It was a week after Summer Solstice, at 9:25 A.M. on Wednesday June 27, that Scott Douglas Cunningham, second-born son of Chester Grant Cunningham and Rose Marie Wilhoit Cunningham, burst into incarnation, weighing in at a hefty nine pounds, four ounces.

Baby Scott was the latest addition to the Cunningham clan, a hardy mix of British and German ancestry, with touches of Irish, French, and Welsh. While it is tempting to derive the surname Cunningham from "Cunning Man," the British male version of "Wise Woman," there is no evidence that this is how the name came into being. Several Scottish Cunninghams were writers, and a couple of them wrote on folk practices, but the relation (if any at all) between these Cunninghams and the branch of the family that eventually produced Scott is unclear.

There is little known of any mystical leanings of bearers of the Cunningham name, but at least one met his death condemned as a Witch. A John Cunningham, also known as John Fian, was called a wizard and implicated in a magical plot to destroy King James. After enduring horrible tortures, this Cunningham was burned as a Witch in 1596 by direct order of the King. But whether or not this Cunningham was an ancestor of Scott Cunningham is not known.

Scott's direct ancestors arrived in the New World early. The earliest confirmed trace is in 1635, when William Burritt and his wife Elizabeth left their home in Glamorganshire, Wales (Welsh Morganwg, or the Territory of Morgan) and sailed to the New World, arriving in Connecticut. William and Elizabeth eventually had ten children. Elizabeth was reckoned a good businesswoman, substantially increasing the estate left in her hands when William passed away.

By the time of the American Revolution, Scott's ancestors were well-established in the Colonies. One branch of the family, the Pointers, moved to Canada and were staunch Loyalists during the Revolutionary War. Later generations crossed America in Conestoga wagons, and cleared fields, rock by rock, to farm.

Dedicated churchgoers, occult practices were frowned upon by most of the Cunningham relations, but two of Scott's female ancestors possessed a bit more than the ordinary five senses. His paternal great-grandmother, Emmy, read tea leaves, bringing a love of tea with her from her native Canada. Scott's great-great grandmother Abby Pointer is written about in *Tapestry*, the family history compiled by Scott's paternal grandmother, Hazel Cunningham: "Abby was a very superstitious woman. She believed implicitly in the signs of the moon. Fridays were unlucky, as were black cats, ladders and such." Abby and her husband planted by the moon, sowing underground crops during the dark of the moon, and plants that grew above ground during the bright, moonlit nights. Abby was emphatic that there were propitious phases of the moon for moving, butchering, and planting. She would never move a broom from one house to another, a bit of lore that Scott included in *The Magical Household*. Abby also insisted that one's purse should be the first thing carried into the new house, to ensure prosperity.

Neither Abby nor her husband Ben Pointer were members of any church, a fact noted by the community around them. When questioned about it, Abby Pointer is quoted by Hazel Cunningham as saying "'Good is good, and bad is bad." and adding that her name on the church book wouldn't change it any, and she could be "just as good as good church-going folks." Hazel notes that Abby, with her red, curling hair, big green eyes, "and a temper to match" would have made a dynamic impact if she had chosen to be active in church circles. Hazel adds that nothing is known of Abby's family ancestry, but Hazel was personally certain it was Irish. The devoutly Methodist Cunningham families did not see fit to record any other of Abby's beliefs or practices. It is tempting to see Abby as a Witch.

On December 9, 1928, near Shelby, Nebraska, Chester Grant Cunningham, Scott's father, was born in a farmhouse on the land Chet's grandfather had first farmed. Hazel Cunningham mentions, without complaint, that it was a challenge hauling water to the house, cooking for the growing family, cleaning, and helping with the rest of the farm tasks. She notes that winters were filled with blizzards, summer with heat, drought, and the occasional plague of locusts. "Springs were promising," she writes, "but harvest brought only disappointment." After another hopeful spring that again ended with the corn crop withering in the fields, the family headed to Oregon in 1937.

In 1948, while at a church camp, Chet Cunningham met Rose Marie Wilhoit. Rose Marie was a Psychology major at Willamette University in Salem, Oregon. Chet served in Korea during the Korean War. After his return, he and Rosie were married on January 18, 1953. They moved to Manhattan where Chet worked on his Master's degree in Journalism at Columbia Graduate School of Journalism. In 1954, they had their first child, Gregory. Scott was born in 1956 after Chet and Rosie moved to Royal Oak, Michigan, where Chet worked for an audio-visual company in nearby Detroit.

When Scott was four years old, Chet and Rosie Cunningham moved from Michigan to San Diego, California, arriving on October 18th, 1960. At that time, San Diego was a relatively quiet Navy town. Mission Valley, then a long, pastoral stretch of farmland and dairies, led inland to the neat, peaceful suburb of San Carlos. Chet and Rosie were attracted by the climate and opportunities that the area offered, and Chet thought California would be an ideal place for expanding his freelance writing career. Their bright, ranch-style house was a welcoming family home. Here Scott and his brother Greg were soon joined by their new baby sister, Christine, and the three grew up under the benevolent nurturing of Chet and Rosie.

The Cunningham children took for it granted that both their parents were home most of the time. Chet worked long hours in his home office, and kept it largely child-free. The mysterious working area of their father was so unknown to the Cunningham children that Gregory, with older-brother mischief, convinced both Christine and Scott that their house contained a secret room. He took them outside where they counted the windows. There were too many, and neither Scott nor Christine knew what part of the house the extra window belonged to. This window was Chet's office, unknown territory to the kids.

The parenting lessons the Cunninghams learned on Gregory only partially applied to Scott. Chet noticed that this second son was more of a loner, but also a showman. At an early age, Scott rearranged the back yard into his version of "Disneyland," where he dragged wagonfuls of paying customers and his bedazzled younger sister past such unnatural wonders as the "Geyser" (a hose stuck up between rocks) and a recreation of "It's a Small World" featuring costume jewelry hanging from the branches of potted plants. Scott treated his audience to a light-and-magic show which was long on flashing lights and short on sleight-of-hand.

Family trips to visit Chet's parents in Oregon provided the family with an opportunity to enjoy nature. Driving north along the coast, the Cunninghams would eschew restaurants and stop to bake clams on the beach. Scott would wander the shore, adding North Coast specimens to his seashell collection. One year when this trip took place at the time of Scott's birthday, Hazel Cunningham baked him a birthday cake and decorated it with finely-detailed marzipan seashells.

From the beginning, Scott enjoyed a special affinity for the natural world around him, a friendship fed by treks up nearby Cowles' Mountain in search of rumored old mines. Though Scott was not then aware of it, Cowles' Mountain is also a sacred site, used in centuries past by the Kumeyaay tribe. They gathered in a circle of stones on the peak at Winter Solstice to watch as a distant peak in the Peninsula Range split the sun apart for a few moments as it rose, making it appear as two globes of light. On the dry slopes, Scott collected rocks and made an extensive study of seashells, determinedly mastering their Latin names with the same thoroughness that he would later master herbs.

Always at one with nature, Scott found at an early age that he could call butterflies and birds to him, or raise the wind to such an extent that the backyard gate would swing open on the force of the wind. He wrote:

> *When I was young, I used to wish the rain away. As I got older,*
> *I would sometimes make it rain in the mountains.*

The Cunningham family owned a cabin, located east of San Diego, near the summit of Mount Laguna in the Cleveland National Forest. The rustic, octagonal cabin sat in a meadow far from the main road, in a grove of tall sugar pines which filled the air with a soft vanilla fragrance. Here, the sound of rain often lulled him to sleep at night. In spring, the wild lupine poured over the hillsides in a river of blue. Winter brought a carpet of snow and a chill that left Scott gazing into the flickering flames in the old stone fireplace. In the thick quiet of the tall trees, Scott became attuned to the subtle forces of nature. Long walks alone, a book his only company, made him comfortable with solitude. He felt the power in the bright white sunlight of high noon in the narrow air of the mountains, and at night, the softly gleaming stars captivated him and set him to dreaming of far away worlds.

Away from the wooded mountains, Scott's powerful love of the ocean drew him to surfing and snorkeling though other sports bored him. Even though he lived many miles inland, he was never spiritually far from the ocean, always feeling echoes of the rolling waves. In "On the Beach," from *Llewellyn's 1985 Astrological Guide to California* he writes:

> *Here in California, perhaps more than anywhere else in the*
> *country, we are attuned with the sea. Even inland, amid deserts*
> *or towering, snow-capped mountains, its presence is felt. Much*
> *of our land was once under water and fossilized shells can be*
> *found in the most unexpected places. On days when the wind is*
> *just right the salty scent of the sea can be detected miles inland,*
> *bringing memories of the days (and nights) spent before it.*

Astral Explorations

Scott enjoyed spontaneous astral projection at an early age, vividly remembering his frequent travels to a secret beach at night, a beach that was dark and glowing with phosphorescent foam. He recalled picking up a shell on one of his many trips to his secret shore, all the while knowing that when he returned home it wouldn't be there.

> *I remember suddenly being back in bed at night and placing the shell on the bed beside me, even though I knew it would vanish when I awoke. Scott later wrote that most of us seem to astral project naturally early in life, before society thrusts down barriers of doubt and materialism. Few are able to enjoy complete freedom and ease of astral projection after youth.*

Mystical events, though rare, intrigued him. Scott saw a ghost in the mirror in his parents' bedroom. A supposed UFO sighting nearby found Scott and his childhood friends eagerly pedaling their bikes to the alleged landing site, fearful, yet fascinated by the risk of a brush with the unknown.

In the quiet community nestled below Cowles' Mountain, a child's only exposure to "witches" was in the Halloween assignments in elementary school. In an assignment for first or second grade, Scott already shows a life-long trait: everything is spelled correctly except for the word "witches," which has been repeatedly erased and spelled over. He would always have trouble using that word. (See photo section.)

As an adult, Scott would listen with shock as his friends recounted difficult early years with challenging families. "I'm the only person I know who had a normal childhood!" Scott frequently admitted. His early writing efforts were particularly encouraged, as he writes in his autobiography:

> *I remember my father coming to me with a piece of paper in his hand, frowning, and saying,*
>   *"You're in a lot of trouble!"*
>   *"Huh? What? Ah?" I said, wondering at his unusual anger.*
>   *He smiled and thrust the paper toward me. "I found this crumpled up under your bed. This is good writing; you shouldn't throw it away!"*

Scott the Radical

Scott's parents were not only supportive of his writing, they also encouraged free speech. Scott writes:

> When I was growing up, I had somewhat liberal parents. At one point during the 1960s my mother and father allowed my brother and I to paint the huge sliding doors to our bedroom closet. We didn't just paint it, though; we covered it with catch phrases of the time ("sock it to me"[1] is a good example); drew flowers, and wrote bold political statements about Vietnam, few of which I understood at the time. Looking back, it was an extraordinary thing for my parents to have allowed us to do.
>
> It was about this time that Timothy Leary went on trial. I'd never touched drugs in my life, but Leary somehow seemed "hip," so one day I added to the multi-colored scenes on the door and wrote down the date of Leary's incarceration with the words, "Ten more years" (I believe that was the length of his sentence).
>
> I couldn't not know about Leary, since the evening news was on during every dinner, and even at that age (twelve or thirteen) I read the papers.[2]
>
> In due time the wall between the bedroom and my father's office was knocked out. The sliding doors were repainted. I forgot all about them.

Scott's sister Christine remembers that the Cunningham table was a happy one, filled with conversation and jokes. Schoolmates who stayed for dinner enjoyed the easy atmosphere of the Cunningham dinnertime, and wished that they shared the same relationship with their own families. Rosie Cunningham loved to cook and the table was always covered with food. In *The Magic In Food*,[3] Scott thanked his mother "who rarely minded me licking the spoon all those long years," and some of the recipes in that book came from family recipe files.

Scott's fears were typical of his generation:

> I was much like any other kid growing up in the 60s in the United States. I was terrified of going to Vietnam and was

constantly seeking escape from the real world, even at that young age. This is why I so readily embraced reading as a method of removing myself from the horrific things that were happening on the other side of the world.

But soon, he would discover that he was not like just any other kid. Scott was about to become a Witch.

1. This was a phrase from the popular television comedy series, *Laugh-In*.
2. Later in his biography, Scott notes: ". . . twenty years later, I accidentally met the remarkably controversial Dr. Leary. It was at an American Booksellers Association convention in Anaheim. Carl Weschcke introduced me to Dr. Leary. He seemed somewhat tired and old for his years, but was there plugging his new book, *What the Woman Wants*. I was tongue-tied and had no idea of what to say to him after we were left alone. He was so infamous that I'm afraid I smiled a lot, looked around the room, and made my escape as quickly as I could. He probably thought I was on drugs.

    "Later, I was ashamed at my behavior. In my youth I'd read Barbara Walter's excellent book, *How to Talk about Practically Anything with Practically Anyone* before interviewing a millionaire for an article that I was writing. That book gave me the confidence to march into his office and treat him like the human being he was. I forgot all this when confronted with Timothy Leary. All the questions that I could have asked him suddenly popped into my mind—hours later. But I never met him again."
3. This book has been restored to its original title, *The Magic of Food* and reprinted by Llewellyn with a new recipe section. Scott's favorite family and magical recipes are included.

Chapter Two

Into the
Circle

ON AN EARLY SEPTEMBER AFTERNOON IN 1971, SCOTT ENTERED THE
Cunningham living room. On the coffee table was his mother's
new Book Club selection, *The Supernatural*,[1] by Douglas Hill and
Pat Williams. Fearful eyes stared up from the dark cover. Scott picked up
the book and began reading, fascinated. In moments he was immersed in
the culture of primitive man, seeing the gods and goddesses of ancient
Egypt, Mesopotamian demons, and ghost sightings, all revealed in full
color. But these ancient spirits were only the beginning. Chapter Five
offered a detailed description of "The Secret Arts"; Chapter Six sent him on
"A Search for Witches." He pored over the pages, committing to memory
the magical hand gestures. At some point later, he tore out the pictures of
Sybil Leek, Gerald Gardner, and others, and placed them in a photo notebook of witchcraft imagery.

The next day, in drama class, Scott met Dorothy Jones. The graceful
teenage Priestess would be his magical teacher and colleague for the next

11

six years. In one account of their first meeting, Scott says that he flashed one of the witchcraft protection signs at her, and she responded.[2] He does not say what led him to believe that she was involved in witchcraft, or if he was just playing around to show off. But the current began to flow between them. Fifteen-year old Dorothy told Scott she had been initiated into a Wiccan tradition at the age of thirteen. She was regularly practicing the Craft at the time she met Scott.

In an early autobiographical fragment written before 1986, Scott elaborates on his introduction to witchcraft:

> *My start on witchcraft did not come to me, it was almost forced on me. I had just read a chapter on witchcraft in a book my mother had got in the mail when that night I saw the movie, "Burn, Witch, Burn" on television on the late movie. The next day I started talking to this girl in my drama room when we started to talk about witchcraft. I don't now remember how we got on the subject, but she later told me that she doesn't usually talk to complete strangers about it, let alone her friends. We tested each other, and found we did know something about it. Our relationship progressed, and we had long telephone conversations about it . . .*

Scott describes this time:

> *I attended my first Wiccan ritual in late September or early October, 1971. It was led by Dorothy (AKA Morgan), who quickly became my first Wiccan teacher.[3] I studied with Dorothy for two years and on August 17th, 1973, received initiation into Wicca. (This form of Wicca, unlike most others today, had no specific name, and had but one "degree" and one initiation. In some ways, it was probably closer to the old style.)*
>
> *Dorothy and I led a coven for a while, but its membership was always haphazard. We soon settled down to working alone together, with various other guests. (We never had more than five present at coven meetings, and usually only the two of us. Such intimate workings were ideal, as far as my training was concerned.)*

Coven records still in my possession show that the last ritual that I performed with Dorothy occurred on October 31, 1977. By this time she was retiring from active coven life, and promptly gave me a new student. I began training G[4]. These lessons and circles continued for well over two years.

Scott wrote about his tradition in 1982:[5]

Once called American Traditionalist . . . the Standing Stones Tradition does not claim to be an ancient order. It was begun in 1971 by Morgan, a Moon Priestess . . . The Standing Stones Tradition was born from the spirit of the Old Ways, from the days when the sight of the full moon hanging majestically in the twilight sky was an awesome sight.

We recognize and revere the life-force of the Universe as represented by a Goddess and a God, whose names cannot be revealed openly here. They are as equal as are all things under the Sun; there is no bias towards the feminine Deity, or to women in general, although Morgan was herself a feminist.

Rather, equal recognition and reverence is paid to both the God, symbolizing the Sun, and the Goddess of the Moon, Earth, and Sea. In coven workings the High Priestess is equal with the High Priest.

The rituals performed in group settings link in with the currents of energy that run everywhere through the Earth. Symbolic or actual standing stones and megalithic circles[6] are "erected" to collect, store, and send forth these energies for magical change.

But the emphasis is not on magic; it is rather on attuning with the Moon and Sun, the Stars, Sea, and the Earth Herself. Magic is simple and uncomplex; it is of the mountains and ocean, of caves and deserts . . . Its tools are the herbs, stones, flowers and trees that surround us; for such are links with the universal power which is the source of all.

Perhaps the best synthesis of the Standing Stones Tradition are the thirteen goals which are handed out to each person coming to us for training and possible entrance:

Thirteen Goals of a Witch

1. *Know yourself.*
2. *Know your craft.*
3. *Learn.*
4. *Apply your learning.*
5. *Achieve balance.*
6. *Resist temptations which negate evolution.*
7. *Keep your thoughts in good order.*
8. *Celebrate Life.*
9. *Attune with the cycles of the universe.*
10. *Breathe and eat correctly.*
11. *Exercise both mind and body.*
12. *Meditate.*
13. *Honor and worship the Gods.*

For our approach to the mysteries, if they may be called that, here are some guidelines from our Book of Shadows:

Seek out wisdom in books, rare manuscripts and cryptic poems, if you wish; but seek it out also in simple stones and fragile herbs and in the cry of wild birds; listen to the whisperings of the wind and the roar of the ocean if you would master Wicca; for it is here that our secrets are preserved.

The Standing Stones Tradition is an open tradition, with no restriction whatsoever regarding sex, race, color, age, sexual orientation, nationality and so on.

There are no initiation ceremonies, but rituals of admission. The only requirements of students is (sic) love of the Gods, dedication, and hard work.

Not all the lessons and circles were solemn, however. In an article originally published in the magazine *New Moon Rising,* Scott describes an evening that did not go so well. Anyone who has spent much time in circle can probably relate to this type of ritual disaster!

I vividly remember a skyclad ritual that we held on October 31, 1973. Four of us were present. We had a pleasant ritual (except when one unruly male covener spun and accidentally walked right into the end of his grand piano—ouch!) and, afterward, sat down for cakes and wine. The cool, highly polished bare wood floor was a great contrast to the hot atmosphere of the circle itself. We blessed the crescent cakes and the wine and had a good grounding.

Then we tried to stand up—and couldn't. Our naked, sweaty bodies had partially melted the shellac on the highly polished floor. We were stuck. It was some time before we could close the circle (no one had thought to bring a shoe horn to ritual).

During this time, Scott became acquainted with Ed and Marilee Snowden. Marilee was giving lectures on magical subjects for a group in San Diego.[7] Scott soon was a welcome guest at the Snowden home. He began attending magical gatherings at their house, the small beginnings of the famous "Hallows" parties annually presented by Marilee. In years to come, he and Marilee would work together extensively in several magical traditions.

Scott kept detailed magical diaries in addition to his extensive notes, files, and notebooks on various magical subjects. Writing had always come easily to him and he kept his diary faithfully, with the exception of a couple of extended gaps which he attempted to recap in a page or two. His entries show a complete immersion in the magical arts. As time went on, Scott also added astrological information on each day's entry and ended each passage with a pentagram. Scott also rejoiced in rain, and every rainfall was carefully recorded in his diary.

Two themes run through almost every entry—the books he was reading or had jubilantly acquired and the herbs and plants he had seen, smelled, gathered, or used magically. Some of these herbal notes contain their own unintentional poetry: "Sweet pea is in bloom, some sorrel in shade, wisteria is out in force." Tracking down hard-to-find incense ingredients brought him true joy, as he writes many years later:

I vividly recall the day eighteen years ago when the package finally arrived. I grabbed it from the UPS person's hands and gleefully ripped away the brown paper.

As I lifted the cardboard flaps enchanting scents of far-flung countries drifted from the box. Inside were the bags of benzoin, frankincense and sandalwood I'd ordered from a New York herb company. At that moment, when I'd finally obtained these once costly treasures, I knew that I'd plunge head-first into magical herbalism and never look back.

That night, with moonlight streaming through my bedroom window and candles gleaming on my worktable, I laboriously ground sandalwood chips to a splintery powder in my mortar and pestle. Next, I crushed the frankincense into a yellow, crystalline mass. Mixing the wood and the resin in a small wooden bowl, I said a few words that seemed right. The moon rose before the eastern window, brightening my room. I lit a charcoal block, set it in my makeshift incense burner and poured a bit of the mixture onto the charcoal.

A dense, fragrant cloud rose like a misty deity from the censer. The bittersweetness enveloped me as I stared at the moon through the smoke of the Lunar Incense I'd created.

While mixing my first incense that night I began to understand the evocative powers of herbs. Since then I've spent almost two decades living with resins, petals, roots, leaves, essential oils, seeds and other aromatic plant materials, crafting incenses, magical amulets, ritual oils, inks, brews and bath mixtures for use in magic.

As I grew from a wide-eyed boy to an adult writer, I infused my magical books with herbal lore, recording what I'd learned and experienced . . .

Scott's parents, although active in their Methodist church, did not actively interfere in Scott's new interest in Witchcraft. Ironically, Scott was introduced to yoga and aura reading while at a church camp led by a Methodist minister. He also noted the lucky purchase of a couple of folk magic books at the church bazaar. It seemed that his path would find him.

Knowing the value of discretion, Scott did not openly flaunt his involvement. For a long time he kept his growing library of magical books hidden, and when he brought the books out into view, he considered it an act of bravery warranting mention in his diary. He also took advantage of a mailing address offered to him by his friend Ed Snowden, Marilee's husband, to receive mail-order witchcraft courses, including those offered by Y Twyleth Teg and the Church of Wicca. He wrote many inquiry letters and sent book orders to authors and others well known in the magical community. Ray Buckland responded cordially to one of Scott's letters, unaware that a decade or so later he would be considering Scott a colleague and friend.

Scott's sister, Christine Ashworth, four years his junior, remembers how excited she was when her older brother invited her to watch him divine by dripping wax onto water and interpreting the images. "It was mysterious and exciting. As his 'little sister,' it was very special to be asked to participate in anything my older brother did. I didn't understand or care that these were 'magical practices;' they were something Scott was willing to share with me, and that mattered above anything else." Divination by wax in water was one of Scott's mainstays, and he did these readings at magical parties such as Marilee Snowden's (now Bigelow) later-famous Hallows parties. Generally, however, Scott took divination very seriously and refused to do unnecessary readings.

When the Cunningham family poured cement for a patio for the cabin in the mountains on August 15, 1972, Scott signed his name and drew a pentagram beside it. Later, he would use the five-pointed star as part of his signature (Figure 1.) when signing his books and letters.

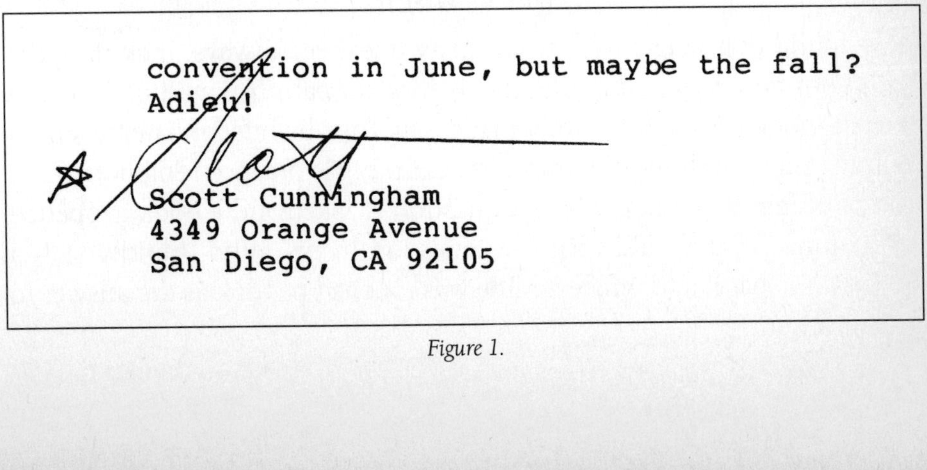

```
conven/ion in June, but maybe the fall?
Adieu!

Scott Cunningham
4349 Orange Avenue
San Diego, CA 92105
```

Figure 1.

Scott writes of another incident showing his parents' support:

> On the occasion of my sixteenth birthday my mother ordered a
> birthday cake without my knowledge. When the bakery asked
> my mother what decorations should be on it, imagine the
> woman's surprise when Mom asked if they had anything dealing
> with witchcraft!

In the early days, Scott notes:

> I didn't do very many spells, but the ones I did do turned out
> spectacularly. Once I did a quick money spell, the next day I got
> a five dollar bill.

This was substantial money to the fifteen-year-old Scott. Since his
magical work started relatively early, he focused on simple spells and was
usually amazed with the results. His understanding of how magic must
first be practical and easy grew out of his early workings. He did healing
and protective spells at the request of his friends. At that time, he did not
hesitate to do a protective spell for someone even if it had not been
requested; after his mother had her purse stolen, he notes that he intended
to do a protective spell for her, presumably without her knowledge. As
time passed, Scott avoided doing spells that were not specifically
requested. As a maturing magician, he no longer believed that he had the
right to interfere in the lives of others, even if he felt that he knew what
was best.

Book Magic

Scott found that magic worked in many unexpected ways, including the
finding of books to guide him on his magical path. An avid collector of
"occult" books, Scott frequently made long trips by bus, or, later, even on
foot, to visit bookstores or libraries miles away. He practiced "bibliomancy,"
a form of folk divination where a question is asked and a book is opened
at random. Scott would form the question in his mind, blindly stab a
finger at the page, and whatever line was touched he took as the answer to
the question.

In a diary from that time, he writes of one memorable book day:

> *On November 23, 1973, I was downtown looking for books. After I had been in a few places, I just suddenly "knew" that I would be getting* What Witches Do *by Stewart Farrar that day. Now, considering that I had been looking for that book since April or May, 1973, I was rather pleased, to say the least. I had often hoped to find it, but always failed. I must have gone to four or five booksellers that day, but no luck.*
>
> *I had almost forgotten the proclamation by the time I was picked up to go to this class on High & Low Magick that evening . . . After about half an hour, Dorothy grabbed my arm and said: "Look! . . . that book he's reading!" Sure enough, there was* What Witches Do, *lying in Michael's lap. We were so ecstatic [about it] that Michael left the room and brought back another copy of it. His wife owned that one: he owned the other. He gave me a copy of* What Witches Do *that night, and I will never fail to listen again.*

Scott took careful notes of other premonitions, particularly two warnings of danger on the same day, November 12, 1973. As with many psychic warnings, he was not able to avoid the expected danger:

> *While I was on the ladder (getting some things from the attic) I told my mother that even if we didn't buy a new ladder this year, I was going to throw this one away. A few minutes later it slipped out from under my feet, leaving me hanging.*

Later that day, in the closed-circuit TV studio at Patrick Henry High School, he gazed up at the heavy television lights, wondering what would happen if those lights fell. A few minutes later, as the cameras were being focused, a microphone fell and hit Scott on the head.

Scott purchased his first Tarot deck soon after these incidents. While Ouija boards were specifically forbidden in the Cunningham household, because of their connection with the raising of spirits, Tarot cards were permitted. Scott decided to purchase a deck after watching a scene in a movie called *The Cat Creature* where the character Hester reads Tarot cards.

By 1974, many of Scott's opinions about the Craft and its practice were already formed. He was collecting and using herb lore in his magical practices with Dorothy and on his own, and was already something of a philosopher on matters of the Craft. In early August of that year, he wrote:

> *I was discoursing today on the matter of Witchcraft. Whether it was possible for a pagan religion to survive during the time of the Persecution without completely dying out, or changing its form, is not for me to wonder at. Nor is it my duty to prove that it did. The facts are that here in the twentieth century* C.E., *there are groves, nests, and covens existing, composed of, somewhat serious practicing persons of pagan religions.*
>
> *I find on the whole the schism in the Craft to be delightful, save those instances (plentiful, I'm afraid) wherein one member of one tradition states that his or her tradition is "The One Right True and Only Way" (my thanks to P.E.I. Bonewicz for coining the phrase).*
>
> *As I wrote a year ago or so: Schism means freedom in the Craft; if one form doesn't speak to you, seek and listen to the music of another, for many groups play different tunes . . . The freedom that gives you the right to choose your religion gives others the right to choose theirs.*

A Magical War in San Diego
Great Wizards and Witches
Rarely show it
I thought so once and
Now I know it.
                —Scott Cunningham

Magical circles and religious organizations in general seem to have more than their fair share of strong egos and combative personalities. San Diego was no exception. An incident which refined Scott's opinions on much of the craft occurred around this time. A few members of the San Diego magical community decided to stir things up by waging a "magical war" partially in jest and partially in earnest. Caught on the fringes of what he felt was utter stupidity, Scott attempted to stay neutral while many of his acquaintances were drawn into the fray. Dorothy, his teacher and covenmate, was requested to provide magical protection to the victim of the attacks, and Scott aided her.

While some genuine magical energy may have been thrown about, most of this "magical war" consisted of loathsome objects left at the houses or on the cars of the intended targets, producing the desired chaos. Perpetrators of this farce were never positively identified, though some members of the magical community avoided several suspects. Unfortunately, the result was a fog of distrust in the San Diego magical community. This atmosphere lingers twenty years later and may contribute to the turbulent nature of many magical groups in the area. In the mid-1970s, Scott wrote that he knew of forty-five covens active in San Diego, an abundance of magical groups for this decade. This, of course, was well before the New Age explosion that began in the early 1980s.

The individuals behind the magical war were supposedly not Wiccan. Though this was not the case, Scott believed it and this belief strengthened Scott's ties to what he perceived as the more gentle, positive path of Wicca as opposed to what he considered to be the more ponderous methods of ceremonial magic. In a 1991 article called "The Wiccan Spirit" for *New Moon Rising* he wrote:

> . . . *Many of us lose the Wiccan spirit by becoming involved with Wiccan disputes . . . Such clashes, when of a personal nature, are rarely known to outsiders. However, when covens are involved, negative feelings often run high. "Wars of the Witches" ensue, and they're rampant across our land. Such bickering is usually underground, and so has only a local effect. Sometimes, though, the war makes its way into print (in letters to Pagan publications). This spreads the spirit of nastiness over thousands of miles, far from its place of origin, and affects an even wider group of Wiccans.*
>
> *Eventually, half of Pagandom knows of the fight. They may not personally know the participants, but all are ready to proffer opinions (despite the fact that few of them, if any, know the actual origin of the clash.) Such opinions can cause division in other covens, which leads to gossip, which leads to new fights, which leads to publication . . .*

Gossip, differing opinions, division—these are common in all human groups, especially those that are religious in nature. Persons often have definite ideas concerning the Goddess and God and ways of worship. They're often prepared to defend their right to their rites, and to denigrate those that observe differing forms of worship. (Usually, however, a personal clash of some kind is the real culprit behind a war. Character assassination isn't reserved for politicians running for office.)

Again, this is quite human, but it is far from the Wiccan spirit. Meaningful dialogue between persons of opposing viewpoints should always be encouraged, but is usually tossed away in favor of gossip. When jealousy tints opinion and leads to an attack, spirituality withers and the perpetrator has lost the spirit of Wicca.

I'm not the first to say this, but it must be said again: we should be defending each other, not attacking each other. Many are in line, waiting their turn to symbolically roast us. We needn't add logs to the fire of words that our enemies busily prepare.

When facing a War of the Witches, remember the spirit of Wicca, encapsulated in the simple phrase: "harm none." Neutrality is best. If others try to sway you, speak of the spirit of Wicca.

If we pay no attention to attacks, they will lose power. If the attackers don't have any fun, they'll do something else and give us all more room.

Yes, we're all unique individuals. Yes, we all have opinions. And yes, we're interested in what the Witch down the street is doing. News of a flurry of angry words between two covens can be exciting at first, but soon pales, since it's ultimately defeating to everyone involved. If we're truly to be Wiccan, we're obliged to attempt to live according to the spirit of our religion.

The next time you hear of a war of words, remember: "harm none."

Elsewhere, he summed up his feelings simply:

> *All magic is self-transformation. Our magical actions alter us forever. If we base our spells and rites on hatred and anger, we'll become hated and angry. If we build our rituals on love and caring, we'll be loved and cared for.*

A Trip to the Pyramids

In 1973, Scott participated in a Christmastime church choir trip to Mexico. Traveling with his mother to commemorate the centennial of a Methodist Church in Mexico City, Scott regarded the trip as opportunity to see another culture. He delighted in the lushness of Mexico City. Vendors along the roadside offered iguanas, holding them up by their tails. His Mexico diary notes that they regrettably missed the Archeological Museum. Archeology was a life-long fascination with him, whether it was in information gleaned from books on various digs, or as entertainment in the form of *Raiders of the Lost Ark*.

The crown of his trip was a visit to the pyramids outside Mexico City. While other members of the group took the massive monuments in stride as relics of a vanished and safely sanitized culture, he was awed by the lingering aura of power and presence. Possibly, this early contact with the remnants of a civilization that had practiced bloody rites also urged him on in his pursuit of a gentler, more positive path of magic. Though impressed by the massive stone buildings, he wrote more about the many flowers and plants he saw in Mexico City than about the monuments themselves.

A Good Age for Unicorns

In school, Scott enjoyed his English classes and frequently wrote on folk-lore or other "safe" magical subjects. This brief paper entitled "A Good Age For Unicorns" received the teacher's note "charming and poetic." and, presumably earned full credit:

> *A good age for Unicorns is one in which there exists a sweetening absence of Red Bulls. Then, too, it must be an age that knows no*

lack of suitable accommodations: i.e., lilac woods, enchanted forests, and assorted wildwoods, well off the beaten track.

But tarry a moment. Let those words die upon the wind. Listen to me: during a time when there is no disbelief in unicorns, when men instinctively glance at rustlings in eternally-virgin forests, and when young maidens still dream in seashell tones of spiralled horns shimmering in the dark; then will you find the good age for unicorns.

And the best age? 'Tis past, and can never be recaptured. One thin slice of our being, that of childlike innocence, has been bound with the chains forged in Time and Age, and only the touch of a unicorn's horn can rend the chains and open the lock, and let us gaze with wonder at the curious beast from the past.[8,9]

Some of Scott's efforts were not as graceful as the above excerpt, although poetic and humorous:

I knew a Witch in England
Who had a magic broom;
At night she'd fly
Across the sky
And then sweep up her room.
Working with her cauldron
She found a magic trick
Her magic stews
And haunted brews
Made everybody sick.

Scott's other interests in his high school years included drama, dance, and advanced piano. He learned Wiccan songs as well as more classical offerings, playing the "Wiccan Grace" and "Hymn to the Sun" at home under the unknowing ears of his parents. At one point, Scott's proficiency in piano led his father to believe he might become a concert pianist. Scott raced through several piano teachers and eventually was tutored at San Diego State University. He became an adept pianist, but this was not fated to be one of his abiding interests. He had no piano during the twelve years he lived on Orange Avenue. On rare occasions he would tickle the ivories at a friend's house and show off his powerful, smooth voice singing Broadway show tunes. Despite his great facility with the piano, he once confessed, "I've always hated pieces with lots of sharps and flats!" which may offer a reason he did not continue his formal piano training.

In drama classes, Scott's natural showmanship found its outlet. He loved participating in high-school plays, and occasionally ventured into small local theater productions. One role he performed was Benvolio in a Gaslamp Quarter production of *Romeo and Juliet*. He also served occasionally as an assistant director, acquiring skills that were very useful for his *Herb Magic* video years later. While his sister Christine danced with the California Ballet Company, he assisted in the behind-the-scenes staging for the productions. He also appeared in a few off-campus dance productions and avidly studied modern dance. For a time, he also seriously considered writing plays, but, aside from a few brief fragments, never completed any.

In 1976, at the urging of his father, Scott began putting together what was to become *Magical Herbalism*. He had in hand his extensive notes and practical experience using herbs magically. Now he began to systematically research and investigate herbs, at first compiling his information by hand on index cards and then taping those to sheets of paper as the data overflowed. His friends in the magical community began to look to him for information, and a raw version of his "Herbal Grimoire" was given to a few of his friends.

But Scott's time could not be devoted entirely to his magical and writing plans. A fragment of a past life would lead him to an unexpected, if temporary, destination.

∾

1. *The Supernatural* by Douglas Hill and Pat Williams, Hawthorne Books, was published originally in 1965, and was later distributed as a Book Club edition.

The book is fairly lurid, well-illustrated with color and black and white photos, and features a number of staged shots for the reader's edification—a naked woman on an altar, a ritual in progress. One photo, however, shows a ritual where the performers are all nice English-looking people dressed in day clothes. The book is generally even-tempered in tone. Though somewhat astonished people do such things, *The Supernatural* is informative and wide-ranging.

Scott might have taken to heart the quotation from W. E. Butler on page 136: "Books on magic seem to be largely made up of quotations from and comments on other books on magic." Although in his compendiums, Scott did the same, he worked hard to ensure that his books also provided fresh, practical information derived from his own experience.

2. The protective signs Scott made to Dorothy were the inverted "sign of the horns" and mano figa found on page 200 of *The Supernatural*.

3. Dorothy writes of her relationship with Scott on page 201–202. (Appendix I: Friends and Readers Remember.)

4. Ginny Therion, whom Scott later initiated into the system of Wicca that he and Dorothy practiced.

5. This material was printed with typographic and other errors which we have corrected here. We have also omitted a statement which Scott later discovered to be false.

6. Recently, a "Stone Circle" was discovered on Cowles Mountain in San Diego and identified as a probable solstice or equinox viewing site once used by native American tribes in the area. This stone circle was relatively small and assembled out of football-sized rocks. Later, the site was ignored and accidentally razed by a maintenance crew installing a rest area.

   Both Morgan and Scott lived near Cowles Mountain, and he mentions in his diary that he did magic on the mountain. While no mention of a stone circle is made, if he and Morgan were "erecting" these circles, as he seems to indicate was part of the practice, it's possible that this controversial stone circle was the work of other "natives" in the area than the Kumeyaay Indians.

   The eastern orientation of the circle, overlooking a flat plateau, would, of course, also have been perfect for watching the rise of the moon from behind the distant mountains.

7. Marilee writes of her relationship with Scott on page 213–214. (Appendix I: Friends and Readers Remember.)

8. The original version says "gaze at wonder" rather than "gaze with wonder." We've changed this apparent typo as I believe "gaze with wonder" was what Scott intended here.

9. Scott's romanticism about unicorns was later replaced by cynicism; he felt that unicorns were overused as a symbol of the New Age and were too cliched to hold any real meaning. Difficult conflicts while he was a member of a coven named for the mythical beast may have contributed to this feeling.

Chapter Three

Into the World

I N 1976, ON A WHIM, SCOTT JOINED THE NAVY. THOUGH AS AN adolescent he feared being drafted for Vietnam, he now voluntarily enlisted and reported for training. Unfortunately, he discovered too late that he had a rather romantic idea of what Navy life would be like. His past life memory of serving in the Navy during World War Two probably was largely responsible for his desire to join up now.

> *When I was in boot camp during my curiously short Navy experience (1976), I made rough notes regarding this book. I also wrote whole chapters by hand late at night on my rack. I began refining it and writing what eventually became* Wicca: A Guide for the Solitary Practitioner *in the mid-1980s.*

Scott tried to be a good recruit. He took extensive notes on every aspect of what was expected of him. Although he was stationed locally, his friends and family flooded him with letters. Before long, Scott realized he had made a mistake.

The highly regimented Navy life did not appeal to him. Where another recruit might have accepted his fate, Scott did not. He began to do magic to obtain his early discharge. Shortly after he joined, budget restrictions offered a chance for new recruits to opt out. He received an honorable discharge after only a couple of months of Navy training.

In 1974, Scott began studies at San Diego State University, spending most of his time in creative writing classes. He attended part-time for several years, but left during his junior year to focus on his writing career.

During this time, Scott held a number of ordinary jobs, most of which he despised. For two weeks, as the junior member of a Jack In the Box night shift, he cleaned grease traps before finally handing in his paper cap. He worked as a data entry clerk at Solar, a major San Diego manufacturer, and spent an enjoyable period working by the ocean at Scripp's Institute of Oceanography as a member of the typing pool. He loved being near the Pacific, and, because he was classed as an "On-call, emergency typist" when there was no work, he was allowed to work on his own writing.

> When I worked at Scripp's Institute of Oceanography in La Jolla (probably in 1976), at the Ocean Systems Laboratory, I spent much of my time reading such works as The Golden Bough and Wicca in front of my IBM Selectric II™ at the lab a few yards from the ocean.

He also enjoyed working at Sea World, a major marine park on the edge of San Diego's Mission Bay. His love of water and of the creatures that inhabit it made his time there pleasant, though he keenly felt the pain of the incarcerated animals.

Scott often generously offered his services to a number of bookstores, filling in when they needed someone. With his quick tongue and ready magical knowledge, he was at his best in the occult and metaphysical stores, where he expertly directed customers to the books they needed. As he worked with customers, Scott became more and more aware that books such as the ones he was working on simply were not available. One letter he wrote in 1978 expresses some of his frustration getting the books he felt were so sorely needed in to the hands of the public, as well as information on how he felt magical herbalism was best defined:

> *. . . I'd be glad to share some herb magic with everyone. It's definitely time that Witches re-learn the old lore; it's fading and dying fast . . .*
>
> *Herb magic is vibrational magic. The flowers, trees, and herbs of our planet emit vibrations. The quality of these vibes determines the herb's usefulness in magic: positive vibrations are used in protective, loving, healing and beneficent rituals; negative vibes are used in cursing, banishing illnesses, and so on. The amount of vibrations present in the herb determines its power; a three year old battery won't light the flashlight like a new battery will. Thus, the fresher an herb is, the more power it contains.*
>
> *Modern science has proved that these powers exist, through the invention and subsequent use of Kirilian photography. It is these "auras" and energy fields which power herbal magic; the magic is in the herbs.*
>
> *Naturally, this power is increased by your own. To enchant an herb, simply tell it what you want it to do. For instance, when picking a sprig of rosemary to help you study, say something like, "I pluck thee, oh spirit of rosemary, that thou shalt aid my concentration and memory." Thus, the herb is infused with your own Intent, and the power of the herb is focused upon your own desire.*
>
> *The magical side of herbalism has for long lain dormant, forgotten. For those who wish to tread the garden path, however, there are wonders waiting at every turn.*
>
> *(T)his is the "secret" of magical herbalism. It has never been said in such plain and simple words, at least not in my experience. I've written two books on the subject—three, actually, including my "herbal grimoire" which is nothing short of a BOS [Book of Shadows] written with the extensive use of herbs in mind—but have never sold any of them. The publishers say, "There isn't a large enough market for this type of book." I agree, there isn't. That's why I've begun sending them out to occult publishers and maybe, through Her grace, I'll get one sold!*[1]

Enchantment in San Diego

In November of 1979, Scott's friend, Ginny, mentioned that there was a new occult store in San Diego, "Ye Olde Enchantment Shoppe." At his first opportunity, Scott went to the small shop on Adams Avenue. He met Judith Wise, one of the owners. There was an immediate rapport between Scott and Judy. She would have a lasting influence on Scott's magical philosophy and training. Before long, Scott was filling in at the bookstore and teaching classes on various subjects. Ultimately, Scott and Judy would "trade initiations" and work together in two systems: Scott's own American Traditionalist, and the Myjestic, a system with roots in rural Oklahoma, Indian lore, and folk magic from Europe. In addition to working magic with her for many years, Scott would continue to teach classes and write articles for Judy throughout his life.

In 1980, Scott and his sister Christine decided the time was right to move out from their parent's house into a place of their own. They selected an upstairs, two-bedroom apartment at 4349 Orange Avenue in East San Diego, overlooking a billboard on which the landlord plastered hardline Bible verses until the televangelist scandals of the 1980s moderated his statements. After a few months, Christine moved in with her fiancé, Tom Ashworth, leaving the apartment to Scott.

Scott was determined to make it on his own, despite financial difficulties. If he needed more money, he worked harder and ate less, practically starving himself. He also did some "book scouting," poring over the cheap book shelves at the Salvation Army thrift stores for volumes he could resell to book dealers. Frequently, Scott would take a space at Kobey's Swap Meet, a huge open-air flea market, held each weekend in the San Diego Sports Arena parking lot. There he sold books, often precious ones from his personal collection, and whatever bric-a-brac he could bear to part with that week.

At one point, Scott drew up plans to sell incenses, oils, spells and other witchy items at the Swap Meet. He never quite moved ahead on this idea. Some of the ideas he discussed for the swap meet Scott later created for the "Crystal Cave" stores owned by his friend Annella Carter. He created several nicely packaged "Spell Kits" for love, health, and money. Each kit contained a tiny bottle of oil compounded by Scott, a special candle, appropriate herbs, and complete instructions. Very few of the kits sold.

Shortly after meeting Judy, another magical individual literally moved into Scott's life: Don Kraig rented Scott's spare room on Leap Year day, February 29, 1980.[2] The next day Scott recorded his reaction: "Don Kraig—interesting! Knows a lot. Doesn't laugh at my jokes."

Scott was attempting a vegetarian diet at this time, and his diary entries are full of food: what he's eaten, what he hasn't, what he should and shouldn't be eating. He writes about this period, appropriately enough, in *The Magic In Food*:

> *I did, indeed, once try a strict vegetarian diet, under the guidance of a long-time vegetarian and ceremonial magician. He taught me how to combine proteins so that I wouldn't undernourish myself. It was an interesting experience avoiding all animal proteins and fat (did you know that lard is an ingredient of Oreo cookies?), but I quickly realized that it wasn't right for me. By the second week of my diet, my head was constantly bumping into the ceiling. Walking became a mystical experience. Colors were brighter, I felt lighter, and my awakened psychic abilities were always present. This was pleasantly surprising, but I soon had an experience that changed my feelings.*
>
> *I was in a friend's occult-supplies shop one night as she was closing. It was just after dark. I stood staring at a painting in my by-now usual "wow, man!" attitude as she turned off the lights. Though plenty of light shone in through the windows from the street, the painting dissolved into blackness. There, where the picture used to be, I saw something that I can't describe.[3] It scared the heck out of me.*
>
> *My friend's store was under physical and psychic bombardment from an evangelical, fundamentalist Christian organization that occupied an adjoining suite. Someone had recently thrown a brick through her store's window. In the inky painting, I saw an image of all the hatred being sent her way. In my completely opened psychic state (which was a direct result of my strict vegetarian diet), this manifestation of negative energy*

*shocked my entire being. I went outside as soon as I could, shook
it off, calmed myself and went about my business.*

*Soon, I went back to my normal diet. Even though I'd been
receiving the proper amount of protein, even though I'd been
taking vitamin and mineral supplements, even though my food
intake was being closely monitored by a vegetarian who'd
followed a similar regimen for over fifteen years, the diet left me
so spiritually and psychically open that I couldn't handle it.*

At this time, Scott was finding that affording food itself was difficult.
One week he subsisted mostly on steamed broccoli, not by intention, but
because it was on sale for only forty-nine cents a pound. Scott notes an
evening where he was taken out by Ed Snowden with a group for a
Chinese dinner, and was given the packaged leftovers to take home. He
notes happily in his diary:

Prosperity ritual attacks again!

Fortunate changes were in the wind. The prosperity rites he
performed were about to "attack" in full force, bringing a richness of
friends and new success.

1. Letter to "Pat" of the Church of Wicca dated January 26, 1978.
2. Don Kraig writes of this time on page 212. (Appendix I: Friends and Readers
   Remember.)
2. Although Scott is evasive here, at the time he thought it was an image of the devil.

Part II

Branching Out

1972–1983

Night be my cloak, the Moon my lamp,
Gathering herbs in the glade.
Sheltered by Oaks, a sweet energy hums
Deep in each root, bud, and blade.
— Scott Cunningham

Chapter Four

The Birth of
Magical Herbalism

THE GIFTS OF THE EARTH WERE NEVER FAR FROM SCOTT'S HANDS, heart, or mind. Constantly crafting magic using herbs, he kept building his loving rapport with the species around him. Walking along a sidewalk where straggly plants reached toward the sun through cracks in the cement, Scott would honor these "weeds" and mention to anyone with him their potential powers in magic. His kitchen overflowed with packets of herbs, spices, and resins. He was continually experimenting.

Scott had been collecting information on herbs since he first began the practice of magic in 1971. Now, he decided that the time had come to make a serious effort at publishing what he knew of the magic of herbs, and he sent out the following "query letter" to many publishers.

Dear Sir,

I am working on a book concerning the magical powers of herbs. This non-fiction book, entitled A Witch's Herbal, is not a cursory look at the topic, but a practical, how-to guide to unlock the powers of herbs.

It is neither cookbook nor medical adviser. It is a book which explores the famous, "forgotten" herbal lore of the Witches.

A Witch's Herbal shows the reader how to use herbs to protect the home, see the future, cure headaches, promote or cool love, attract wealth, find sexual happiness and improve the mind. The practical applications of the powers of herbs are limitless.

It is written for the housewife, the truckdriver, the executive and the secretary. It is a practical book, a complete guide to magical herbalism, and it's (sic) time has arrived, with the lingering popularity of the occult (especially in the fiction category) and the boom in herbs.

I'd like to send you three sample chapters and a chapter-by-chapter outline for your attention.

I hope that this fits into your editorial needs, and that I will be hearing from you soon.

But early responses to his query letters and, later, reviews of sample material were not encouraging.

New American Library, March 21, 1978 "*. . . we are not looking for an herb book of any type.*"

Lyle Stuart, March 27, 1978 "*. . . (We) are not considering any new manuscripts for the foreseeable future. This policy applies to the Lyle Stuart imprint as well as to books published by our Citadel Press and University Books, Inc.*"

Avon Books, April 5, 1978 "*Your proposal is very good. . . but I'm afraid the book is a little too special for us and I don't see a way we could do it.*"

St. Martin's Press, July 27, 1978 "*Our editorial committee has decided that we cannot add this title to our list at this time.*"

Warner Books Inc. (undated) *"Dear Writer, We regret that we cannot use the material which you suggested for the current Warner Books line."*

Stein and Day (undated) *". . . we do not feel that it is right for our list at this time."*

Samuel Weiser *"Dear Mr. Cunningham, Thanks very much for your letter of June 28th concerning your manuscript* Magical Herbalism: Secrets of the Witches. *It sounds very interesting but . . . we are so backlogged in our publishing schedule that we are not able to consider any new projects. We do want to thank you for thinking of us and wish you well in your work."*

Scott's notes on other publishers are more succinct:

David Mc Kay . . . No 7/20

Grosset & Dunlap . . . No 7/20

Coward, McCann, Geohegan . . . No 7/17

A letter from Prentice-Hall, who gave *A Witch's Herbal* serious consideration, was more personal and included a suggestion for a change in title.

I found the lore in your Witch's Herbal *prospectus most interesting, but don't feel our firm could market it as successfully as some of our competitors. For one thing, there seems to be a preponderance of ritual over results; our books need extensive case histories to illustrate how the reader can derive his benefits. I also feel that this book cries out for illustrations from old herbals, and could be best handled by a house with an extensive gardening line.*

The editor mentions the prevailing attitude toward Wicca and related subjects in publishing companies at that time:

Witchcraft in general is rather low in the roster of occult topics, and so The Magic of Herbs *is a title that might appeal to a wider audience. Hope these suggestions are of some help.*

Finally, a positive response came from Carl Weschscke at Llewellyn Publications. He would accept the book, along with some revisions and additional material, such as a section on baneful herbs. Scott had omitted any potentially negative material in his original version, fearing that discussing baneful herbs might incite their misuse. In 1979, Scott met with Sandra Weschcke, who was visiting San Diego with her son Gabriel. On Carl's suggestion, she had dinner with their new author, and found him charming. Later, he met with Carl when the Weschckes again visited San Diego. Even so, *Magical Herbalism*'s path to publication was still a rocky one. The manuscript was finally completed in 1980 and Llewellyn released it in 1982.

Scott's own account of his efforts to sell *A Witch's Herbal* shed light on why he didn't go directly to Llewellyn:

> Magical Herbalism *began as* A Witch's Herbal. *I sent out dozens of query letters to publishers throughout the United States and even Britain. Most publishers thought that there wasn't enough interest in the subject matter to buy the book.*
>
> *Finally, as a last, desperate resort, I sent a query letter to Carl Weschcke[1] (I picked Llewellyn last because I knew that they didn't pay advances[2]) in 1979. He asked to see my outline and three sample chapters. I sent these to him; a year later I sent him the entire mss., after having incorporated some of his suggestions (such as the appendix of "baneful herbs"). They finally published it in 1982. (I was amazed and delighted when this book was published in Dutch in 1984; reading the Dutch translation, however, gave me a headache—not nearly close enough to German to be intelligible.)*
>
> *In 1982, I self-published a pamphlet entitled* A Formula Book of Magical Incenses and Oils.[3] *This 13-page pamphlet eventually became the seeds of* The Magic of Incense, Oils and Brews.
>
> *Before* Magical Herbalism *was published, I was working on* The Encyclopedia of Magical Herbs *and another book that eventually became* Earth Power.
>
> *David Harrington read aloud one of the chapters of this book on one night and made it sound as if I was a country preacher. I toned it down a bit after hearing it in that fashion.*

A Book is Born

In the Spring of 1982, *Magical Herbalism* was about to be released. Carl and Sandra Weschcke invited Scott to attend the American Booksellers Association (ABA) convention that June in Anaheim, California. Scott looked forward to seeing Carl and Sandra again, but hesitated to attend. He was already fighting a particularly nasty cold, he knew the ABA would be crowded, and he was wondering if the book would be ready on time. If Scott had any lingering doubts about his career as a writer, attending the ABA must have helped. He was warmly greeted by Carl and Sandra in their hotel suite near the Convention Center. Carl had a special surprise for Scott: the first author's copy of *Magical Herbalism*.

The wait was finally over.

Carl and Sandra Weschcke found Scott's combination of nervousness, wit, and intelligence enchanting. Their rapport grew. Scott's relationship with the Weschckes would range from playing ball with Gabriel, to sending off forceful letters to Carl if he thought Llewellyn was moving in the wrong direction. Though Carl and Sandra did not always agree with his viewpoint, Scott's opinions were always considered. His influence was felt at Llewellyn even in areas that did not directly affect him.

The ABA itself was overwhelming. The Anaheim location across from Disneyland was appropriate, since this was a Disneyland for lovers of the written word. Aisle after aisle was filled with display booths of hundreds of publishers, all presenting their newest works. It was hard to walk down an aisle and not come away loaded with giveaways, ranging from new hardback books to coffee mugs or bookbags. Scott described the ABA as "Trick-or-Treat for literary people," and came home weighted down with bags of books.

Inspired by his visit to the ABA, Scott surged ahead in his magical writing. A few months later, in December of 1982, Scott finished *Earth Power*. It was promptly accepted by Llewellyn and published in 1983. He began working on the *Encyclopedia of Magical Herbalism*, wrapping it up in November of 1983. *Magical Herbalism* was selling well, and had just entered its third printing. Scott, however, was still broke. There were still periods when there would be no income from royalties, due to the unpredictability of book orders. Scott was doing extensive research for his planned *Mesopotamian Magic* book.

Although Scott had been a published author for several years, he still was thinking of looking for supplemental work, especially during months when he barely had enough to eat. The long effort to guide *Magical Herbalism* into print made him doubtful that his occult writing would ever be enough to support him. As of 1984, his income from all sources, including his car articles, Spur novels, and Llewellyn books was only $500 a month. He polished his resume in 1982.

Scott Cunningham
4349 Orange Avenue
San Diego, California 92105

Summary of Skills: *Researching, orga-nizing, and writing non-fiction magazine articles. Researching and writing monthly columns. Composing advertising copy. Writing full-length novels.*

Summary of Achievements: *Numerous published articles. Three columns. Sixteen published novels.*

Education: *San Diego State University, 1974-1977. Major: English.*

Additional Skills: *70 WPM typing. Photographer (black and white). Transcrip-tion. Operation of photocopying equipment. Proofreading.*

Personal Data: *Birth date: 6/27/56. Marital status: single.*

At this time, most of Scott's income was derived from the mass-market novels he was writing at the rate of about one every four or five weeks. His top output in one day was an amazing eighty-two pages of completed text.

Scott did not regard these novels as great literature, but he felt that he did a competent job with them. Many of them are still in print ten years later and some were recently reprinted in special double-editions. Here's a taste of one of his Spur McCoy novels that provided the income to let him write his magical books:

> The man's weight around his arm felt like it was about to snap his knees. Groaning, Spur yanked, pulled and shoved a blubbering Enoch Salt toward Sheriff Tex Frank's office.
>
> Salt drowsed along the way, his big body slumping down, further hindering their progress. Each time the man's chin hit his chest McCoy backhanded him, rousing Salt for another half-block or so.
>
> It took him nearly ten minutes to clear the distance between the Red Ace Saloon and the sheriff's office. He finally halted before the closed door, yanked the knob and kicked it open.
>
> He shoved Enoch Salt forward. The big man stumbled, blinked at the bright light and melted into a heap of pulsing flesh at Tex Frank's feet.
>
> "Brought you some company," Spur said.

Written under the pen name of "Dirk Fletcher," the Spur novels are sexy, violent stories set in the Old West. The series was created by Chet Cunningham as a way to provide Scott with a regular writing income, such as his father had enjoyed writing other series. Chet developed the series concept, sold it, and then he and Scott both wrote the novels for the series. The Spur novels were enjoyable and easy to read but Scott's friends paid attention primarily to see what mischief Scott had done. He was notorious for parodying his friends by using their first or last names. Women friends particularly suffered, since most of the women in the Spur books were prostitutes or criminals. Male friends might fare better and be cast as another lawman, but they, too, were more frequently recognized as outlaws.

Many aspiring writers, presenting one or another "explanation" to Scott why they had not yet written, would find him inspirational yet unsympathetic. He had earned his right to write what he wanted through years of crafting articles and books so boring to him he could hardly stay awake at the typewriter. He was impatient with anyone waiting for the ideal conditions to work.

Classes

Although thousands of people would later attend classes taught by Scott Cunningham, his 1980 classes in San Diego were usually poorly attended, perhaps an illustration of the old adage: "No man is a prophet in his own country." This situation changed when his roommate, Don Kraig, arranged for Scott to teach in northern San Diego county. This class was very well attended and, for the first time, Scott was warmly welcomed by a group of strangers, many of them well-educated in the magical arts, who knew and respected him through his published works. Llewellyn was also beginning to actively promote its authors, and set up opportunities for Scott to reach his public. In October 1986, Carl and Sandra flew Scott back to Minneapolis to take advantage of the media's usual hunger for "witchy" shows around Halloween. For several days, Scott could hardly open his mouth to speak without a camera or a microphone recording his words. He appeared on a show for Group W cable, appeared on "Twin Cities Live," and did interviews on KUOM radio and Geoff Charles show on KSTP talk radio. In between, he went to Selena Fox's Circle Sanctuary, did a booksigning, and taught a workshop on Natural Magic.

Tours and Teaching

Scott writes in his autobiography about his teaching experiences:

> I taught my first class in 1980, at a store known as Ye Olde Enchantment Shop in San Diego. After that first terrifying ordeal, about which I can remember little, I taught several more times at the store.
> In 1983, at Don Kraig's urging, I taught at a store about forty minutes north of San Diego. After that the sky was the limit. A

later trip took me to Los Angeles, where I spoke at a store there. Soon afterward I did my first class at Eye of the Cat in Long Beach. Then, at various times, I taught in Costa Mesa (California), San Francisco, San Jose, Oakland, Las Vegas, Denver, Springs, Kansas City (Kansas) Norman (Oklahoma), Sandusky (Ohio), Cleveland, Detroit, Metairie (Louisiana), Baton Rouge, Bloomfield (New Jersey), New York City and Buffalo (New York), and probably many other places of which I have no memory.

I never have relished teaching, and I'm not very good at it. I seem to have some ability to transfer my knowledge to others through this technique (thanks to my acting training), but I've never had the true need to teach.

I've done my best at various times throughout the last decade to meet with people and to show them some of the ways that I've learned, but teaching has never been my métier.

Individual classes were never a problem. I showed up, taught, met some nice people, and left. However, tours were another matter. They always left me exhausted. I remember one time, after being on the road for nearly three weeks, looking up at the sky and being thrilled that I was actually below the clouds for a change.

Here's one example of a typical Cunningham junket from 1989:

April 13: Arrive Detroit
April 14: Four hour workshop
April 15: Lecture
April 16: Lecture at "Curiosities"
April 17: Booksigning
April 18: To Sandusky, Ohio. Booksigning.
April 19: Class: Magical Aromatherapy; Magical Foods
April 20: To Minneapolis/St.Paul. Booksigning.
April 21: Lecture
April 22: Workshop
April 23: Free
April 24: Return home

In a flyer dated March 2, 1981, one of these classes, "Wicca," is described: ". . . a class in the ancient, pre-Christian religion of Wicca will begin. Enrollment will be limited to seven people. There is no charge for the class, except for a small amount for printed materials (about two dollars). The class will be held in the home of its teacher, Arthur, which is located near the Shoppe." The curriculum for the course, lasting seven consecutive Monday nights, promised to cover "The Basics of Wicca: The Gods, the Elements, Reincarnation, The Power, The Tools of Wicca, The Magic Circle, The Sabbats, Magic, Herbalism, Polarity, and the Wiccan Way." In addition, practical instruction would be given in "Meditation, Concentration, Relaxation, Visualization, Clairvoyance, Healing, Magical Breathing Techniques and Protection." Completion of the course would lead to an advanced course and, possibly, to initiation into Wicca.

Scott, teaching under the name of Arthur, is described as "High Priest of American Traditionalist Wicca and an initiate in three other traditions besides his own . . ."[4]

This class announcement ends with "Wicca: The Religion of the Past— The Religion of the Future. Blessed Be."

Scott also taught many classes at Lucy Brown's Magick Bookstore in National City, as well as appearing at most of the metaphysical and New Age bookstores in San Diego at one time or another. As his book grew popular, requests for classes rose, and it was a rare week that he wasn't teaching some aspect of magic somewhere.

Along with his new success in teaching classes, Scott began to receive fan mail from readers of his book *Magical Herbalism*. He found the letters flattering and surprising. He tried to answer all he received until the number grew too overwhelming. Scott still read each letter carefully, and took his readers' comments to heart.

Scott was delighted with most of the letters he received, and when he received one which indicated that the writer had a genuine interest or need for extra information, he would send back page after page of material. One reader sent him a letter asking for the magical uses of twenty different stones she wanted to know about. He researched some answers and replied to others out of his own knowledge, sending back the information in a long letter.

Other letters disturbed and depressed him. Each month, he would receive a handful of letters from people who had supposedly read his books, but completely missed his meanings. One reader would ask how to put a curse on someone, or would blame all life's challenges on some wicked curse aimed at them, asking Scott to remove the bad magic or do magical battle on their behalf. In the early years, Scott responded to these letters, patiently restating his position on the natural, positive powers of magic and suggesting ways these people could help themselves. When he believed readers were facing genuine danger, he would often call them and give some no-nonsense advice, referring them to the appropriate agencies for help. Many times, he received letters that were beyond the scope of gentle transformative magic, and required more physical intervention.

In one column written for "Ask Scott," his regular article for the *Llewellyn New Times*, he responds to a letter that asked him why he suggested that another reader get physical, not magical, help for her problems. He reiterated some of his basic beliefs about magic:

- *We create our futures every second that we live.*
- *We must take responsibility for our lives.*
- *Magic is not a cure-all; it is a tool that is used in conjunction with other tools.*
- *Magic is effective only if the magician allows it to be effective; only if she or he wants and needs positive change.*
- *Magic doesn't work overnight.*

. . . The techniques of self-transformation contained in magic books will be effective only if they are conscientiously applied. Some may well read such books for their "entertainment" value, just as some people watch exercise videos but never move from the breakfast table.

However, magical techniques are effective if they're properly applied, with the certain knowledge that they will work, backed up by a true, lasting desire and need to change.

Some books are, of course, written by charlatans to make money, but books of this nature are published in every field (especially weight-loss). Most metaphysical writers know that their techniques are effective and certainly don't write them for the amusement of others.

. . . Few of us claim to have all the answers. Indeed: magic isn't an answer. It's a tool that, correctly applied, may create answers.

. . . You have no way of knowing this, C., but I've spent my share of time phoning and writing to many, many desperate persons. I've talked them out of committing suicide, urged them to leave a husband who beats them, tried to convince them that drug use is no answer, and supported their desire to receive help for alcoholism.

I've referred these persons to help centers, crisis telephone lines, battered women's shelters, hospitals, M.D.'s, psychologists and counselors—and have never charged a dime for my large phone bills, or tried to sell such persons my books.

When a person writes to me in despair, I try to direct them to the tools that will give them the most help, in the quickest amount of time. I don't tell them to light candles or toss herbs over their shoulder if they're being beaten by a mate. I urge them to get more immediate and human help—from sources such as those mentioned in the above paragraph.

Many turn to magic out of desperation. Magic, however, is not a panacea. It cannot immediately remove decades of self-abuse, incorrect decisions, anti-evolutionary behavior and untrained thought. It is a tool which can eventually lead to great change, but it isn't supernatural.

You wish to be healed? Do a healing spell—but also listen to doctors, take the correct medication, and really, truly want and need to be healed. Too many of us enjoy the luxury of illness: days off from work and other responsibilities, being the center of attention, basking in the concern and care of loved ones. if you're sick and wish to continue being sick, no spell or drug will cure you. Even doctors agree with this. However, if you need and wish to be healed, you will be.

. . . You can rub the lamp until your arm falls off and no genie will pop out to solve all of your problems. Put down that

lamp, examine your life, and discover what's inconsistent with your goals. When you discover this, use magic as a tool to facilitate positive change, if you wish, but also use other resources: counselors, doctors, lawyers, financial consultants, employment centers, shelters, crisis lines. Continuous positive thinking is also a key.

Magic can be effective only when it's used by a person familiar with its techniques, and when it's backed up with the necessary changes that also must be made within the magician.

1. Carl Llewellyn Weschcke, owner and active head of Llewellyn Worldwide. At the time, Carl was handling submissions personally.
2. Llewellyn did pay advances, but not to first-time authors.
3. See Appendix for the complete text of this booklet.
4. "His own" tradition referred to the American Traditionalist system which he had created. Much of the original *Book of Shadows* for this system was included in *Wicca: A Guide for the Solitary Practitioner* as the *Standing Stones Book of Shadows*. Scott also distributed a training manual for the American Traditionalist system.

Chapter Five

A Genie
Breaks a Bottle

I N 1980, SCOTT WAS SPENDING MUCH OF HIS TIME TRANSCRIBING THE magical instructions and insights provided by Ruth Phillips to a friend of his, Mel Fuller. Phillips was the last surviving member of a traditional Scottish family system that had never before been written down. Phillips was sending the surviving information and additional material that she was discovering intuitively on tape to Mel. Scott was already studying a Celtic system with Fuller, the Reorganized Traditional Gwythonic Order, and he was delighted to be involved with the creation, or at least the standardization, of another new system. Scott accepted the task of converting the taped instructions to words on paper. He looked at his transcription duties as a sacred service.

I (David Harrington) recall the events that led to my first meeting with Scott. I had been seeking magical paths for a long time, approaching and then retreating from the path, with unsatisfactory results. The beginning of my own magical journey started in High School where I met this raven-haired girl whose ancestors were Gypsies from Lithuania. We dabbled with the Ouija board, her aunt read the cards for us as well as our tea leaves, and we bought and read *Fate* magazine faithfully. I also remember buying and devouring the book *Diary of a Witch*, the life and times of the famous Witch Sybil Leek. What a wonderful time this was, not only my first love with a girl, but also my first love with magic. Then came Vietnam and the magic was gone, not only for me, but for countless others.

When I got discharged from the service I moved to San Diego to start anew. Finding a job, setting up a household, and making new friends soon filled up most of my time. I still occasionally picked up a copy of *Fate* magazine, but I could not recapture that happier time. As the seventies came to a close I felt an emptiness that could not be explained. Looking back I now realize I was soul hungry.

Then, one evening at a pool tournament, I met Mel. For the first time in years I was talking to someone who knew where I was coming from. Soon we were kneedeep in a conversation that was liberally sprinkled with magic. As time passed Mel and I became good friends. Mel's house became a peaceful oasis for me and I always looked forward to the quiet times I spent there.

One evening I called Mel to see if I could come over to visit. He said sure, there was another friend visiting that he wanted me to meet. I was hesitant, as I am painfully shy at times and it's hard for me to meet new people. Mel assured me I would be comfortable around this person, so I went. When I got there I was introduced to Scott Cunningham.

Scott was an imposing figure. He could literally fill a room with his body and his personality. His wit was sharp and a well-aimed word could cut through the air with crackling energy. As Scott surged forth, I retreated. I did not stay long. I later learned Scott sometimes used this tactic when he himself was uncomfortable.

The next day I called Mel and told him I did not like Scott at all and to please never put us together again in any situation. There was a small chuckle from the other end of the phone as Mel told me that Scott had just called him to say the same about me.

I still visited Mel, and on occasion I would see Scott. Out of respect for Mel we were civil to each other and would even exchange a few words.

Mel's work took him out of town frequently, and he often asked Scott to housesit for him while he was away.

On one of those occasions my phone rang late at night and it was Scott on the other end. This was strange since Scott had never called me before, and he sounded upset. It seemed that in the middle of the night while Scott slept, two glass decanters on the bedroom dresser suddenly exploded, sending glass and liquids all over the room. This unnerved Scott, as it would anyone. He found my phone number among Mel's things and called me to relieve the tension of this weird situation. I imagined he may have just wanted to hear a human voice in the middle of the night.

We talked for hours on that dark night and somewhere along the course of that conversation my life was changed forever. Now when I visited, I was disappointed if Scott wasn't there. That call in the middle of the night had broken the magical ice, and Scott and I became friends. We were both very shy people, but we just projected it differently.

I knew that Scott had written many articles for magazines and was hoping to have a book published. One day in 1981, Mel called and said to come over because there was a special occasion to celebrate. When I got to the house, there was Scott with a huge grin on his face, his first published book, *Curse of Valkyrie House*, in his hands. Celebrate we did. I knew Scott was also working on a more serious work dealing with herbs and magic, later to be published by Llewellyn Publishing as *Magical Herbalism*.

At this time, all of our conversations dealing with magic were very general. As the three of us became closer friends and since I spent so much time with them, it could not be hidden any longer. One day they just sat me down and told me bluntly that they were both Witches. I was flabbergasted. The only contact I had with real Witches was reading about Sybil Leek and the stereotypical Witch one sees on a broom at Halloween. These two men in front of me did not fit into either category.

Then they explained what a Witch was, described the religion of Wicca, and told me both men as well as women could be Witches. They still wanted to be my friends but they wanted me to know the truth. They also told me that this was not a recruitment and that only one's heart could lead to this religion and way of life.

If strangers had told me this, I would have fled instantly. But these two people were trusted friends and I knew no evil lived in their hearts, so there must be something positive to this thing called Wicca. As months passed, I asked many questions about this religion, and found in time this path was for me. Both of them told me to wait and to make sure this was the right choice for me, as this was a serious decision and could not be taken lightly. They told me to wait a year and a day. I did, and the answer was a firm yes. It was decided that Scott was to be my teacher because of conflicts with Mel's work schedule. Slowly, I went through the three degrees of our tradition. Scott was a generous and gentle teacher and his guidance into the craft was a loving journey.

Scott believed that there should be no limitations on one's magical growth, especially when it came to the written word. Books, books, and more books were given to me and I studied them avidly. Most of these books dealt with Wicca and magic combined with books on archeology, folk tales, astrology, and more.

After finishing a required text, Scott would light some candles, brew some mint tea and we would sit down and discuss whatever subject the book had covered. His knowledge was vast and he could converse intelligently on almost any subject. Many evenings the wick would burn low in the candle as we talked well past the witching hour.

Scott thought that magic and worship should not be constrained within a structure or "concrete cave" as he laughingly referred to modern housing. So, it was decided that some of my lessons were to be taught outside, with the Elements surrounding us. I was glad of this, since after months of study and research and experimentation I knew that magic practiced out in nature could be a powerful experience.

These training sites were as widespread and as varied as Scott's imagination and our transportation allowed. At times I would find myself with him in the desert, the mountains, at the beach or even on an island. All of these places were accessible from San Diego in a matter of hours.

One of these first excursions took place in the Anza-Borrego desert about an hour and a half from San Diego. Scott had heard of a rumored fossil site near an old desert town called Ocotillo Wells. The fossils had supposedly been uncovered in a recent sand storm, and Scott wanted to find and explore the site. So off we went.

It was early morning on a spring day when we pulled into the sleepy town of Ocotillo Wells. The thermometer was already creeping to the eighty degree mark. The town itself consisted of a few weathered buildings facing each other across a cracked and sunbaked road. After some inquiry we were told of a place where fossils might be found.

The road ended at the edge of town so we found a safe place for the car, put on our backpacks and stepped into the desert which had been an ancient sea, millions of years ago. The weather was balmy and the air was pungent with earthy desert scents. Our destination was a low ridge of hills that spilled into the desert about a mile away. Around mid-morning we reached our goal. At first we didn't see a thing. Then it hit us like a thunderbolt—the fossils were at our very feet, just as they had been left ages ago when this prehistoric ocean had dried into desert. As we knelt down we discovered fossilized sand dollars, clam shells, and beautiful corals. We were absolutely spellbound with the beauty of these ancient relics of another age. The fossils were in pristine condition due to the protecting sands that had covered them for eons. And here we were possibly the first humans to stand at this spot on this ancient sea bed with its treasure scattered at our feet. Talk about energy—the very air hummed with it! After walking and collecting a bit we miraculously came upon a small stream where we decided to rest. While we sat by the gentle waters Scott told me some of the lore and uses of fossils in magic. He said that fossils were most protective when placed in the home or carried on the person. While going through the finds of the day, Scott held up a spectacular fossilized sand dollar that he had found. He told me that sand dollars which show a natural five-pointed design are often found on Wiccan altars, are linked with the pentagram, and are held in high regard.

Scott also showed me his rite of collecting. He told me that when collecting specimens out in nature to show reverence at all times and take only what is needed. He cautioned me to not rape or plunder the earth, for to do so is to ravage the Goddess herself.

Scott taught by example, and on many occasions I have seen him reverently asking the earth for some of her substance. Even then, Scott would take only a small conservative amount and always leave an offering. Frequently, the offering was copal incense. Scott was an early environmentalist and felt that incense was a perfect offering since it was biodegradable. Another favorite offering was a bright shiny quarter. The roundness of the quarter and the silver color reminded him of the moon, and he often tossed these in wishing wells.

While we rested by the stream and talked, a wind came up and gained strength. We left the stream and headed back toward the car. As we looked behind us, the new wind was already blowing the sands back over the ancient sea, reclaiming once more this most magical place.

On crisp fall days, Scott's attention turned toward the mountains east of San Diego. Usually, our destination was the rustic mining town of Julian, high up in the Cleveland National Forest. The drive to Julian was always a pleasure as it passed through some of the most scenic areas in San Diego county. From Scott's apartment we would travel north about thirty miles and then head inland on Highway 67. We would pass the San Diego Wild Animal Park, where we could see antelopes, zebras, and gazelles grazing peacefully on the rolling hillsides. After the park the road opens onto green farmlands dotted with fine old country homes. Our first stop on these field trips was at the small town of Santa Ysabel where we would pause at Dudley's, a huge roadside bakery, and enjoy homemade bearclaws with steaming cups of coffee.

One of the most memorable of these trips took place in early November. Coming out of Dudley's Bakery, our eyes were caught by a gleaming white building in the distance. Deciding to explore, we got into the car and headed toward it. It was a small Spanish-style church made of adobe brick, layered over with a glaze of bright white stucco. By happenstance we had stumbled onto the landmark for which Santa Ysabel is named—the Santa Ysabel Mission—a "helper-mission" founded in 1818 to handle converts in an area too remote to allow them to attend services at the main mission. Scott noted a sign welcoming visitors, so we went inside.

The interior of the mission was beautiful. The walls and ceilings were covered by colorful folk-art murals depicting animals, flowers, and soaring birds. The murals had been designed and painted by local Indian and Mexican artisans.

Leaving the sanctuary by a side door, we stepped outside into a court-yard, and found to our surprise that it was the mission cemetery. It was unlike any cemetery I had ever seen before. On the graves were paper-maché flowers in vivid shades of orange, blue and green. Glowing candles marked the boundaries of each grave and on the headstones were foods of different kinds. I turned to Scott with a hundred questions, but he silenced me with a gesture and answered quietly, "Dave, I'll answer your questions when we get back to the car."

I wasn't surprised at Scott's reticence to begin a lesson in the presence of the grave rituals around us. One of Scott's ethics was not to disturb other people's space, especially when it came to their individual religious practices. He abhorred the idea of barging in and making oneself a nuisance among others' sacred sites. If you were invited, that was another matter, but even then he felt it was essential that you should show the utmost respect and reverence at all times.

Here at Santa Ysabel was a perfect example of this ethic in action, because Scott realized we had accidentally come upon someone's private devotions and it would have been disrespectful to stay and treat this as a tourist attraction. Once we were safely back in the car and heading again to the mountains, Scott explained to me what we had come upon in the churchyard. On the second of November, Mexicans come together to celebrate the "Dia De Los Muertos," or, literally, the "Day of the Dead." This custom is no longer widespread, even in Mexico, but here in this tiny pocket of California the traditions of this holiday are still handed on. On this November day, families gather at the cemetery to commune with their departed ones. This is not a sad time but a joyful one for it is believed on this day the world of the living and the world of the dead are quite close and each is aware of the other. The family members dress in their most colorful finery and meet at the graveside to clean and repair the site while strolling mariachi bands play festive music. Later, as the sun goes down and night falls, flowers, food, and candles are laid upon the grave both for the living and the dead to enjoy. Scott summed up with his opinion that "Dia De Los Muertos" was a very magical and healthy way to deal with the death experience. And of course, he added, it paralleled the Celtic day of "Samhain" which falls around the same date, as well as other festivals of the dead around the world.

As Scott unfolded this tale, we left the flatlands and climbed the winding road toward Julian. The highway cuts through steep mountain passes covered over by majestic pine. The air at this altitude was crisp and clear and the sky on this day was a vivid blue, the color of cornflowers. Scenic viewspots were scattered along the way, and Scott liked to use these as a starting point to identify and collect herbs indigenous to the mountains. On this occasion, he had spied some white sage growing off the road, so we stopped to collect some. We went down into a nearby ravine, since Scott was adamant that we collect herbs that were not contaminated with roadside dust and pollutants.

As was his habit, he picked only a few leaves from each bush. While we gathered leaves and smelled the tangy fragrance of the herb, Scott explained how it is used in purification ceremonies and is especially good for use in purifying the home. He told me to dry the sage naturally and then crumble it onto smouldering charcoal bricks. This releases the plant's energies. When any negativity creeps into an area, this will cleanse it immediately.

After collecting a small bag of leaves and leaving a small offering, we headed back to continue our journey. Suddenly off to the side, we saw a strange sight—about four feet from our foot path there stood a medium-sized shrub completely covered in bright red. Stranger still, the bush seemed to be alive and moving. With some caution, we approached to get a better look. When we realized what it was, a smile swept both our faces, for the bush was covered by thousands upon thousands of ladybugs. As we stood there, some took flight and one landed on Scott's t-shirt. He gently removed the bright red bug and put the tiny creature onto his hand. Taking a closer look, I noticed this one was a little bit different, for this ladybug was spotted with orange. Scott told me that these are the ladybugs you make a wish upon in folklore. Just then a gentle breeze came and the ladybug took to the air.

We hiked back to the car and resumed our journey. Soon we were in the town of Julian, California, founded in 1869 after gold was found in the area. The gold is long gone and the town now relies on tourism for its existence. The streets are lined with many of the original buildings from the gold rush days, with hitching posts, horse troughs, and cigar store Indian statues to match. It's easy to picture yourself back in the West during the late 1880s. Scott liked to stroll around the town exploring the shops. One regular stop was the old-fashioned candy store where he would buy rock candy by the bagful. The candle store naturally held his interest as he watched the candles being dipped by hand from a dipping wheel and then hung to dry. But his favorite place to visit was the folk art store filled with Amish quilts, Pennsylvania Dutch hex signs, apple head dolls, homemade potpourris, intricate wheat weavings, trivets, and cast iron cauldrons. As we looked through these treasures, Scott would tell me of their history and magical meanings. Here in Julian, more than in any other place, the seeds were planted for the books we would do together, *The Magical Household* and *Spellcrafts*.

Summer and winters were spent near the ocean. Living in San Diego makes this easy because all roads lead to the beach. This was the perfect environment for Scott, for he loved water. Water soothed him both spiritually and physically, especially the sea. Scott believed the waters from the oceans and all they touched to be doubly blessed. In Wiccan traditions, salt and water are added together to magically cleanse and consecrate. Here, then, in the sea, these two ingredients are naturally blended together creating a sacred place ready for magic to begin.

On a clear swept beach in the summer, Scott taught me the rune signs by taking a pointed piece of driftwood and inscribing the mystical symbols into the wet sand. Also on this natural blackboard, I would learn the witch's alphabet and various pictographs. One of Scott's favorite pictographs was the double trident (Figure 2) which he used for prosperity spells.

Scott liked to beachcomb in the summer. A good place for doing this in San Diego is Imperial Beach, close to the border of Mexico. Here he introduced me to an amazing sight, Mummy Island. Off the coast of Imperial Beach is a chain of islands called the Coronados. Set among them is a small isle in the shape of a mummy lying on its back. With Mummy Island as our backdrop we would hunt for shells and Scott would continue to

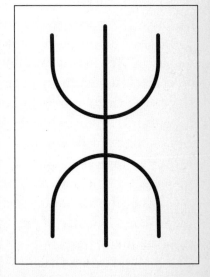

Figure 2. Scott's favorite pictograph of the double trident used for prosperity spells.

instruct me for the final initiation into our tradition as my apprentice years came to a close.

As a young boy, Scott collected shells and was very knowledgeable about them. He liked to have them on display in his home and also used them on his altar sites. Some of his favorites were sand dollars, moon shells, and the tiny conical shell called the chinaman's hat. Scott introduced me to mermaid tears, another treasure of the sea. These are small pieces of broken glass that have been worn down to a smooth beveled edge caused by the constant agitation of the sand and sea. Being so long in the ocean the glass has become oxidized forming a glazed patina. Most mermaid tears come in green, brown, and blue, but if you're lucky you might find a prized red one. Tears of the mermaid are rather elusive but Scott seemed to have an affinity for finding these jewel-like treasures, and he used them in spell bottles and charm bags.

The most magical spot Scott and I came across near the sea was indirectly found for us by the art department of Llewellyn Publications. Scott had finished the manuscript for his book *Earth Power* and the art department thought it would be a good idea if Scott would take photographs of the subject matter contained in the forthcoming book. These photos would be the basis for the illustrations by the Llewellyn artists.

So one Saturday, Scott rang me up and asked if I would join him on this project. We decided that the photos should be taken outside since the book dealt with magic out in nature, and since it was winter we headed to the beach. We knew we would need quiet and solitude so we decided on Point Loma, a high rocky peninsula jutting out from the mainland of San Diego. The view from Point Loma is spectacular, with the peaceful calm bay of San Diego on one side, while on the other the unrestrained ocean crashes on the rocky beach below.

At the tip of the peninsula is the Cabrillo lighthouse, built in 1854. This area is a state park and the old lighthouse is now a museum. Not far from this historical landmark is a steep winding road feeding down to the beach. The character of the land and sea here resembles the eastern seaboard states, very unlike the typical Southern California coastline usually found in San Diego.

On this day, Scott brought a large sack of materials to use in the photo shoot. Among them was this huge handmade broom. As we unloaded the car we were cheered by the solitude on the beach. For about two hours, Scott laid out designs and patterns to photograph, and he used me as a model for some of the photos.

By the beginning of the third hour, Scott was pleased with the day's results and called the session to a halt. We packed all the witchy paraphernalia back into the sack when Scott suddenly handed me the broom. With a mischievous look in his eyes, Scott said "Do you know what would be fun?"

"What?" I asked.

"Why don't you go to that outcropping of rock over there and get astride the broom. From this camera angle you'll look like you're flying." I refused. But, finally, Scott talked me into posing on the broom. Scott could be very persuasive when he wanted to be and soon I found myself on that damn broom pointed toward the ocean. Scott was so intent on taking this candid shot, and I was so busy balancing on the broom next to the cliff edge, that neither of us noticed we now had an audience.

"Excuse me, gentlemen, may I have a word with you?" We turned around and found ourselves face to face with a uniformed Park Ranger. I quickly dismounted from the broom with the sudden agility of a gold-medal gymnast and stood there beside Scott, hoping that a large wave would take us both out to sea and away from this embarrassing situation. We listened, a captive audience, while the Park Ranger revealed that he had been watching us, through binoculars, from his post up on top of the ridge. We had provided his entertainment for the entire length of the shoot. The problem, he lectured, was that only tourist photos were allowed to be taken on the grounds of the state park. Anything for potential publication—and here his eyes narrowed at us—was forbidden without the proper permits. He had the authority to confiscate our film if he desired.

But Scott, who ordinarily was an extremely honest individual, saw that this situation might not warrant perfect candor. "School project!" he protested quickly. "We're, uh, shooting this for a class, not for publication." He swallowed. Technically the photos were to be used only as illustration guides for Llewellyn's artists to follow. The Ranger was silent for a moment, looked us over, decided that we looked more like goofy college kids than professional photographers, and let us go. We packed up the car and went to the beach, laughing at our close escape and our confrontation with authority.

Then suddenly, we were struck silent. Another step down the narrow cliffside path had taken us around a small bend, and below us was an enchanting cove. We continued down the path onto the stony beach which was filled with a rainbow of ocean-smoothed rocks. One caught Scott's eye and he bent down to retrieve it. As he lifted the stone skyward, I could see there was a small round hole in the rock.

"Dave—look. It's a holey stone." He gave me the stone and I looked at it. Scott had never found one of these before. Most tales of holey stones, also known as hagstones, came from England. As I gazed at the rock, Scott told me their lore. "You can use these for scrying. Look through the hole and let your mind go blank. You're supposed to see visions through the opening."

They could also be used for protection, kept in the house or hung over doorways. We were delighted to find a source for these holed stones, magical objects that are from nature, not bought from a store.

This cove became one of our most treasured spots, and we named it, for us, "Hagstone Cove."

One evening not long after this day, Scott came to me. "Are you ready?" he said. I didn't know what he was talking about, but I went with him to the car and we drove off under the light of the full moon. He took me to the same beach where we had done the rite for Sybil Leek. We walked down onto the sand, and Scott told me why he had brought me here tonight. Like the full moon above, I had come full circle, and the priest training me had decided that the time had come for my initiation into the third degree of the Ancient Pictish Gaelic Way. We performed the rites. Though our years of formal training had ended, the years of our friendship were just beginning.

❧

Part III

Leaf and Bud

1983–1989

Chapter Six

Hawai'i

WHERE OTHERS MIGHT HEAR OF MAGICAL ISLANDS AND THINK OF sunken Atlantis, or even Tir nan Og, to Scott's heart, the most magical islands rose up from the Pacific waters. Scott's love of Hawai'i began when his parents took a trip to the islands and sent him back tantalizing postcards of pristine beaches, exotic plants, and glowing sunsets. His first visit was a life-changing experience. Although he felt a resonance with several ancient cultures, none of these compared with the power of his attraction to Hawai'i.

As soon as Scott was an adult, he planned to visit Hawai'i for himself and see the islands. He and Marilee Bigelow shared several trips together, including his first trip in 1984. This trip was a surprise for both of them. Ruth Phillips, the magical teacher behind the APGW system which both Scott and Marilee loved, was very ill and it was not clear if she would recover. Scott and Marilee wanted to see her while she was still on this plane of existence.

It was Scott's first chance to meet the woman he had corresponded with and worked with for so long. Ruth was an important influence on Scott's magical life and the magical lives of many others. She was an extraordinary woman of mixed Scottish and Hawai'ian lineage. Before moving to Hawai'i, Ruth held workshops on Wicca with her colleague and contemporary Sybil Leek while they were both in Sacramento, California. Ruth continued giving workshops in Hawai'i. Scott and Ruth's shared love of Hawai'i and Wicca brought them together. She was also a practitioner and teacher of an old Scottish family system of Wicca that became Scott's major religious influence and was a catalyst in helping him begin his study of ancient Hawai'ian magic. Scott and Ruthie always looked forward to being together and would hob-nob for hours on subjects centering on Hawai'i and Wicca.

Scott recorded his and Marilee's whirlwind visit in his diary.

April 18, 1984

We got onto Flight 119 on United to Honolulu. After spending the night at Marilee's house her mother took us to the airport. We flew to L.A., then Hawai'i. We only bought the tickets yesterday, in surprise, because Ruthie Phillips is so sick . . . We'll be sleeping on Ron and Sandy's living room floor, so it won't exactly be luxury, but we're still here, anyway!

After driving around in circles for most of an hour in downtown Honolulu, we finally found Queen's Medical Center . . . and saw Ruthie . . . (A)fter staying a while we went out the Pali highway and stopped at the lookout . . . The Pali Lookout was wonderful and very, very windy. I also walked around all day in a daze—first I couldn't believe that I was coming here, then I couldn't believe I was here.

Downtown Honolulu is dirty and awful, crowded and horrendously noisy, awful traffic, a welter of one-way streets and tourist traps. We went out the Pali and I couldn't believe how lush and tropical everything was and is. We saw marvelous things! . . . [After getting lost in downtown Honolulu, Marilee and Scott finally arrived at their hosts', Ron and Sandy.] *Ron and I talked Hawai'ian plants all night. Heaven!*

We went to bed about 1:00 A.M., laying sleeping bags onto futons. Nice. Dog barks outside, children crying, etc. kept us up for a while. Rain and wind came and went outside, but one storm was so intense (yet brief) I was sure we would be blown and washed away.

Later, I (David Harrington) would accompany Scott to Hawai'i on several occasions, but initially, I had no desire to visit the fiftieth state. Scott, however, was enamored with Hawai'i. He was enchanted by her flowers, her plants, her native peoples, but especially the land which to him was the embodiment of the Goddess Pele.

I once asked Scott who had introduced him to Hawai'i and he told me his parents had. In the 1970s his mother and father took a trip to Hawai'i. Before they left they had made arrangements with Scott to pick them up at the airport on their return home. When the time came, Scott went to Lindbergh Field to meet his parents. When the plane landed and the passengers disembarked, Scott first noticed their bright aloha wear but what really captured his attention was the exotic and perfumed *leis* they were wearing around their necks and carrying in their hands. Later Scott would tell me,

> *Dave, right then and there I felt the* mana[1] *of Hawai'i emitting from those beautiful flowers nested in the colorful leis and knew someday I would have to go see where such beauty was created.*

In the 1980s Scott would realize his dream to see Hawai'i for himself, not once but many times. When he could, Scott visited the islands with friends but if this was not possible he visited Hawai'i alone. At first I could not share this new passion with Scott and I think this disappointed him somewhat.

During the Vietnam War years I was an enlisted man in the U.S. Navy. For me, Hawai'i was just Pearl Harbor: a place to refuel our warships before we went into battle. When I was discharged from the service, I promised myself never to return to the islands. Scott knew about this and did not press me on the Hawai'ian issue. He had other ways to persuade his stubborn student.

Scott was always a very generous person, and so when he brought me gifts from Hawai'i, I thought it was nothing more than his usual desire to share things he valued with others. At first, it started innocently enough with colorful postcards of the different islands he visited showing up in my mailbox. When he got back from these trips, he would call me up and ask if he could come over for a visit. When he arrived at my home, his arms would be loaded down with bags filled with Hawai'ian goodies. The first thing he would hand me would be a plumeria lei. The plumeria flower was sacred to the Hawaiian Moon Goddess Hina and he surrounded himself with the five-petalled, moon-colored blossoms whenever he could.

Reaching into his bag, he would then hand me Hawai'ian foodstuffs, taro chips made from the taro root, mango and guava sodas, passion fruit cookies, banana twinkies, and, my favorite, chocolate covered macadamia nuts—yum! Also out of these bags Scott would bring forth Polynesian designed T-shirts, calendars, *tikis*[2], *kapas*[3], and books on the Hawai'ian culture.

After this gifting, Scott would show me photographs he had taken of his latest adventures. He was an accomplished photographer and his pictures were a delight to the eye. After Scott left for home, I would place the flowers on my altar, put on one of the T-shirts, eat some Hawai'ian food and find a prominent place in my home for the various treasures I had gotten. While doing this, I was still convinced Hawai'i was not for me, But the spell had been cast and I didn't even know it.

When Scott was home we would talk on the phone almost every day. We both loved word play and would banter back and forth various words and phrases. Knowing my curious nature, Scott would occasionally drop Hawai'ian words in our conversations. As planned, I would ask the meaning and the correct way to pronounce the new word. Soon I was learning and speaking basic Hawai'ian words. Scott was delighted.

Eventually, Scott told me of his plans to write a book about Hawai'i. This was the first I had heard about this and my interest was piqued. He was not sure what direction he wanted to take in his new book, but he was sure it would be on Old Hawai'i. Scott then told me he was planning a visit to the islands. This was to be a research trip for the new project. He wanted to find, explore, and catalogue Hawai'ian archeological sites on the various islands. He then asked me if I would care to join him. Knowing my obsession with archeology and research, he knew my answer would finally be a positive one.

In two weeks time Scott and I boarded a plane bound for Hawai'i. In about five hours, we spotted the Hawai'ian island of Oahu, our destination. From the air this green island looks like an emerald set into an aquamarine sea. Soon we were over the island and the plane was banking its wings to make our approach to Honolulu airport. Suddenly, Scott told me to look down. When I did, my heart did a flip-flop, for almost grazing the underbelly of the craft was the extinct volcano Diamond Head. As I pulled my seatbelt tighter I knew this trip was going to be no ordinary experience.

After a safe landing, we disembarked and found ourselves in the busy beehive of the Honolulu airport. To gather our wits and find our land legs, Scott led us to an open-air courtyard styled after a Chinese garden. Here, under a flaming Dragon's Blood tree, Scott gave me my first lesson on Hawai'i, the air itself. The flora of the islands is more colorful and aromatic than on the mainland, due to the rich volcanic soil and high humidity. So for a time we blocked out the busy airport noise and just sat there and drank in the fragrant air.

Soon we were in a rental car heading for Waikiki, about thirty minutes from the Honolulu airport. We found our hotel among the forest of tall concrete buildings that line the beach, and checked in. After settling in to our rooms, we decided to take a walk along the Waikiki waterfront. When we stepped out on the beach it was sunset. To our left stood the volcano Diamond Head, now a darkened silhouette. The skies had taken on the colors and hues of a lava flow. There was no doubt that a fire Goddess dwelled here.

The Honolulu and Waikiki side of Oahu is fairly crowded due to development and tourism, and very little remains of Old Hawai'i there now. But if you look close you can find traces of this ancient past, and sometimes these relics show up in the most surprising of places. In fact, not four blocks from our hotel, right in the heart of Waikiki beach, Scott introduced me to the "Wizard Stones." The old story goes that in the 1500s four healing magicians visited Oahu from Tahiti. Their names were Kapaemahu, Kahaloa, Kapuna and Kinohi. While on this Hawai'ian isle the four performed miraculous healing ceremonies. Before leaving back to their home in Tahiti, the magicians took four standing stones and imbued them with great healing mana. Since the "Wizard Stones" are now placed on a busy section of Waikiki beach, Scott would get up at 4:30 A.M. so he could be alone with the magicians and do his personal magics with them.

Also in this area, tucked above Honolulu is the charming *heiau*[4], Keaiwa. This temple site sits in an open glade surrounded by lush pine trees and blooming hibiscus. The overall feeling here is one of peace and contentment. On a bright blue day with the warm trade winds blowing Scott and I visited this lovely spot. The complex can still be entered and as we strolled through the grounds we noticed that offerings were still being left by faithful pilgrims, flowered leis, coins, photographs, tobacco, and tiny bottles of rum. Before we left this still much alive sacred site Scott showed me the rite of the *ki*[5] leaf blessing. As Scott taught me in the student years we asked permission of the ki for one of its leaves, then, placing a small offering at the base of the plant, we collected one leaf. Scott then reached down and picked up a small lava pebble. Placing this in the middle of the leaf he bundled the package tight. With a blessing on his lips he secreted this offering into a niche of the black volcanic wall of the heiau. I quickly adopted this spell, partially because the materials used in the blessing return naturally back into the earth with the passage of time.

Keaiwa would be the first of many heiaus I would explore with Scott and always standing guard on these sites was the faithful ki.

To get away from the hustle and bustle of Honolulu and Waikiki Scott would lead us to the other side of the island to the famous North Shore. This is Oahu at its best with gigantic waves crashing upon golden beaches on one side of the main highway while on the other is jade green jungle creeping up into the misty mountains. The North Shore is also home to the beautiful Waimea Falls Park, a natural valley carved out of the verdant mountain side eons ago.

An ancient Hawai'ian community once thrived in Waimea Valley and artifacts of these early inhabitants can still be found. The Park can be entered for a small fee and once inside you find Hawai'i as it must have appeared long ago. Well-placed garden trails are laid out on the valley's floor allowing guests to walk and view the fantastic flora of the islands. Red torch ginger, multi-oranged heliconias, hot pink hibiscus, purple-hued orchids, everywhere you look is flowered in color. In fact, over 2,500 species of plants grow and bloom here. Scott the herbalist was in his element finding and cataloguing the exotic treasures Waimea held.

Not only does the flora live here but also the fauna and along the way you encounter them: iridescent jungle fowl, the *nene*[6] geese, flamingos, green geckos, and, if you're lucky, you may get a glimpse of the elusive mongoose.

As the trails lead in to the valley you come upon local Hawai'ians performing games, rituals, and dances of their ancestors. The *hula* here is shown in the old way, with the music of the dance provided by chants and percussion. I had already seen the "hula" that was done for the tourists. Now, here, Scott wanted me to experience the hula as it was danced in Old Hawai'i. Finding a seat close to the black volcanic stone hula platform, we waited for the ritual to begin. Softly and slowly the drums began to beat in a rhythmic fashion, when, almost magically, a bronzed warrior appeared on the platform above us, wearing a *malo*,[7] with fern fronds tied around each wrist and ankle and with a headband to match. Bending down, the dancer lifted a large *conch*[8] shell that had been at his feet and, raising it to his lips, he blew. As the rich baritone of this instrument thundered across the valley, beautiful Hawai'ian maidens danced in procession upon the stage, chanting prayers to the hula Goddess *Laka*.

Now the drums grew louder and the dancers' bodies were caught up into the rhythm and story of the ancient Polynesian legends expressed in their hula. The chants and drums now reached a crescendo and when the last drum beat fell the dancers silently left the platform like so many phantoms joining the mist that was now rising from the floor of the valley.

After the dancers' dramatic departure, I looked over at Scott and we both laughed. The intensity of the hula had left us both with "chicken skin," a Hawai'ian idiom for goose bumps. Dark blue and purple shadows were now spilling down the valley's slopes and it was time for Waimea Falls Park to close. Leaving the serene place behind, refreshed, we headed back to our hotel in Waikiki.

After a visit with Ruth Phillips, it was time to leave Oahu and fly to Madame Pele's home, Big Island Hawai'i.

The flight to the Big Island takes about forty-five minutes and soon we were landing at Kona's Keahole Airport. This island is the youngest of the

Hawai'ian chain and still growing from the eruptions of Kilauea, residence of Pele. The drive to Kailua-Kona, our destination, passes through black volcanic terrain as bleak and as stark as a lunar landscape. The Goddess shows herself at all times on this, Her island.

Arriving at the seaside village of Kailua-Kona we stowed our gear at a local hotel and set out to explore this tiny but exquisite town. The village rests at the base of Mt. Hualalai that gives way to a natural bay enclosed by a man-made seawall. Inside the enclosure under tall swaying King palms are narrow cobblestone streets, fronted with structures built during Hawai'i's Colonial days. As you walk through the village of Kona you can almost believe you're in a pirate's cove during the swashbuckling days.

After our walk about we returned to where we were staying, the historic King Kamehameha Hotel. Here in 1812, King Kamehameha built his principal residence and rebuilt the Ahuena Heiau that was on the grounds. This heiau has been carefully reconstructed with exact copies of its original buildings and *Ki'i*.[9] The temple grounds are torchlit at night and from the hotel rooms, the view evokes images of the ancient times.

The day after we arrived on the Big Island we headed for the hearth and home of the fire Goddess, Kilauea Volcano. The Polynesians tell the tale that in the mist of time Pele and her volcanic brothers lived in *Kahiki*, [10] but Na-maka-o-ka-ha'i, their sister the sea Goddess, was constantly badgering them by trying to put out their fires with her element water. So Pele built a huge outrigger canoe for herself and her fire clan and sailed toward Hawai'i to find peace and a new home. But peace was not to be had because Na-maka-o-ka-ha'i followed close behind. Pele and her brothers first landed on Ni'hau. Here, she took her digging stick and tried to carve out a home for their fire but immediately, their sea sister covered them. This maddening situation happened again on Kauai, O'ahu, and Maui. Finally, on the Big Island of Hawai'i Pele was able to thwart her sister. This was the largest island on the chain and Pele was able to go deep into the interior where the ocean could not reach and dig a deep fire pit at Kilauea for her fire family.

It was to be a full day so we got up early. As we were loading the camera equipment into the car, I glanced up at the sky and noticed that thick fog was quickly rolling in. When I voiced this concern to Scott, he became excited, for it was not fog, he explained, but "Vog." Vog was a mixture of soot and ash that rises into the sky when a volcano erupts. Pele was awake. We quickly got in the car and headed for volcano country.

Since we did not plan to stay long on Hawai'i, Scott decided to take the coast road so I could get a feel of what this island was about. In an hour, we were passing the quaint and charming town of Hilo. Outside of Hilo we stopped for provisions at a rustic store made from weathered board and corrugated tin. The store had a covered wooden porch lined with old rain barrels filled with tropical cut flowers that were for sale. Scott quietly and intently inspected and selected an armload of flowers which he purchased. When we got back to the car he carefully found a safe place for the exotic bouquet.

Around lunch we stopped at Kaimu Black Sand Beach. This is truly an incredible sight, for the beach as far as you can see is completely made up of black volcanic sand. I quickly reached down and grabbed a handful of this magical substance and was surprised it was the same texture as regular beach sand. Before we knew it we had kicked off our shoes and were soon engrossed in beachcombing. The black sand was hypnotic and I was soon lost to the outside world. When I looked up, Scott was just a speck on the horizon.

Shaking myself out of this stupor I started walking back toward Scott. When I got near, it seemed he was standing over the bleached bones of a large dinosaur. In fact, it proved to be pieces of white coral that had been washed ashore. Using the coral for his paintbrush and the black sand for his canvas, Scott began laying out Hawai'ian pictographs. The result was dramatic.[11]

Early in the afternoon we arrived at Hawai'i's Volcanoes National Park, the place of Pele. Her land is the land of the fantastic, huge cinder cones, mineral deposits moulded in bizarre shapes, steam vents, lava tubes, even a primeval forest of giant ferns. We spent the rest of the day exploring these sites.

The most memorable part of the day and possibly, of the whole trip, began when Scott went back to the car and retrieved the flowers he had purchased earlier. Now I knew what the flowers were for. With the floral tribute cradled in his arms, Scott reverently approached the rim of the volcano Kilauea. As he bent down and placed the flowers on the lip of

Pele's smoking caldera, I moved away so he could be alone with the Goddess.

Walking away, I began to understand this Hawai'ian adventure. I knew now what the attraction of these magical isles were to Scott. The mother Goddess was alive and well here, it was that simple. Here in the Polynesian world her form was in the shape of Pele and her temple was not just a building but an entire chain of islands. And all who dwelled on Hawai'i respected and acknowledged the Goddess.

Later, driving back to the Kona coast with Scott at the wheel, I told him of my musings. Taking his eyes off the road a moment he answered with a wide grin. Without a word between us I knew finally why this enchanted land had captured his heart, for now it had captured mine.

The next morning we said goodbye to the Big Island and Madame Pele and boarded a plane for Kauai, the garden isle, Scott's most favored place on this earth.

In an hour's time we were above Kauai, coming in for a landing. Already I was marveling, for from the air this beautiful island is in the shape of a gigantic hibiscus flower. Scott quickly agreed with my observation and added that Kauai is at times referred to as the hibiscus isle.

Scott favored Kauai because of its lush tropical setting and the famous waterfalls found throughout the island. Here, Scott allowed himself to rest and collect his thoughts, notes, and research materials; Kauai was his place of rest and refuge. The island also piqued Scott's curiosity because in ancient myth this was the first stop Pele the fire Goddess made on her journey to Kilauea.

On the last day on Kauai, Scott took us to the mystical spot where the fire Goddess Pele first tried to dig her fire pit. The fire pit is a huge cave carved into a rugged mountain side; the cave is filled with water from a natural spring. As we hiked toward the cave, we started collecting plumeria blossoms that had fallen on the ground from trees clutched tightly to the cliff side. Almost as if following an ancient rite we knelt down at the entrance of the cavern and dropped the sweet scented petals into the water. As the flowers slowly disappeared into the darkness of the cave, we said Aloha to this great Hawaiian adventure which neither of us would forget soon.

Encountering Pele

Though Scott was inspired by all of Hawai'i, Pele touched him very strongly. During his trip to Hawai'i in November of 1989, he wrote:

I can taste Pele in the back of my throat. Smell her, see her in the furrowed, cracked landscape, red molten rock, steam, and smoke. Feel her in the texture of lava. Hear her in the hiss of boiling sea water.

My relationship with Pele began in 1984. While staying with friends of mine in Kane-ohe, Oahu, we spoke one night about Her. Pele, I learned, is more than a volcano Goddess. She is more than a wrathful deity consuming all that gets in Her path.

Pele, as the ruler of volcanoes is a true Mother Goddess. From her fiery home flows new land. Her most recent eruption, which began on the Big Island in 1987, continues to extend the size of Hawai'i's landmass.

For many in Hawai'i today, Pele is more than a myth. She is a living, sentient being, a Goddess of fire and fertility—the Goddess.

Though the old Hawai'ian religion collapsed, as a universal system of beliefs and practices in the islands in 1819, traces of it live on.

And finally, Pele herself still walks the land and lives in Hale-mau-mau.

Some see her in the smoke issuing from vents.[12] Some see Pele in the dancing lava fountains, or in the patterns of Her lava.

Pele sometimes appears as an old, gray-haired woman, but also as a young, attractive woman. A modern myth states that she sometimes hitchhikes, only to disappear after riding along. A small white dog may also be Pele—the mythological literature is filled of stories of Pele testing persons by changing her appearance. Her worship continues today in both formal and informal forms. Many persons whose homes have been spared in the recent lava flows in Royal Gardens, Isle of Ha-wa-ii, state that they gave offerings to Her and prayed that she would divert her fiery destruction.

A visit to the lookout over Hale-mau-mau reveals an abundance of offerings scattered over the rim of the crater. Incense stalks, broken bottles of gin and money are modern innovations, but the older offerings, leis, fruit, ohelo berries, le kua ohia and more are also seen. Many others have been thrown into the depression and cannot be seen.

No matter what your spiritual beliefs may be, Hale-mau-mau is an awesome place. On the floor of Kilauea crater itself it stretches [many] feet across. Eerie lava rocks plunge downward. Beneath them, abstract markings ripple along its surface. The smell of sulfur, which blasts into your nostrils and lungs on the way to the look out, becomes familiar. Civilization fades within Pele's realm. Even the disbelievers who snicker at the sight of persons making offerings to the Goddess must feel something.

This becomes ever more real during a visit to an eruption site. The day I went, the twenty-three mile trip down Chain of Craters road was a pilgrimage. Stops to see the rare Pele's hair and fantastic lava formations climaxed at the first glimpses of Pele—a column of white steam/smoke billowing up from the water and being buffeted by the wind.

The ground looked quiet, but we saw signs of Pele's recent march—the charred remains of a coconut palm tree, its trunks half [flung] out from the perfect mold let by the molten lava. The nearby sight of dead trees that marked the prior existence of Wauhala visitor's center.

Three other columns of steam rose in the surrounding area, marking more underground volcanic activity. The clouds of vog (volcanic fog) zipped past us at eye-level and gave the sensation of incredible speed.

And in the air but [illegible] wing-like glassine objects blew up from the crashing sea and fluttered overhead.

Upon capturing one of these shimmering objects and showing it to a ranger, I learned that they were the product of hot lava hitting cool sea water. Impossibly fragile, transparent, light brown, they crumpled as they hit the lava rocks.

I love you, Pele. I will be back to visit your home, to smell you,
to see you, to taste you, to feel and love you. I will be back because
I have seen Hawai'i, know Hawai'i, and because it is Pele.

In the same diary, Scott recorded two prayers invoking Pele:

O Pele ko'u akua,
He ali'i no la'a uli,
No la'a kea.
'O Pele ko'u akua,
Miha ka lani,
Miha ka honua

Pele is my goddess,
a chiefess of sacred darkness
And of sacred light.
Pele is my goddess,
Quiet reigns in the heavens,
And reigns over the earth.

E ho'oulu ana i Kini o ke akua,
Ka lehu o ke akua,
Ka mano o ke akua;
E ulu, e ulu, Kini o ke Akua!

Ulu Pele!
Ulu Kane me Kanaloa!
Ulu Laka me Hina!
Ulu ku me Lono!
E ola nou, e!

amama wale! Ua noa!

In notes for a class he taught on Hawai'ian magic at the Isis Bookstore in Denver, he translated this prayer:

We now invoke the 40,000 Gods,
The 400,000 Gods,
The 4,000,000 Gods.
Come, come, you 40,000 Gods and Goddesses!
Come Pele!

Come Kane with Kanaloa!
Come Laka with Hina!
Come Ku with Lono!
We hail you now!
The Kapu is lifted, we are free!

The beauty of the islands brought out the poet in Scott. With Pele as his muse, even his diary entries flowed with beautiful imagery:

February 6, 1991 about 6:30 A.M.
Before dawn on Kauai. Coconut palms tower around me. The sky is gradually lightening. Indescribable birdcalls punctuate the cool morning air. As dawn draws nearer, the incredible green of this island intensifies. A patch of red earth glows at the top of a nearby ridge. Nearby, the ocean laps at a coral sand beach. Birds unfurl themselves in the lagoon, awakening—like the earth itself—glorifying the dawn. Lauhala—spider lillies—coral trees.

About 7:45 A.M.
Choruses of birds greet the shining sun.

Earlier, the sun slowly rose above the horizon on Hanamaula *Beach, bathing the clouds above and behind me with red light. The sunrise shows the volcanic origins of this island.*

A loud mynah bird chirps its call, perched on a coconut branch nearby. Birds of every description lace through the skies.

Pele Honua Mea—Pele of the red Earth—live on in her long-ago works here. Hine-of-the-spiny-corals resides nearby.

Kanaloa slaps against the beach.

Wakea and Papa—of the forests—stand on the hillside. Ku (?) of the coconut—is here too.

Hina and Ku—of all medicinal plants—are also present.

Lono resides nearby in verdant patches of vegetables.

The akua are still present. They still exist in the timeless "ways of nature" that thrive on this paradise, the garden Island of Kauai.

February 14, 1991

To see orange ilima *rambling over cliffs near the sea . . .* ferns *gracing lava fields . . .* noni *fruits hidden beneath foliage . . .* ko *on the side of the road . . .* maile *vines gracing a jungle . . . sacred* ohe *rustling in the wind . . .* maia *and* ulu *and* niu *rising above . . .* pohuehue *cresting a sand dune . . .* naupaka *brightening a beach . . .* ki *guarding homes and* heiau *. . . is to see Hawai'i.*

February 7, 1992

To understand the Hawai'ian akua, *it's necessary to understand nature. Rain. Sun. Chlorophyll. Ocean currents. Wind. Vulcanism. The behavior of birds, mammals, and sea creatures. Such expressions of nature weren't thought of as expressing the gods; they were the* akua, *the* 'aumakua, kupua *and the 400,000 deities—the* ikini *of the* akua. *The Haw* akua *aren't to be found in buildings, or even in books. They're found in the sacred* aina *of Hawai'i nei.*

The best way to know the akua *is to come here. To see water gushing forth where Kane and Kanaloa thrust their digging sticks into the earth in search of water for their* aina.[14] *To see a coconut tree, one like that which Hina climbed up to go to the* mahina. *(moon). To walk upon lava which Pele spewed forth from Her fiery home. To see the plants:* pala pala'a *fern (Mi'iaka);* Kalo *(Kane/kamepua'a);* Ohia *(Ku);* 'ohelo *(Pele); the fish; the birds; the totality of the Hawai'ian experience.*

As Scott wrote, he began to form this entry as a rough draft for an article:

If this, at present, is unlikely, (nothing is impossible), look at nature in your own area. See the timeless forces at work—the cycles of germination, flowering, fruiting and decay; the seasons passing in glorious succession. Feel the wind; the heat of the sun; the cool light of the moon. Realize that these same processes were the ones that impelled the Hawai'ians—and their distant Polynesian forebears—to realize the emenence of deity: to know the akua.

The akua are not gone. They still walk among the rain forests; swim and surf on the beaches; still drink awa. The Rainbows arch overhead as signs from the akua. They fight. They love. They flee. They unite—and it is these actions which formed Hawai'i. More importantly, they yet reside within the Hawai'ian people themselves.

February 2, 1994

Each island is complete, and yet—each is also part of a patchwork quilt. Hawai'i is the red earth and greenery of Kauai. It's also the black lava and waterfalls of Hawai'i, the valleys of Mau'i, the hustle of O'ahu, the tranquility of Moloka'i and Lana'i. The surging blue Pacific stitches them together.

From the air, the islands seem small and quite near to each other. On the ground this isn't so. But, culturally and geographically, they're united.

To see but one of the islands is to see but a tiny part of the beautiful quilt that is Hawai'i.

On this trip, Scott also noted in his journal information about the fishhook amulet he wore:

On Maui, on June 27, 198? I held up a makau *to the heavens. It matched the constellation of Scorpio that hung in the sky. Scorpio, in Hawai'i, was known as Maui's fishhook. Hawai'ian name:* Hoku-ula . . .

I wear a fishhook today as a symbol of my respect for traditional Hawai'ian culture.

Like the resurgence of popularity in miniature reproductions of makini *(gourd helmets), the fishhook is an ancient yet contemporary emblem of Hawai'i's rich cultural past.*[15]

Scott also drafted notes for an article with the ponderous title of *Aspects of Contemporary Incidence of Hawai'ian Religion* which transformed itself into a passionate paean to the living power of the islands:

Are the old ways gone? Have the akua survived the onslaught of western religion, technology, and ideals?

Ask the woman who prays to Ku when she hikes in the mountains. Ask the countless home owners who plant and maintain fences of ki around their homes for protection. Ask the hundreds—thousands—of persons who, each day, leave offerings at heiau and sacred sites.

Ask the local who proudly hangs a makini from the rear-view mirror of his car, or the folks who secretly keep an old aumakua figure in their homes.

It is alive! It's in the aina, and the land instills respect for the old ways, even in those who conform in other ways to "conventional" religion.

1. *Mana*—the innate spiritual energy of Hawaii.
2. *Tikis*—Hawaiian ancestral figures, often carved from wood.
3. *Kapas*—Hawaiian barkcloth fabric paintings.
4. *Heiau*—ancient Hawaiian temple complex.
5. *Ki (Dreacaena terminalis)*—Commonly known today as the ti, pronounced "tee." Sold in gift shops throughout the islands.
6. *Nene goose*—endangered Hawaiian State bird.
7. *Malo*—Hawaiian loin cloth.
8. *Conch*—spiral shell used as a summoning instrument.
9. *Ki'i*—representations of the Gods, Goddesses and aumakua (ancestral spirits) fashioned of wood or stone. Often (mis) pronounced "tiki."
10. *Kahiki*—ancient name for Tahiti.
11. Six months after our visit to Hawaii this beautiful beach was completely destroyed by a lava flow from nearby Kilauea.
12. One trip to Hawaii Scott went to the Big Island to visit Madame Pele's house, the volcano, Kileua. He would always bring armloads of flowers to throw into the crater as an offering to the Goddess. On this occasion, when he visited Her, he wanted to ask Pele for a favor. He had been trying to stop smoking for a long time without much success. He didn't believe that the Gods and Goddesses should be casually used for "let's make a wish," but he had exhausted his own efforts and felt the genuine need for divine help. But when he returned to the mainland, he was still smoking. At first he was puzzled as to why his prayer had failed. Then he realized— he had asked the Goddess of smoking volcanoes, fiery cauldrons, and hissing lava to help him give up a symbol of Her own element—fire.
14. *Aina*—the land.
15. Scott wrote about the fishhook he wore in a diary excerpt he apparently intended to use as an article. On his birthday, June 27, one year, he held a *makau* up to the

heavens at night. It matched the constellation of Scorpio, which, in Hawaiian, was known as Maui's fishhook. "I wear a fishhook today as a symbol of my respect for traditional Hawaiian culture." he simply stated.

Chapter Seven

High Priest and Grand Jester

In jesting guise but ye are wise
who know what the jest is worth.

—Rudyard Kipling

THE PRESENCE OF SCOTT CUNNINGHAM IN A CIRCLE WAS A BLESSING and a curse. It was a blessing because few others had such an easy hand with power and extensive knowledge combined with a very genuine reverence for and devotion to the deities. It was a curse because few others were so openly intolerant of game playing and inattentiveness to what Scott regarded as the essentials of Wiccan worship. At the same time, he would not hesitate to refuse to worship at what he regarded as false Wiccan idols: the unbroken tradition of worship "from neolithic times," the word-for-word infallibility of the *Books of Shadows* (including obvious typographical errors and misspellings), and the right of the High Priestesses to call worshippers to her own shrine, (not necessarily identical with that of the Goddess these High Priestesses purported to serve).

While Scott recognized that all humans possess a "divine spark," he was adamant that humans are not on the same level as the deities. He was

81

opposed to members of the coven clergy commanding obedience, and even more opposed to the idea that one could order the gods and goddesses around in the course of a rite. In *Living Wicca*, he states:

> *Few people enjoy being commanded; no Goddesses or Gods enjoy it. Such "prayers" have no place in Wicca.*

With unusual force, he goes on to say:

> *This statement doesn't mean that it only has no place in my form of Wicca; it's universal. It isn't dependent upon your personal conception of the Goddess and God; it's dependent upon the nature of things: the Goddess and God are bigger than us. End of discussion.*

Scott advocated the right of students and neophytes to question the High Priestess and High Priest. Although many *Books of Shadows* specifically granted this right to coveners, in practice many High Priestesses and High Priests avoided or resented this type of questioning. (Of course, some of these same *Books of Shadows* granted the equivalent of Catholic "papal infallibility" to priests and priestesses, essentially stating that nothing they said or did could be wrong.) Some regarded any question, no matter how legitimate, as a reflection of doubt of their authority. And few were willing to answer "I don't know, I'll look it up," when queried about obscure passages or difficult information in their BOS.

In some cases, it was impossible for Scott to remain in groups that offended his sense of Wiccan right and wrong. In one situation, Scott and a number of others left a coven in support of one member who was blacklisted for the crime of asking too many questions in what was regarded by the coven leader as an insufficiently respectful manner. The sarcastic wit that could be so entertaining could turn devastating when Scott was confronted with these situations.

At the same time, Scott was almost alone in recognizing the more healing uses of humor in circle. Where the usual response to mishaps in circle was shocked silence, fear, or angry accusations, Scott prescribed a less daunting response—laughter. This was often interpreted as irreverence, but, as Scott describes in his article "Circle Stories" from *New Moon Rising*, Vol. 4, No. 3, he had good reason for levity at these moments:

Most Wiccans have "circle stories;" i.e., tales of events that have unexpectedly occurred during ritual. Some of these experiences may be deeply moving and highly spiritual, such as a visible appearance of the Goddess within the circle as She is called.

Others may be rather magical: points of light flying through the air; candle flames dipping or growing incredibly high; cauldrons boiling with no fire beneath them.

Still other circle stories, however, may be of a totally different nature. It's these that are most often shared with other Wiccan friends who appreciate a good laugh.

Yes, a laugh. Despite our best intentions, mishaps do occur within circles. Though they can happen in a solo rite, they're most common during coven meetings. With eight or ten (or more) persons in a small space, surrounded by candles and sharp knives and big swords and hot censers and lots of things that shouldn't be touched or knocked over, accidents do occur. When they do, the healthiest Wiccan thing to do is to laugh, let that energy subside, and begin again.

What are some examples of circle stories? I've already written of one memorable night. There were only five of us in the circle. Everything was going smoothly—until I mispronounced the name of the elemental ruler of Earth–until the huge labrys fell from the side of the altar, narrowly missing a foot . . . until we banged our heads into the lamp hanging over the altar. By the time the third mishap occurred we were weak from laughter.

There are other circle stories. Once I was being initiated into a tradition that I'd studied for about a year. I was kept in a rear bedroom with the other neophytes while the initiates cast the circle in the living room. One by one the neophytes were led out.

Finally, I was alone. The messenger arrived for me. She was a vision of gentle power in a flowing white robe. I took her curious expression to be an indication of her highly spiritual state.

Anyway, the messenger rigged me into the "cable-tow" and led me into the circle. After various actions were performed there, it was time to unbind me. Her razor-sharp white-handled knife glistened in the candle flames. She knelt and cut the cord that secured my ankles. Unfortunately, her hand slipped at just the wrong time; the knife dug into my ankle. I laughed. It was a memorable rite . . .

There are many other circle stories. How many robes have gone up in flames when their wearers bent too close to the altar candles (or the bonfire)? How many skyclad Wiccans have accidentally backed into burning censers? I've heard tales of high priestesses trying to bless wine—and ramming their athames into their High Priest's hands. I've heard of fingernails bursting into flames in ritual (greatly impressing the coveners in attendance).

I've heard of matches that wouldn't light, charcoal blocks that refused to take a flame, incense that wouldn't burn. High Priests and High Priestesses may accidentally switch parts during rituals. Coveners trip over their feet during sacred dances. On one memorable night, two Wiccans suddenly decided to leap a bonfire at precisely the same second from opposite directions—and barely missed smacking into each other in midair over the roaring flames.

Ours is, indeed, a religion of spirituality and magic, but it shouldn't be completely solemn. You show me a ritual where a Wiccan casts a square "circle," knocks over the altar and gets dizzy from the incense smoke and I'll show you a Goddess that's laughing with Her children.

So what if we forget to bring the matches? So what if we suddenly can't remember how to pronounce all those difficult goddess names? So what if our crescent cakes are so rubbery that we play a game of handball with the extras after ritual? So what if the incense smells like a dead horse? Such experiences happen to the best of us—at some time, at some place.

Scott also rejected the idea that mishaps reflected on the competency of those performing the rituals.

Proficiency in Wiccan ritual doesn't ensure that no circle mishaps will occur. Chaos will always have its day. When it rears its smiling little head, we're faced with a choice: will we allow this absurd incident (accidentally lighting the flowers instead of the candles; cutting a big 'Z' on a covener's robe with that incredibly heavy sword; banging a toe into the cauldron) to ruin our ritual? Will we get angry and end the circle? Or will we accept the humor of the moment, enjoy it, let it pass, and get on with things?

The choice is yours, but here's some things to think about: every Wiccan that I know agrees that Wicca is a religion with solemn moments, not a solemn religion. Rituals should be filled with light and love as well as invocations and ritual actions and the proficient use of tools. When something so absurd, so incredibly funny occurs, laugh! That's probably why it happened in the first place: too much solemnity was bogging down the ritual. (Some folks say that there are no accidents—that everything happens for a reason.)

And so, the next time you spill the red wine on your best white robe, you forget that forty-seven-page Gaelic invocation, and you accidentally torch your Book of Shadows half-way through the ritual, smile—and realize that you'll soon have another circle story to share with others.

Scott's personal religious style also made for differences with others. He tended to be quiet when in actual contact with the deity forces. When others would be invoking or creating a verbal dialogue with the forces, he would be silently feeling the contact in his innermost soul. The type of ritual where everyone was urged or required to make a spoken comment to the God or Goddess while lighting a candle or making another offering was difficult for him. He also felt that this practice made many rituals unduly long, and that it was difficult or nearly impossible to maintain functional power in rites involving dozens of people who were expected to stand "at attention" while everyone had their say. This was one reason Scott avoided large group rituals. He writes:

I've been to just a few Wiccan and Pagan gatherings. I don't like crowds, which is perhaps the best reason for not attending such functions. However, I did the Heartland Pagan Festival and the Harvest Moon Celebration, plus a few others. I simply don't like them. I'm not a tribal person; drums give me stomachaches; I need to be alone (which is impossible when you're with 300 other persons, half of whom seem to be intent on tracking my every step, even at 1:00 A.M. on my way to the john).

Scott personally was successful in contacting the deities and even seeing their forms. In the afterword of his "Deity Concepts" chapter in *Living Wicca*, he comes close to apologizing for his own facility in knowing the presence of the Goddess:

I've got this nagging thought that my references to seeing the Goddess and God may make some of you feel left out . . . By the word "see," I don't mean that, while completely awake, we look up and notice that the Goddess is physically standing in the room before us. Visitations of that magnitude are so rare that we needn't wait around for them.

We have better opportunities for seeing the Goddess and God during alternate states of consciousness. In the circle, when we're in ritual consciousness, we're far more likely to see Them. We may also get glimpses, as I've already said, during dreams and meditations.

The first time I saw the Goddess was in a circle. I was seated before the altar and was meditating on Her. It can happen, but don't expect to use your eyes to see the forms of the Goddess and God. Realize, too, that the forms in which They come to you may be quite different from those that They present to others.

In the autumn of 1982, a critical break occurred. After a year of leading a coven of the Ancient Pictish Gaelic Way (APGW), Scott left abruptly. His diary notes:

My "break" from Wicca came in '82 October when, after a year of leading a coven (of five persons) in the APGW I was more

than fed up! "Living room wicca!" I was heard to say. Put the
pagan back in the countryside and the heathen back on the
heath! Put Nature back into it, for it is supposed to be a religion
honoring it!

> *Egos get too big, it becomes a chore to do circle, etc. . . .*

> *I still communicate (write, telephone) with Ruth (Myjestic*
> *Queen) and Ruthie Phillips (APGW, ROTG, Myjestic, etc.) but*
> *not as often as in the past.*

> *I've settled down somewhat since then (over a year ago) but*
> *not quite completely.*

Scott still kept in touch with the elders of the traditions but, as he
notes, not as frequently. In the future, he would occasionally join with
others for ritual (including most of those in the group he once led), and he
and David performed many rites outdoors. But from that point forward,
Scott was on his own magically. He was now a Solitary Practitioner in
spirit even when he joined to worship and work magic with others.

Sarcasm and Satire

The snow on the tall, white mountain gleamed in the sunlight. The portal
to the castle was open, and milling throngs of people eagerly awaited the
day's magical pleasures. Initiates would be led through darkness, splashed
with water, spun around dizzily until all sense of direction was lost,
whirled past spirits dancing to unearthly music and, finally, granted a
vision of the Goddess Herself appearing in the sky to bless Her children.

Scott could find paganism and evidence of the Goddess everywhere.
We talked about the "pagan" elements of Disneyland, particularly those
relating (possibly!) to Isis. He wrote up some thoughts on the subject in
his diary:

Contemporary Isian Worship in Anaheim, California
I. *Isis is Alive*
    A. *Various forms, geared toward consumption.*
    B. *Millions worship (visit) Her home*
       in Anaheim yearly.

  C. *Isian-influenced masked/costumed figures*
   featured in religious processions ("parades")
 II. *Forms of Isis*
  A. *Enchantresses—Tinkerbelle, Fairy Godmother*
  B. *Mother—Bambi's Mom*
  C. *Celestial—Fireworks (symbolic)*
 III. *Places of Isian Worship in Anaheim*
  A. *Sleeping Beauty's Castle*
  B. *Snow White's Well/Fountain*
  C. *"Matterhorn" (Religious object of worship*
   from which Isis in Her "Tinkerbelle" aspect
   descends to bless Her children.)
 IV. *Votive Offerings*
  A. *Plates (obviously symbolic of the Moon)*
   inscribed with vivid, polychromatic images
   of Isian aspects.
  B. *Small Ceramic Images*
   1. *Tinkerbelle*
   2. *Bambi (obviously associated with Horus)*
   3. *Snow White*
   4. *Sleeping Beauty, etc.*

  Although Scott wrote these notes up in fun, he was faithful to the "worship." He always visited Snow White's well and threw in a coin. Two of the chants he created after this visit in 1990 found their way into *Earth, Air, Fire and Water:*

Chants to Accompany Coins Tossed into Well

A Penny for Loving
(The use of a penny in this spell may need a bit of explanation. Older pennies are made from copper, and copper is the metal of the planet Venus and of the element of Water, both loving energies. That's why a penny is used here.)

  To smooth the path of a rocky relationship, visualize you and your mate enjoying happy times, giving full attention to your love. Pour this energy into the penny that you hold in your projective hand. Then toss the penny over your right shoulder into the well while saying:

> Coin of the realm;
> Metal of Venus;
> Ensure that naught will
> Come between us
> Strengthen our love
> This magical day
> This is our will
> And this is the way!

A Money Wishing Well Spell

Hold any coin in your projective hand. Visualize yourself enjoying the fruits of prosperity. See yourself as a more monied person. Charge the coin with this energy.

Still holding the coin, say the following:

> Coin of the realm,
> Silver and gold,
> Return to me
> One hundredfold

Toss the coin into the well and continue:

> I call Water
> To charge my spell
> Now here within
> This magic well.

Scott was not always so whimsical in his viewpoints. He was an adept, sharp-witted satirist and enjoyed creating "Wiccan" versions of movies and plays, with the hope of one day filming his low-budget versions. One of the more complete scenarios was his version of *West Side Story* entitled *Wicca Side Story*. In Scott's version, the rival gangs warring over turf are replaced by rival "covens," (though one group is in fact a group of solitaries). Although he probably did not expect that this would see print, he prefaced it with a disclaimer as if anticipating the furor that would later greet his writings on Wicca.

Wicca Side Story

Note: All names, organizations, and individuals mentioned in this work are fictional. Any resemblance to any actual individuals or organizations, if any, is purely coincidental.

Wicca Side Story is not an attack on the Wiccan Community. It is presented in the spirit of fun and love.

Synopsis of Plot:

Sunrise. Trees rise above a grassy swarth with skyscrapers rising in the far distance. The Gardenings (a long-established Wiccan tradition) are staking out their turf, a remote section of Central Park in New York City. Just hours after their Spring Solstice Solitary rituals, LOKI, a "wild" Solitary, leads the male Solitaries in singing of the wonders of their tradition. Meanwhile, in another park of the park, SELENA and the Gardening women sing of theirs (WHEN YOU'RE A WITCH).

An altercation between the Gardenings and the Solitaries occurs when some Solitaries wander onto Gardening turf in the early morning-light (I LIKE IT BEST IN A COVEN, YEAH!)

This potentially explosive situation ends in a stalemate when LUGH (pronounced, "Loo") a long-time Solitary, meets the eyes of SELENA, a young Witch in the Gardening tradition. They come to an understanding—and something more.

Afterward, SELENA whirls around in a daze following her initiation into the Third Degree into the Gardening Tradition. Three female coveners watch on, amused (I FEEL WITCHY).

LOKI finds DIVINA (a beginning Solitary) making a poppet of SELENA, whom she despises because of her stuck-up attitude. "Just a few stitches around the mouth," DIVINA says. LOKI warns DIVINA that she is treading on dangerous magical ground (IT'S BANE).

CASSANDRA, SELENA'S sister and a long-time (but currently non-active) Gardening High Priestess, is psychically aware of SELENA's attraction to LUGH. She warns SELENA of the possible dangers of falling in love with a Solitary (A WITCH LIKE THAT).

That afternoon, the Solitaries call a meeting with the Gardenings. They've decided to form a "Grand Council" with representatives of both traditions to work out their differences. LOKI is as suspicious of SELENA'S real plans as SELENA is of LOKI's and even LUGH's, though he doesn't realize this. They set up the Grand Council meeting for that evening, following a "interdenominational circle gathering."

In preparing for the first truly democratic ritual with the Gardenings, LUGH sings of his excitement of the ritual to come (TONIGHT).

Tonight
Tonight
Won't be just any rite
Tonight we'll draw the Moon from above!

Tonight
Tonight
Upon the sacred site
We'll make music and magic and love!

Today
The Goddess is so real
A God is how I'll feel
Within the ring of light!

Oh Moon,
Grow bright
And send your power down to our rite . . .
Tonight!

That night, in the park, SELENA avoids speaking with LUGH. He's hurt and doesn't understand; after all, this is a non-denominational circle. The Grand Council meeting never takes place. At the beginning of the "democratic" ritual DIVINA nastily pushes LUGH out of the circle, believing it will cause him "astral damage." LUGH feigns a state of shock so as to finally confront SELENA, who is bending over him, and ask what's bugging her.

The Gardenings and Solitaries wander off, leaving LUGH and SELENA alone together. As he's still feigning "astral damage," LUGH and SELENA sing of a utopian Wiccan community that knows no strife between traditions (SOME WITCH).

SELENA:
There's a Witch somewhere
I know, a Witch somewhere
Gardening or Solitaire
Waits for us—
Somewhere.

LUGH:
There's a Witch somewhere
Some Witch that's really rare,
Priest or Priestess who doesn't care
What clothes you do or
You do not wear—

BOTH:
Some Witch,
Somehow
Will find a way of forgiving
The other traditions for living.
Some Witch.

BOTH:
There's a Witch somewhere
Some Witch who'll take the dare,
Your tradition? Ah, he won't care.
Find that Witch and we're halfway there.
Somewhere!
Somehow!
Some Witch!

After the song, DIVINA comes back and apologizes to SELENA for "killing" LUGH. He jumps up and they call back *the rest of their respective groups to have a good, old-fashioned bust-your-stomach feast. (WHEN YOU'RE A WITCH REPRISE)*

Ironically, Scott himself fulfilled much of the ideal which he had his characters sing about in *Some Witch*.

Scott also started work on a Wiccan version of *A Chorus Line*. It was titled, somewhat predictably, *A Coven Line*. Here's an excerpt:

Stage: *bare living room walls, bright, harsh lights, mirrors, altars, cauldrons, other ritual equipment lying strewn about. Several NEOPHYTES stand around nervously, fingering their freshly-bought pentacles and athames. This is a coven audition for the Witch-gypsies, those brave young (and not-so-young) souls who journey from coven to coven, hoping to find the one true right and only tradition. They are dressed in a brilliant blaze of multi-colored robes, saris, tabards, the ubiquitous lingerie, tights, and so on.*

HAGMAN: *I want everyone in circle. Okay, we'll go over the last combination. Ready? A five, six, seven, eight!*

He brandishes an athame— an everyday working knife, not one of those flashy super-deluxe ritual items.

HAGMAN: *Up, down, right, left, down up! Again! Up, down, right, left, strong arms! Again! Up, down, right, left, down, up!*

Again! Up, down, right, left, down, up! Good! Going on and . . .

The gypsies nervously match his moves, standing with backs firm, heads held high, eyes rigidly drilling into the pentagrams they are sketching. But some arms are lazy, some slashing, some faces are smiling, some grim. Hagman and the kids watch themselves in the mirrors as they audition for the unseen, near legendary High Priest— a hard case, hard-line Wiccan named, (of all things), SACH.

HAGMAN: *Get those arms up! Do it like you mean it!*

Music appears out of nowhere, matching their movements— just a piano at first, then more, much more. As the music builds to increase some of the gypsies begin making their movements larger, fuller, more dramatic, until the whole cast is trying to outdo each other in pentagrams. Spins, kicks, flexed backs and flipped hats add to the spectacle . . . As they do so, each gypsy tries to impress the unseen high priest—who is sitting in an apparent direction, although we never see him.

Scott hoped that there might one day be a pagan theater group willing to perform his works, and that there might be a market, however limited, for humorous video works produced for the pagan community.

✑

Chapter Eight

The Magical and the Medical

ONE MORNING IN SEPTEMBER OF 1983, WHILE SHAVING, SCOTT FOUND a mysterious lump on his neck. Instinctively[1] knowing that this was something he could not ignore, he immediately went to a doctor. After tests, his fears were confirmed. At the age of twenty-seven, Scott was suffering from lymphoma, a particularly virulent and often deadly form of cancer. The prognosis was not good and his chances for long-term survival were considered slim. He immediately began a course of treatment which included surgery, radiation, and chemotherapy.

Scott still wrote furiously every day, and spent his long hours at the hospital mentally revising in-progress works. He wrote:

> *I remember lying in the dark on a gurney in a hospital room, waiting to go in for a biopsy,[2] listening to the rain thrashing outside the room's windows and trying to determine the correct method of arranging the elemental information and spells that I'd written.*

Magical Healing

Scott augmented orthodox treatments with healing rituals and spells, and also employed extensive visualization. He viewed the film *Tron* repeatedly, which he mentally adapted as a scenario for his own cancer battle. He lost his hair and combated the daily nausea with the help of federally approved marijuana which was provided to him, pre-rolled and neatly packaged, by prescription under a later discontinued program.

A document found among his papers probably dates from this time, though it is also possible these affirmations could have been adopted shortly after his first bout with meningitis in 1990:

Affirmations:

I can and will heal myself.

I will heal myself through magic, meditation, chanting, through diet, vitamins, exercise, through positive thinking, visualization, through doctor's advice and help.

I can and will heal myself, for I have too much to do yet on this place, in this life.

I must bring the rest of my magic out in print for all the world to see.

I must bring the rest of my herbal magic in print for all the world to see.

I must bring the world of Wicca to its feet in surprise by bringing Beyond Wicca to the world.

I must bring myself to the highest spiritual peak that I can.

I have students and readers depending on me, and I won't let them down.

Neither will I let me down. I can and will heal myself!

If for no other reason than because I have the power to perform this feat.

Nothing is miraculous for the well-armed.

I know that mind has an effect on the body, and I know that evil, dark, negative thinking produces evil, dark, negative results.

I will keep my thoughts clean and pure, my actions well-honed
and productive, my words kind and gentle.

I shall serve as an example to others.

I know that to do this I must change my life, and my world.

And this I shall and will do, because I can and will heal myself!

This is my will, so mote it be!

Scott made a miraculous recovery from the lymphoma. His checkups at the hospital dropped in frequency, from once a month to once every three months, finally to twice a year. Each time he went in he was concerned what the doctors would find. All of his friends dreaded the frequent visits and were relieved when he'd toss off a casual comment, "Everything seems to be okay . . . they don't want to see me for another two months." The slightest illness or indigestion set everyone wondering if the cancer was coming back. He hated the sympathetic attention and refused to dwell on the possibilities. He trusted his doctors and rejected extra information on lymphoma or alternative methods of treatment.

He hurled himself into his writing, setting a breakneck pace that did not slacken for the rest of his life. If time was short, then work must be consistently productive.

A Magical Heroine—Sybil Leek

Shortly after Scott survived the lymphoma, another passing reminded him of the preciousness of life. Sybil Leek was one of Scott's heroines in the magical community, and her passing affected him deeply. Two elders of the magical traditions he had been initiated into had known Sybil, but Scott had never contacted her personally, perhaps because he was in awe of her. At one point, Scott hoped to write a biography of Sybil, but unfortunately this never came to pass. His eulogy for her was published in *The Shadow's Edge* article: "Sybil Leek—An Appreciation."[3]

> *As announced in "Summonings" in the previous issue Sybil Leek*
> *passed away last October just before Samhain. When I learned*
> *this I was deeply saddened and felt that some sort of apprecia-*
> *tion of the lady was in order.*

Much has been said concerning the Witch of the New Forest, —the popular press on both sides of the Atlantic made headline-generating copy concerning her exploits for nearly a decade—and criticism has been directed toward her methods of instructing the public in the ways of Wicca and the Occult.

However, no one can question Ms. Leek's profound impact on the United States, when in 1968, her autobiography was published. Diary of a Witch opened the eyes of a Vietnam War-torn country to a way of life far different from that which was generally known. The book, filled with tales of magic, astrology and gypsy lore, shot to the top of the best-selling charts and remained there long enough to set the framework of the later "occult explosion" of the late 60's and early 70's.

She was, clearly, a larger than life figure, and she made much of her eccentricities. Tales of her pets (such as her snake, Miss Sashima; iguana, Mr. Verde-Verdi; and her jackdaw, Mr. Hotfoot Jackson); her inability to drive; her preference for flowing robes and purple stockings—these seemed to be her tools for attracting attention to herself in order to present some truths about her religion.

It has been stated (just as it has [been said] of Gerald Gardner, Alex Sanders, and others) that Sybil went public with her religion for the money. This is absurd. Yes, she was rich in her later years, but this was due to her extraordinary business sense. In 1972 she owned nine companies involved in manufacturing sailboats and jewelry, among other things. She wrote books on the occult but few authors grow rich from royalties, and lecture fees often barely cover transportation costs.

When she said (as she once did) that all her success was due to Witchcraft, I think she meant that the principles and magical techniques of Wicca, if properly applied, can bring about anything.

She did not make money from being a public Witch—it probably hurt her more in the business world than helped her—but she did a tremendous amount of good in bringing to a whole generation the basic precepts of the Old Ways.

She will be remembered mostly for her books. Although estimates differ as to the actual number of her volumes, she clearly produced over forty works. These range in subject from beauty to astrology, cooking to antiques, bicycles to Wicca.

In fact, although known as a Witch, she wrote only three books remotely related to Wicca. These are Diary of a Witch *(Prentice-Hall, 1968);* The Complete Art of Witchcraft *(World, 1971); and the almost unknown* The Jackdaw and The Witch *(Prentice-Hall, 1965, originally published in England as* Mr. Hotfoot Jackson*).*

I know of few people who have read The Complete Art of Witchcraft *who can criticize the basic information it contains. True, different traditions of Wicca place emphasis on different areas, and Sybil's is no different, but the principles outlined so clearly and lovingly in this book (which is still in print a decade after its original publication) are universal.*

I learned from a personal friend of Sybil's that she actually wrote The Complete Art of Witchcraft *years before it was published. All the houses she approached wouldn't accept the book. "Add more sex," they said. "Throw in some evil spells." She resisted and her patience was well worth the final product.*

In her life Sybil Leek withstood hate mail, physical attacks on her person, family and home, sermons preached against her in pulpits around the country, slanderous news stories and the ignorance of most people with whom she came into contact. In the last years of her life she became rather isolated. She rarely lectured or made personal appearances. Her writing was limited to an occasional book and a regular column in The Globe, *a weekly tabloid.*

She was criticized for writing for a "gossip" newspaper, but obviously she enjoyed the work and one thing a writer needs is steady work.

I am sure that there will be controversy surrounding Sybil Leek for some years to come. This doesn't concern me. If she opened just one person's eyes to the Old Ways nothing else matters.

Scott performed a seaside ritual for the passing of Sybil with David Harrington. David describes the ceremony: Shortly after we discovered Hagstone Cove, word came to us that the famed English witch Dame Sybil Leek had passed on. This saddened Scott and me, for she had played an important role in our magical growth. So to lessen the pain that we felt we decided to do a ceremony in her honor.

We drove to a secluded stretch of beach off of Torrey Pines State Park, near La Jolla, on a dark night with the moon above. With our backpacks filled with wood we walked about a mile down the beach to do our rite away from prying eyes. We came to a perfect spot, with a high sandstone cliff behind us and the crashing surf in front of us. We dug a deep fire pit. While I put the wood in the pit Scott scattered aromatic herbs onto the symbolic pyre. Soon flames were licking the wood as sparks from the bonfire spiraled toward the moon. While we watched the fire we shared our personal feelings on this great lady and then fell into a light meditation brought on by the rhythmic sound of the waves. After meditating, we ended this spell of peaceful parting by picking up fire-brands and throwing them into the ocean. As the torches hissed into the water, the rite was done.

The Birth of Earth Power

Scott was perpetually writing, both on paper and in his mind. Once he had decided to move forward on a specific book, he was absolutely dedicated to that task until it was finished. He rarely wrote a draft and then set it aside. His usual method of work was to write a complete draft of the book and then immediately begin a full rewrite draft. Depending on the publication schedule, he often offered to his friends an opportunity to review what he had written, and he took the comments of those he trusted very deeply. He even tried to "standardize" the format of his friends' reactions and streamline the process, as he writes in his autobiography:

> I made up a "Reader's Response Sheet" for my friends to use as they read the mss. of what became Earth Power (one of the original titles was Natural Magic).
>
> Here's the original set of questions, circa 1981:

1. *How would you describe the tone of the book as a whole:*
   a. *Earthy*
   b. *Mystical*
   c. *Pagan*
   d. *Witchy*
   e. *Other_____*
2. *Which chapters, if any, didn't seem to fit into the book, for whatever reasons?*
3. *Did any of the information, spells or techniques in the book seem to go against the idea that magic is natural, and that it should never be done to harm?*
   a. *Yes. If so, what specifically:_____*
   b. *No_____*
4. *What chapters did you enjoy the most?*
5. *What chapters did you enjoy the least?*
6. *Did the presentation of the spells seem to encourage their actual performance?*
   a. *Yes*
   b. *No*
7. *What would you omit from the book?*
8. *What area of magic should be added to the book?*
9. *Was the book complete in scope for a general introduction?*
   a. *Yes*
   b. *No*
10. *Which word should be used to describe the practitioner of magic in this book:*
    a. *Witch*
    b. *Magician*
    c. *Both*
    d. *Other_____*
11. *What is your basic feeling about the book's contents:*
    a. *A good introduction*
    b. *Simplistic*
    c. *Advanced*

     d.   *Too advanced*
     e.   *Not enough information*
     f.   *May mislead*
12. *Could you recommend an appropriate name for this book, other than* Green Magic, Natural Magic, *or* Wiccan Magic?

My great concern regarding the book's content and focus should be put into the proper perspective: no books like it had ever been published at the time.

Although *Wicca: A Guide for the Solitary Practitioner* and *Living Wicca* were later regarded as controversial, even "heretical," books by many members of the magical community, this controversy actually had its seeds in the immensely popular *Earth Power*. In *Earth Power*, Scott simultaneously demystified magic and conveyed its power in vivid words that inspired many to perform their first acts of magic. He proved that magic was simple, even quite mundane, yet he also showed the richness, beauty, and magical power present in simple objects.

Where many newcomers to magical practice spend great sums of time and money in pursuit of the perfect magical tool, Scott showed that these tools, formed and charged by the power of Nature, were all around, free to those who were wise enough to recognize them.

Before *Earth Power* was published, few books described natural magic even in passing. Most of the "occult" books available were based on ceremonial magic using specially prepared tools in complex rituals. Some authors stated that the difficulty of performing these rites correctly would increase the effect of the ritual when it was finally mastered. Simple, natural magic was disdained, and was more likely to be dismissed as "folk superstition" even by writers more adept at ritualized forms of magic.

In Witchcraft and Wicca books, the natural powers of the world around us were often presented as much less important than adherence to the rites and rituals of a specific group. The idea that anyone could simply go to nature and easily draw magical power from it was foreign to most of the published authors. Only a few Witches, secure in their own knowledge and power, were willing to hint how very easy it could all be. In addition, many books on witchcraft were still spending several chapters defending the right of Witchcraft to exist and attempting to undo the image of witches as inherently evil, usually leaving little room for practical working information.

When *Earth Power* arrived, the New Age explosion was just beginning. Few people knew or cared about the inherent powers of quartz crystal, other than, perhaps, as a way of powering a primitive radio. Herbs were admired for their physical health benefits, not their magical uses. While no one can be given sole credit for this change in attitude, Scott definitely paved the way for a greater acceptance of the power of natural objects and their ability to be used to positively affect our lives. His books became standard Wiccan "reference books" that provide solid information for the magical practitioner to use in developing new magics.

A listing of the books Scott recommended to one student in 1979 gives an idea of what materials were available then, as well as which ones Scott found most valuable for beginning students at that time:

The Best Thirteen Books on the Craft— Beginning Booklist (Published in English)

Aradia, or the Gospel of the Witches —C. G. Leland, 1897
The God of the Witches—Margaret Murray, 1934
Witchcraft Today—Gerald Gardner, 1955
The Meaning of Witchcraft—Gerald Gardner, 1959
Witches: Investigating an Ancient Religion—
    T. C. Lethbridge, 1962
Witchcraft: The Sixth Sense and Us—Justine Glass, 1965
The White Goddess—Robert Graves, 1966
What Witches Do—Stewart Farrar, 1971
Echoes of Magic—C.A. Burland, 197?
The Roots of Witchcraft—Michael Harrison 1973
An ABC of Witchcraft Past and Present—
    Doreen Valiente, 1973
Witchcraft for Tomorrow—Doreen Valiente, 1978
The Spiral Dance—Starhawk, 1979
Supplemental: Witch Blood!—Patricia Crowther
The Complete Art of Witchcraft—Sybil Leek
King of the Witches—June Johns

The Truth About Witchcraft—Hans Holzer
The Twelve Maidens—Stewart Farrar ("Fiction")
A Book of Pagan Rituals—Paganway

A Return to Magical Herbs

Magical Herbalism remained a bestseller for Llewellyn, and soon Scott decided it was time that he provided the extensive encyclopedia material that he had originally planned to include in *Magical Herbalism*. He discussed the writing of this book in an article for the *Llewellyn's New Times*.[4]

> *After* Magical Herbalism *was published I realized that my herb magic notebooks (the results of experimentation, research and teachings) were fairly bursting with information, much of which wasn't included in* Magical Herbalism.
>
> *I thought idly about doing a revision of* Magical Herbalism, *incorporating the new information, then thought better of it. Instead I'd write a new book, with individual descriptions of the plants, plus supplementary material to make it complete. Thus, a year later,* The Encyclopedia *was born.*
>
> *After I'd finished it, I realized that creating a separate book was far wiser than trying to blend the 240-page* Magical Herbalism *with [the] 350-page encyclopedia. The end result would have been massive.*
>
> *But why did I write* The Encyclopedia? *Why did I spend a year of my life on that book? Because I love herbs, plants, and green things, I enjoy sniffing the biting scent of mint, staring with wonder at a sunflower's spiral formed of seeds, and lying on cool grass.*
>
> *Early on, I combined my interests in magic with herbs and plants, and so herb magic became my forte. This wasn't a conscious decision on my part; although my first teacher was an herbalist, I was never pushed in that direction. It just seemed natural.*
>
> *Experimenting with one incense led to creating another, and then another. Blending oils became a habit, and the ritual of drinking herbal teas had its magical overtones. After a few*

years I noticed that hardly a day passed during which I didn't practice some form of herb magic—rubbing an essential oil onto my body, setting incense smoldering, mixing up protective sachets, piling herbs around natural-hued candles with wishes of health, money and peace. This became second-nature to me, and slowly I realized that I had become a natural herbalist. . . .

In the book I've included fruits and vegetables, nuts, spices, seaweeds, flowers, ferns, and as many other different types of plants as space allowed. As surprising as it may seem, a whole magical world awaits you at the produce store and at the garden shop.

In writing The Encyclopedia *I suppose I wished to further the practice of herb magic, if only because it is safe, simple, and above all—effective (if properly done). Far from "high magic," the complex rituals of ceremonial magic, herbs need little pageantry to get things done.*

Some people scoff at the idea of herb magic, at the notion that plants could possess powers that can be tapped and directed through magic. But just as some plants possess demonstrable medicinal properties, from which many healing drugs were originally extracted, so, too, do subtler, psychic powers abound in the plants around us.

If we can shut out the mechanized world and concentrate on herbs, they'll sing their secrets to us. By carrying a seed in your pocket, adding an herb-filled washcloth to the tub or drinking an herbal tea, you set magical powers in motion to benefit your life. Herb magic is that simple.

Fortunately, herb magic doesn't involve the invocation of "demons," nor the ingestion of poisonous draughts. I have included some of the so-called "baneful" (death-producing) herbs in The Encyclopedia *because the book couldn't be considered comprehensive without them. Besides, they are part of the magical herbalist's heritage. I strongly warn against using any poisonous herbs, no matter how enticing their traditional powers may seem to be. They will kill you without mercy!*

> *It's safer to stick with the homey herbs and flowers that grow in gardens and the countryside, even the cities. In the midst of busy streets and in the worst parts of towns I've found plantain, fleabane, mustard, mallow, chickweed, dandelion and a host of other plants flourishing, all useful in magic and absolutely free!*
>
> *Herb magic isn't an arm-chair art—it is one which is learned through doing. In performing the rites the herbs reveal their secrets—thus, anyone can learn herb magic.*
>
> *It is my hope that* The Encyclopedia *will stimulate more to investigate the mysteries and powers of herbs and plants.*

However, outside of the publicity-oriented article quoted above, Scott was a bit more blunt about the creation of this book:

> The Encyclopedia of Magical Herbs *was one of those books that never seemed to end. By the time I began typing it up, I'd filled two fat notebooks with several hundreds of pages of herbal information. One day I finally decided, "Enough!" and wrote the book. Every time I retyped TEOMH (no computers in those days), I thought I'd never get through the "A" section of the herbs. Someone at Llewellyn decided to call it* Cunningham's Encyclopedia of Magic Herbs; *that certainly wasn't my idea. (I'd like to expand and enlarge this book, but the task is rather daunting.)*

However daunting Scott found some aspects of writing, this didn't stop him from moving into a new medium—video.

1. His immediate action may also have been prompted by his long-held belief that he would die young, at age twenty-six. He connected this belief to the memory of his most recent past life, when he had died in a fall from a carrier's deck during World War II.
2. This was during the period when he began undergoing treatment for lymphoma.
3. *The Shadow's Edge*, Spring/Summer, 1983, Vol. 4, No. 3.
4. "Green Magic" article from *Llewellyn's New Times*, #852, April, 1985.

Chapter Nine

The Making of Herb Magic

SCOTT CUNNINGHAM STOOD STOICALLY BEHIND THE TABLE LADEN with herbs. He was visibly sweating under the hot studio lights. Though not apparent to anyone else, I (deTraci Regula) noticed the slight tightening around his eyes that meant that he was in pain from his injured foot. The night before we were to shoot the studio sequences, Scott broke a small figurine at his house and promptly stepped onto the broken shards, leaving him with a bad cut on his foot. In between takes at the studio, we were also changing the bandages on Scott's foot. Fortunately, the studio sequences did not require him to move around very much, since he was limping noticeably. But he never let his injured foot hold up production.

The production had been fraught with challenges, but we had managed to conquer each one. I went forward to wipe off his forehead and tap him with the hated powderpuff to cut down the shine from the lights.

"This wasn't in my contract!" he called out derisively. "Where's my agent?"

"He called and said he was running off to South America with all your money. Sorry—you're stuck on this set."

Our teasing banter was typical. We both loved humor and bad jokes and laughed together at puns that no one else caught. It was hard to believe that our friendship almost never happened.

I first set eyes on Scott Cunningham on a hot spring day in 1982, over a table covered with swords, spear heads, daggers, wheellock pistols and chastity belts. Marilee Bigelow (then Snowden) said with a flourish, "This is Scott Cunningham." In my own mangled version of Elizabethan dialect, I greeted him and tried not to stare at the t-shirted, scrawny, nearly bald individual in front of me. By the accepted rules of the Renaissance Pleasure Faire, he was out of costume and therefore automatically a "turkey," practically beneath notice, if not worthy of true contempt. After introductions, he disappeared into the crowd swiftly. It was never Scott's way to impose himself where he wasn't wanted and the reception at the booth was not exactly warm. I didn't know—or care—who he was.

His name rang no bells with me. I was acquainted with Marilee, who had known Scott for years. She had mentioned her friend Scott, the author, and suggested that I would probably want to talk with him about writing. I did not yet own a copy of *Magical Herbalism*, which had just been published.

In the bacchanalian madness of those old Spring Faires, my non-meeting with Scott didn't cross my mind again.

Some time later, Marilee mentioned that she had shown Scott a story of mine that she liked, suggesting that he should read it. Scott had glanced at the faint typing (I was perpetually using a ribbon until the typing resembled shadows) and refused to consider reading such an ill-prepared manuscript. He had a few words, which I no doubt heard in tactfully edited form, about maintaining some standard of professionalism if I wanted any of my work read.

Ouch.

And my third remembered Scott encounter hardly seemed any more fortuitous, but it completely changed our relationship.

Paganism, Wicca, High Magick share many things with more common (i.e., Judeo-Christian) religions. Most of these things are positive—caring, a sense of community, a base of ethics, a relationship with deity. Unfortunately, it seems that all religions and religious clergy and leaders can fall prey to a devout egomaniacism, and a fair number of High Priestesses and High Priests put themselves higher in their own minds than perhaps they should. This is compounded by the fact that those seeking guidance frequently are very willing to accept someone else's total authority, and less than utter despotism somehow doesn't feel as worthy of admiration and respect.

I was waiting for a mutual coven member to show up for an appointment. We were going to consecrate a few dozen candles so that they would be ready for use in the coming year's rituals. Scott was present. My covenmate was late and I was growing more and more irritated. I had as usual, over-scheduled myself so that each wasted minute seemed like an incredibly rude intrusion on my own personal time. My coven-mate and I were both the same degree in that system, but I already was a Priestess of Isis. In extremely petty fashion, as I was roundly criticizing my missing covenmate, I even dragged that in. The tardiness was taking on the proportions of a major sin, against the system we were working, against the Goddess herself, and certainly against Her representative—me!

"He shouldn't just ignore an appointment to do sacred work, it's his duty . . . and besides, I'm a High Priestess in my own right!"

Scott looked at me earnestly, nodding.

"Yes, certainly, he shouldn't do this, after all, you're a High Priestess in your own right!"

I stopped, a strange feeling in my stomach, devastated. But all Scott had done was to repeat my own foolish words back at me, even supposedly agreeing with me! But the tone, the flash in his eye as he put one more pompous priestess-in-training in her place! Scott was a magician with the written word, but he was a swordsman with the spoken word. I jolted, swallowed . . . and shut up, utterly ashamed. More than ten years later, whenever I begin to climb on my high horse about anything in magic I remember those words . . . and pause. I wish I could say I have never again allowed my own self-importance to run away with me as it did that evening, but for the many times the memory of those words has halted my speech or turned it in another direction, I am grateful.

Oddly enough, that was the beginning of our true friendship. I realized that I had in a sense surrendered a part of myself to Scott and given him the right (his own right!) to correct me. His was an opinion to which I must listen.

Shortly after that, we shared another special experience together. It was a crisp winter night in 1982, when Scott with Ed and Marilee Snowden arrived at my door. Bundling up against the 3:00 A.M. chill, we crowded into Ed's car. Our destination was the observatory on Palomar mountain. We had an appointment with Halley's Comet, now in the last stages of its streak across the sky. The busy glow of the lights of San Diego veiled it from our sight, and only a journey into the mountains would reveal it to our eager eyes. We pulled out of the city onto the dark, winding roads leading into the mountains. Bright snow lined the roadways, startling with its whiteness in the dark night. I had never seen snow before. We rolled on into the night, ears popping with the changes in altitude, as we hurried to reach the observatory in time to see the comet before the light of dawn erased it from the sky.

Ed pulled over to the side of the road and Marilee pulled out a roadmap. Scott and I looked at each other, anxious. We were already running late; the excursion was supposed to start at 2:00 A.M. Everyone's attention focused on the roadmap, alternate routes, whether or not we were lost, whether or not we could reach the observatory in time or if we should turn back and wait for another night. Scott stared out the window at the night sky. Then he reached for my binoculars lying on the seat between us. He put them to his eyes.

"Hey, I think I can see the comet!" He handed the binoculars to me. There, low in the sky, was a cone-shaped smear with a brighter bead of light pointing south. "It is the comet!" We passed the binoculars around for a moment, Ed found his bearings and the car shot forward over the road. The dark mountains soon curtained the comet from our eyes.

When we reached Palomar observatory and parked, we found dozens of people walking toward us on the path leading from the observatory. We scrambled out of the car and crunched over the snow. With each step, the high altitude and the cold pulled the breath from us lowlanders. Finally, we reached the cluster of domes marking the observatory. We were too late. The observatory had closed its Halley viewing for the day; the rising sun, still obscured from our view, had washed away the comet with its own light.

While the rest of us were voicing our disappointment, Scott went off by himself and knelt on the snow, inscribing magical figures into it to "fix" their influence on his life. We gathered around him to see what he was doing. He cheerfully taught us this new snow spell and our frustration at missing the view of the comet from the Palomar telescope melted away.

Without Scott and his special vision, we would have been blind to the comet. Focused only on the destination, the rest of us would have missed the point of the journey and the magic of the night. It was the clearest example I had ever known of how the road itself, not the destination, may be the most important part of a journey. Scott found magic everywhere, and shared it freely with all who would listen.

Our friendship deepened when, in 1983, I opened a bookstore which was my personal lesson in how not to run a small business. Located on an obscure street with no parking, no walk-by traffic, and no capital to invest in stock, it was a doomed venture. Scott was very supportive about the store and repeatedly volunteered to watch the shop. I paid him in books. He offered to teach a class, which I advertised with a few flyers haphazardly distributed around town. Nobody showed up. It was a relief for us both and we pooled our money and went to dinner.

A few times we locked up the shop and walked to the shore in Pacific Beach. One day we ate at a Mexican restaurant and afterwards, Scott felt ill. He immediately planned to see his doctor and I knew that he suspected that it was not merely an upset stomach but something heralding the return of the lymphoma. This terrified me because a few nights past I had had a horribly detailed dream of his impending death, so alarming that I skipped recording it, not willing to give power to the images by writing them down. But the dream had stunned me so that I brooded on it for days. Now we stood at the top of the cliffs looking down on a beach covered with palm-sized dark stones. The water rushed in over them and retreated with a gobbling sound. Scott said we should record the sound as a sound effect for one of low-budget movies we were always planning to shoot. But as I listened to the sound of the waters receding and draining away through the rocks, I felt as if Scott would soon be pulled from me, and that the time we spent together would be precious. I loved Scott, and it was only by a sharp act of will that I managed to channel the emotion into our various projects.

One of the great pleasures for Scott as he grew successful was to be able to go into a bookstore and buy new or used books off the shelf without much concern for their price. We shared a love of bookstores, and when we went to them together, the booksellers rejoiced. We would goad each other into buying books. "I think you really need that book—you should get it!" If either of us still hesitated, usually the protest, "But if you buy it, then I can use it too!" would settle it. One of our favorite bookhunting grounds was Jeff Bohannon's Safari Books on Adams Avenue in San Diego. I stumbled into this bookstore one windy Autumn night, cautiously entering a long deserted corridor leading to the bookstore in the rear. Excited by what I found—a new bookstore with wonderful books at what could only be termed introductory prices—I called Scott and told him about it. He went a few days later and was hooked, and we often went there together. Jeff Bohannon, the owner, kept a special eye out for books for both of us. We kept an eye out for him, too, well aware of the difficulties a new bookstore could face. In the early days of this store, we were both afraid it might not survive and we spent as much as we could afford there. Another good reason for book buying—as if we needed one. I remember Scott calling me one night. "Jeff's having a hard time making the rent this month. Get over there and buy as many books as possible!" Under these conditions, both our book collections ballooned.

At other times we sold books back and forth when we knew the other needed money, and after a while we possessed books in common whose ownership was a little vague. *Food: The Gift of Osiris* was a beautiful two-volume set that Scott originally purchased. In a financially flush moment, when Scott needed money, I bought it from him for twenty-five dollars. Then he borrowed or bought it back, then I borrowed or bought it back, then I lent it again for his food magic book, then it came back to me, and so on.

We also loved to go to the movies, and when we found a film we liked, we'd see it again and again. The "Monday Dollar Day" was our usual haunt, and we would count up our coins in those lean years, dividing them into piles for gas money, admission, and, if we were lucky, popcorn. A particular favorite was *Romancing the Stone*. For a while, we saw that film almost every week. We thoroughly enjoyed it, and we began to study it as an example of screenwriting. Once we took a stopwatch and made notes of every key scene to learn how the film was paced. Another time we snuck in a small tape recorder and taped the audio track. We both virtually memorized the dialogue, and both of us would spring lines from the movie on the other when some real-life situation resembled, however slightly, the action in the film.

At the time, the majority of Scott's income was still derived from mass-market Westerns which he wrote competently, but without much relish. I was starting to turn my attention to screenwriting at about the same time that Scott's father, Chet, was also making efforts in that area. Scott was very aware of the power of the media. Late one night, we were talking on the phone, tossing around some ideas and generally stirring the fires of writing in both of us. He used to quit writing fairly early because he was afraid of disturbing his neighbors in the apartment on Orange Street. So I invited him over to spend a night writing. This was in the days before either of us had made the switch to computers. He hauled over his old red IBM, I fired up my black one, and for a few hours we both pounded away at our screenplays. These were productive nights: the sound of someone else clacking away on a fresh project at a hundred words a minute a few feet away is inspiring.

Scott's screenplay that night was designed to be a low-budget film that we could produce ourselves. The heroine was a witchy woman selling magical items at Kobey's Swap Meet in San Diego. An enchanted bottle holding an evil spirit is accidentally sold, leading to various disasters. We both agreed the idea had possibilities. I worked on some project of mine, now forgotten, and we wrote until dawn.

A few weeks later I asked Scott if he intended to continue with his swap meet story. He told me he had abandoned the idea. When I asked why, he told me that he'd decided the idea was too negative and that more stories on evil spirits were the last thing the world needed to see or hear. He did not want to unintentionally make it possible for negativity to gain a foothold anywhere.

Our love of movies, and plans for low-budget extravaganzas, led to the production of *Herb Magic*.

In late 1986, with the video revolution underway, Scott and I decided to put together a herb magic video. We both attended local community access classes so that we could be certified to use the equipment at the cable station. However, restrictions on using this equipment for commercial purposes stymied us. I continued studying television production, and the following spring, we decided we were ready to make our mark on the video world. We threw ourselves into the planning of every aspect of production. With his long-standing love of films and extensive reading of behind-the-scenes stories of film production, Scott was a natural. In addition to writing the script, Scott made endless lists of props and other items which we endlessly revised. Finally, after carefully planning virtually every shot of the production, Scott became troubled by a clause in his contract with Llewellyn which essentially prohibited him from using any information presented in his books in any other medium. He approached Carl Weschcke for permission to do the video, which would include similar material to his *Magical Herbalism*.

As it happened, Llewellyn had been interested in producing video programs for a long time, but had been put off by the high budgets presented to them, often tens of thousands of dollars for a short program. This was in the days before high-end consumer cameras brought down the costs of video production in general. Scott and I calculated that we could do our video for about $1500. Since we had been planning to bankroll the project ourselves, there was no slack in the budget. Llewellyn heard our remarkably low estimate and offered to fund our production costs. The company would own the final product, but we would receive a royalty on copies sold. In addition, Llewellyn would have script approval and control over various aspects of the production. Since we knew it would take a long time for us to raise the money on our own, we gladly accepted Llewellyn's offer. We arranged with Kent Taylor of Taylor Herb Farms[1] in Vista, California to shoot at their site. Many people mistakenly assume that the vast herb farm was Scott's personal garden.

Scott, although an excellent impromptu speaker, was insecure about improvising anything during the videotaping of *Herb Magic*, and insisted on using cue cards throughout the production. While this did ensure that everything was taped exactly as scripted, it gave a stilted feel to some of the sequences. In the studio sequences, we intended to use a teleprompter but equipment problems with that required us to make giant cue cards instead. We later used these on location at the herb farm, where gusty winds and glaring sun added their own special problems.

Scott was a willing performer, and he kept all of us amused with his wisecracks between scenes. Our tight budget and shooting schedule prevented us from doing many repeat "takes" on given scenes, but he was always game to try and get it a little better. After the second take, Scott's creative energy would tend to fall, and additional takes usually were disappointing. We decided to keep moving straight through as much of the material as possible. Generally, on location, we shot a second take of everything to protect us in case there was any technical problem with the videotape itself, but much of what made it into *Herb Magic* was first-take material. The studio sequences were largely shot straight through. Part of the studio management was upset that we had negotiated a very inexpensive deal with the sales staff for our studio time, and endless obstacles were placed in our way in an effort to drive us into overtime. Some of these barriers included a "missing" camera, which required us to do the show with only two cameras, instead of the planned three, a technical director supplied by the studio who had never done a multiple-camera show before, and a missing "switcher" operator. Luckily, we were familiar with the "switcher," which is a device that switches between different cameras, provides dissolves between shots, and mixes the video with the generated titles, so we were able to switch the show in spite of the absent crew member.

In addition, we discovered that one of our production assistants was a recently reborn Christian. Although astounded to find herself on the crew of a production dealing with magic, she simply told us she would pray for us and, as agreed, worked hard for us through the rest of the production. During the stress of television production, any benevolent prayers are always welcome.

Most of the studio sequence holds together despite these problems. One objectionable moment has a little charming humor of its own. Most people know that charcoal incense rarely lights easily, particularly when you really want it to. Not so this time. This incense had delusions of stardom. Clouds of grey smoke billowed up, almost completely obscuring Scott, who had to wave the smoke out of his face.

Funny things would happen, of course, as they usually do on any production. We shot one sequence in a shady greenhouse filled with hanging ivy plants. As it happened, during this one sequence Scott kept stumbling over a phrase, and we shot it five or six times. My attention was drawn to the misspoken words, and it wasn't until we were in the edit bay that we noticed an artistic problem with the shot. There was Scott, walking toward the camera, with a large potted ivy plant hanging directly behind his head. The shady lighting enhanced the effect of Scott sporting a large green Afro-style haircut. This "Green Man" material never made it into the final tape, though it alone probably took more time taping than any other scene.

We also ran into pagan "technical" difficulties during the sequence when Scott shows how to draw a prosperity sigil on paper, then burn it to release the energies of the spell. On the first take, the match blew out. On the second take, the match stayed lit but the paper wouldn't burn. Then, on the third take, the paper charred slightly but wouldn't take a flame. Fourth take, the match blew out again. Fifth take, the match wouldn't light. And so on. We wished the spark which had made the incense billow up so dramatically in the studio would return to ignite this shot. Finally, we decided to just shoot the match igniting the paper and use that as a "cut-away" shot that we would insert into one of the better takes. This is what ended up in the final product, but the effort spent in getting that dratted thing to light again ate up a considerable amount of time, while other sequences which were more complicated went much more quickly. That tiny flame was probably the most expensive "special effect" in the entire program!

Nature did not always work against us on the outdoor shoot, however. The herb farm offered several peacocks as unpaid extras. We taped quite a bit of the lovely birds, but their best moment came on camera when Scott was demonstrating how to harvest herbs, and the peacocks came right up to him. It was a magical moment.

This same sequence supposedly helped us in generating interest at the Japanese company which bought the tape rights for Japan. Scott used and recommended a crescent-shaped harvesting knife which they recognized as a traditional Japanese blade. While it was not our intention to do "product placement" or promotion for the Japanese or anyone else, this accidental inclusion of the Japanese tool apparently helped in selling the distribution rights. After the Japanese version came out, Scott and I would joke that we were at least doing our part to offset the trade deficit between the United States and Japan. We particularly enjoyed watching the version which has the Japanese translation dubbed over Scott's voice.

Ironically, Scott was not happy with the book on which the videotape *Herb Magic* was loosely based.

> *Since 1971, I'd been collecting and creating recipes for incense, bath salts, oils, and other magical concoctions. In 1985 I put many of these together into a book entitled (I think)* The Magical Formulary. *Llewellyn published it in 1986 as* The Magic of Incense, Oil, and Brews. *I wasn't happy with the project; it wasn't indexed, and was rather short. I worried that some readers might think I was resting on my laurels. Still, the book sold fairly well. (I was worried that I'd been writing too many herb books.)*

Scott hoped that the videotape would augment the material in the book and get the information to his readers. This was the only book of Scott's which was later extensively revised and republished, as Scott recounts below:

> *In the winter of 1987 and the spring of 1988, after being assured by Llewellyn that I actually could write a new version of one of my books (I had always been told that this was too expensive to even consider), I wrote* The Complete Book of Incense, Oils and Brews, *thereby addressing many of the problems I felt were present in* The Magic of Incenses, Oils, and Brews. *It was fun, and it was a lot of hard work, and I'd never made so many inks and incenses and powders and ritual soaps and tinctures in my life. I was quite pleased with the final results. It was published in 1989, and* The Magic of Incense *was allowed to go out of print.*

After recovering from the production of *Herb Magic*, Scott was eager to do other video programs. Two of his friends, Annella and David Carter, then owners of The Crystal Cave in Claremont, California, decided to take advantage of the video explosion to create a marketing presentation.

This was the *Merchants of the Mystic Arts Video Catalogue* of the Crystal Cave's witchcraft and other supplies. Even with a script by Scott, beautifully shot by Peter Oliver (using much better equipment than we had for *Herb Magic*), narrated by Scott and de Traci, and a soundtrack of beautiful music kindly provided by Melissa Morgan from her "Invocation of Isis" tape, this project was a resounding failure. Annella and David offered the video catalog and only sold one or two of the hundreds of tapes prepared.

The most lasting effect of the video production was a craving Scott developed for fried bananas. Annella introduced the video crew to this Chinese dessert at an Asian diner near her store in Pomona. From that day on, Scott sought out fried bananas at every Chinese restaurant we visited.[2]

Scott also completed a video script for a *Crystal Magic*, and some footage for this program was shot by us in conjunction with Peter Oliver Productions. Unfortunately, this project was never completed. We also intended to do a "What is Wicca" video, but, again, other projects more immediately connected with paying the rent and putting food on the table interfered.

Buckland's Video

Back in 1984, Raymond and Tara Buckland had moved to San Diego and quickly became friends with Scott, often having him to dinner at their home in Pacific Beach. Ray, or "Buck" as his friends called him, and Scott had much in common. They were both writing for Llewellyn, both were ardently popularizing Wicca, and both tended to be a bit iconoclastic, unafraid of tweaking the pointed hats of other witches.

Buck was one of the first to "come out of the broom closet," publicly proclaiming himself to be a witch in the early 1960s. With the publication of *The Tree*, Buck had also spoken out against the narrowness of "traditional" Wicca and made it accessible to more people than ever before. Scott and Buck could "talk shop" on many levels, and the evenings spent together were enjoyable ones. Publicity tours occasionally paired them together on the road. There was a friendly competition between them, and both Ray's *Complete Book of Witchcraft* and Scott's *Wicca: A Guide for the Solitary Practitioner* stayed at the top of the Llewellyn bestseller list. Buck's erudite, professorial teaching style contrasted sharply with Scott's casual, lighthearted approach.

Buck also shared Scott's love of the movies. After *Herb Magic* was finished, Buck suggested to Llewellyn that he would like to do a video for them as well, and *Witchcraft—Yesterday and Today* was born.

During the videotaping of Ray Buckland's *Witchcraft—Yesterday and Today* videotape, Scott worked to ensure that the production went smoothly and he was responsible for finding the locations used in the program. One moment did not go so smoothly. After a very long day of taping, the neighbors next door brought in a disk jockey for a rave party. In a short time about a hundred partygoers arrived, mostly young kids wearing gang clothing. We had one more scene to shoot at that location, and the noise became so loud it was interfering. Scott volunteered to go next door and beg a few minutes of silence from the rowdy neighbors. We heard the noise level drop, knew he had succeeded, and commenced shooting. At that moment Scott, unaware that we were rolling tape, loudly shouted from the doorway, "Is that quiet enough?" Buck, after twelve hours of taping, was not amused. His fierce glare practically erased the videotape. But we stopped, had a good laugh, and completed our shooting just before the kids next door couldn't wait any longer and cranked up the volume again.

Seeing Stars

Inspired by the on-the-set atmosphere while shooting the videos, Scott once again toyed with the idea of writing for film. He still created satirical pieces based on movies in his spare time, but there was less and less "spare time" as he became more successful. Although tempted, he never really invested the time into screenwriting. He was still easily starstruck, though he was beginning to enjoy a measure of fame himself. Scott was always amazed when people would gather around him, attracted by his celebrity within the craft. He collected movie memorabilia from popular films, particularly enjoying Harrison Ford and most films from George Lucas and Steven Spielberg. He was intrigued by the magnetism of famous individuals, and by the effect of fame itself. He was aware of its power and its power to corrupt. Scott stated more than once, as his books became successful and he became well-known, he "could've been a guru," offering expensive retreats and workshops to loyal followers willing to go to the ends of the earth at his word. This prospect appalled him, and he constantly fought to remind his readers and listeners that the power they needed was already within them, and he was only one guide among many.

A chapter from his unfinished autobiography sums up his feelings. He writes about his contact with the movie industry.

Fame Doesn't Mean Anything But Fame

. . . . Like millions of others, I was enamored of Hollywood and of movie stars. Even after I began to frequently visit Hollywood and it became somewhat commonplace, I always kept my eyes peeled for glimpses of celebrities. I loved seeing the front gate to Paramount, the Hollywood sign, etc. Since my father's agent was located at Hollywood and Vine, and I frequently accompanied him on trips to the city, I got to know the area fairly well.

One day my father had a meeting in Century City. Of course I begged to go with him. It was something to do with some publisher. I was immediately bored with the famous writers in the room and begged to be allowed to go out and explore the Century City shopping center. My father quickly agreed.

As soon as I stepped out of the lobby, I noticed that grandstands were being set up. I walked around the shopping center but, because I had no money and have always been "reluctant" to "bother" shopkeepers, I didn't actually go into any of the stores. I kept my eye on the grandstands that were being built on the other side of the street across from the center.

I finally stopped and asked someone what was happening. "They're having the West Coast premier of Bette Midler's new movie The Rose *here tonight."*

I couldn't believe it. I raced up to my father, explained what I was doing, and raced back down. As soon as a few other people had sat in the grandstands, I immediately went and sat there, resolved not to move before I saw a movie star.

Soon, thousands of persons were all over. The press was out in force. Private security officers and policemen were everywhere. A rock band played exceedingly loud (and lousy) music across the street.

Near dusk, the great search lights circled the sky. It was a beautifully warm California summer night.

The limousines began pulling up. I sat entranced: here was the glamour of Hollywood that I'd always heard about. Star after star emerged from those long, gleaming cars, so many that I can only remember a few today: Faye Dunaway and Raquel Welch stand out in my mind.

Everyone was elegantly dressed. The scene seemed so unreal. Flashbulbs popping, limousines gracefully arriving and departing, even a man in front of a microphone announcing the arrivals (I don't know if it was Army Archerd, but I assumed that it was).[3] It seemed that half of Hollywood had come to see the film that would eventually earn Bette Midler an Academy Award for Best Actress.

Finally, as the sun began to set, the star herself arrived. She was dazzling, wearing a very, very low-cut sequined gown, smiling, waving and blowing kisses. I sat there on those grandstands completely mesmerized. This was my dream of Hollywood—and I was seeing it in Century City.

It was then (after attending a premiere in Century City), at the age of twenty four, that I began to seriously think about fame. I knew that it could be created in a number of ways (positive actions; negative actions; sheer publicity; accident) but I still didn't know what it was. After the first flush of publicity and all that, what did these persons have that kept the spotlight trained in their direction (or, perhaps, that kept their internal spotlights brightly shining)?

I realized that it had something to do with energy—I'd learned that much from my early acting experiences. I'd learned that to hold an audience during a performance, it was necessary to be brutally honest, and to send as much internal power into the role as was possible and as was necessary. This *energy, if properly sent (i.e., if the acting is good), bombards the audience. The audience returns this energy to the actors on the stage with its attention, laughter, gasps of horror and applause. Actors incapable of sending this energy to the audience receive little or none in return.*

Maybe, then, actors and other famous persons seemed to be so luminous when in the spotlight because they'd learned to turn on that energy when needed, even when they weren't acting or making speeches. Somehow, I decided, energy had to be involved with fame.

The famous people that I've met—the truly famous ones— all exuded this energy. Natalie [Wood] was mesmerizing, even with a shirt over her head. [See page 124.] Steve Allen was humble and aloof, but riveted my eyes as long as he was in the same room with me (during a book signing party in Newport Beach). Some famous people might be famous simply because they have been for so many years.

One of the first things my readers ask me when we meet is, "What's it like being famous?" I usually make a joke, but some- times I tell them that I'm not famous and never will be, for I'll never have that star presence that separates we mortals from the immortals.

I realize that I'm well-known in some circles. After all, I have 500,000 books in print;[4] have done a video tape and have sat through who-knows-how-many interviews for radio, television, newspapers and magazines. I'm occasionally recognized on the street, in stores and even in pharmacies, both here in San Diego and elsewhere across the country. Fortunately, though, this is rare, and I'm able to enjoy my privacy.

Sometimes I wish that I could write a real best-seller; one that would shock the world by rising to the top of the charts. Such dreams of fame (and, of course, fortune) don't last long, and I always go back to whatever book is presently at hand. I may love meeting famous persons, but I've accumulated a bit of wisdom in this life: fame doesn't mean anything but fame.

In an earlier section of Scott's autobiographical material, he recounts another brush with celebrity:

In 1975, I'd been working the summer season at Sea World in San Diego. The work was difficult at times, since it involved lugging around huge boxes from the warehouse to the various gift shops in the park, but I enjoyed arriving there early in the morning and waking up the exotic birds. I spent stolen hours standing by the dolphin pool, watching the sea lions, the killer whales and enjoying the lush plantings that then covered much of the grounds. (When Harcourt Brace Jovanovich bought Sea World, they ripped out 90% of the landscaping and covered it with concrete. Despite what I may think about their use of animals for entertainment, HBJ completely ruined Sea World for me.)

On one memorable day, I was as usual walking to a gift shop to see if they had anything for me to do. As I approached the shop, I saw Robert Wagner, Natalie Wood, two children and a few body guards approaching the same shop. I was shocked at Robert's appearance: he wasn't lensing a film at that particular period, and his hair was obviously laced with grey. He looked years older. Natalie was, of course, stunning and seemed to be enjoying herself.

Somehow or another, he became separated from the group. Foolishly, I asked him for an autograph, since I'd spent many hours watching his television show.[5] (I was 19 at the time.) He looked at me, smiled and said, "Oh, wow, I don't think I should with all these people around. Maybe later." It was obvious to me that he was a bit perturbed that I'd approached him in public. I blanched. Their party moved away.

About a half hour later I was once again walking to that gift shop with a small box of something or another. I waved at the employees and rapidly walked toward the stock room in the back. I still don't know why no one attempted to stop me.

For some reason, there was an anteroom between the gift shop and the stockroom. It was about six feet square and contained a broom and a bottled water dispenser.

I opened the door to the anteroom and froze. There was gorgeous Natalie Wood, alone. She stood in her skirt, her blouse hanging on a door knob, struggling to get a Sea World t-shirt over her head. I stood still for a second or two, not quite comprehending that she was wearing only her bra but transfixed by the sight of this movie star. The beautiful, flawless white skin of her torso was sharply contrasted by her black bra. I couldn't move, speak, or think.

In a second she slipped the shirt over her head and smiled at me, completely unembarrassed (she was, after all, an actress and must have been through endless costume fittings). I made a hasty retreat, hid behind a counter until she left the store, then collapsed against one of the employees.

"Why didn't you tell me that Natalie Wood was trying on a Sea World t-shirt in there?" I managed to ask. "I walked in and she was in her bra!"

I still remembered Natalie's beautiful skin. I remember her getting into the t-shirt and shaking her head to rearrange her lustrous hair. I remembered her smiling at me as if nothing untoward had happened. And yet, I can't remember what reason my fellow employees had given me for not even trying to stop my entering that room.

Years later, I was crushed to learn of her death during the filming of Brainstorm, *especially since she'd been drowned and her fear of the water was famous. Though I certainly didn't know her, I felt that we'd shared a rather peculiar moment, one of those impossible events that can be waiting around every corner.*

Later Scott had an opportunity to be involved with a motion picture production in another way. He wrote:

Perhaps my most curious involvement with motion pictures was with Carolco. One day in 1990 I received a call from the prop master of an upcoming Oliver Stone movie which at that time was known simply as "The Doors Project." She had gotten my phone number from a mutual friend in Denver. Anyway, she told me that they were doing this movie and wondered if I'd be interested in renting them some props—namely, 100 to 200 occult and metaphysical books, all of which had to have been written before 1970. They were to be used to dress the set of Jim Morrison's Witch girlfriend's apartment, circa 1970.

I was confused about all this and told the woman that I didn't think I could rent any of my books. She hung up. About an hour later I said, "Scott, what have you done?" I spent an hour on the phone, calling all over Hollywood, and finally tracked her down at Carolco, who gave me the number of the Doors project offices.

I agreed. The rent would be for $200. I would ship them the books via an overnight service. They would keep them for a month and ship them back to me with the check.

I spent the next day poring though my book collection. I ended up with about 150 books, including works by Margaret Murray, Gerald Gardner, Charles Godfrey Leland, Crowley and others. I threw in a good selection of Eastern mysticism texts to boot (and because I'd run out of other suitable books.)

Impressed that the Oscar-winning director had wanted his movie to be as accurate as possible, I sent off the books—each of which was marked with my initials and phone number on a small Post-It™ note inside each cover. I was worried that I might lose a few books, so I got the woman's word that they would be well-treated and would not be lost. I also included a list of the books and the actual "replacement cost" of each should it be lost.

Two months went by. They still hadn't filmed the apartment scene. Then, while I was on tour on the East coast, I went into the hospital. By the time I got back from Boston, I called the production company again. By this time it had been four months. The woman nervously said that they'd lost a few of the books.

A few weeks later I had nearly all of them back. They'd only lost a few, and these were inconsequential paperbacks that are available in any used book store. I got my $200 plus and they got props for their movie.

When I finally saw the movie (named The Doors), I kept waiting for the apartment scene. Just as I'd figured, it was *darkly lit and weirdly photographed. We never saw the books on the screen.*

Since I've written in this chapter about famous persons and movie stars, I might as well tell you about my other brief fling with movie-making. It must have been 1975 or 1976. A motion picture production company was in town filming a movie. They were filming only at night on the campus of a local college. A friend of mine who was attending the college called me one day and asked if I wanted to be in the movie.

"I want top billing," I told him.

He laughed and said that they needed extras. The movie was starring David MacCallum and was some kind of horror movie. I thought it would be fun and instantly agreed. He said to me that I was supposed to dress "like a student," and to be sure to bring some books to carry around—and not expect to get paid.

I showed up at the set at about 9:00 P.M. the first night. I quickly learned from experience just how boring motion picture production truly is. Nothing in my limited acting experience had prepared me for this. We must have done twenty or thirty takes of the same scene that first night. This scene consisted of forty college students running down a long hall and stopping in front of a glass door, screaming and looking as terrified as we possibly could. I usually finagled my way to the front of the pack and did some pretty convincing banging on the glass door. Some vicious dogs were supposedly chasing us.

I seem to remember the director being very patient with us and he finally got the shot. David MacCallum finally came to the set, looked around, and went to his honeywagon (portable dressing room). He looked far shorter than he had on The Man From UNCLE.

The highlight of that first night was dinner. I've never had such a wonderful meal. The stars, of course, had their own dinner, but us extras dug into massive containers of piping hot food on a chow line set up by the caterers. I ate so much that I have no idea how I once again ran through that corridor after dinner—the director wanted another camera angle of the scene.

I quickly learned that this was a very low budget film. They were saving money by shooting at a real college but, since school was in session, they were shooting the entire thing at night. For the exterior shots, they lit up huge, smoking arc lights that were so powerful that they literally changed night into day for the scenes on the campus commons. I've always thought this was amazing—how many times have I watched a cheap movie or a television show in which scenes were shot "day for night." Here was the reverse.

Guess what we did on that college campus commons? That's right—we ran across it, back and forth, all night long, while David MacCallum wisely stayed in his honeywagon.

There were many boring moments in my two-night long acting career, but I enjoyed watching the dogs being run through their moves. They were handsome big black creatures that were quite sweet off camera. In the movie, these innocent pups were supposed to eat about fifty people.

I had a bit of fun and ate enormously well for two nights.

On the third night of shooting, though, my parents were coming back from Hawai'i and I went to pick them up at the airport. I left my Hollywood "career" behind me.

By the way, if you're wondering what the name of this film was, it was Dogs. The movie was a complete disaster. I've never even been able to sit all the way through it. Dogs is available on video tape at your nearest store, but I don't urge you to see it. I think, as is often the case, that I ended up on the cutting room floor.

1. Sadly, this herb farm no longer exists.
2. We also received a number of comments on the small joke included at the very end of the tape: Is this sirius? The production company name, Ast-Sothis, refers to the aspect of Isis associated with the star the Egyptians called Sopdet or Sothis, also known as Sirius. The Egyptians loved punning and our meaning was "Is this Isis? Is this the Dog Star?" Llewellyn received letters demanding to know what the meaning

of this was. One person misread the "sirius" as "serious" and wondered if the joke was meant as a disclaimer on everything that preceded it. So much for bad puns!

3. A famous Hollywood columnist.

4. As of this writing, Scott's books in print total approximately 1.2 million.

5. Probably "Hart to Hart"

Part IV

Blossoming

1988—1990

O stars whirling through the sky above;
  O power hiding from the light;
O black curling on the darkened land;
  O secrets biding in the night;
O ebon treasures of the drowsing Earth;
  O haunting forces of the deep;
O misty measures of the circling sky;
  O daunting splendors that you keep;
Come to me with your shadowed kiss!
  Fill me with your mystic power!
Come to me with your arcane might!
  Be here at this midnight hour!

—Chant to increase the power of a spell
from *Llewellyn's 1993 Magickal Almanac.*

Chapter Ten

Collections and Collaborations

Most writers' lives are solitary. Scott's was no exception. Rising in the early morning, he would often be at the typewriter by first daylight. Furiously puffing cigarettes and chugging down Coca-cola, he pushed to get his bread-and-butter writing out of the way first. Each month he churned out four columns on various aspects of car repair. Though these articles were carefully researched and verified, running for years in some markets, Scott himself had little interest or experience in car repair. His skills as a researcher carried him through. He was amused by the fact that these anonymous articles ran under the pictures and by-lines of experienced mechanics and car dealership owners.

In addition to these articles, Scott was usually racing to complete a mass-market novel before the deadline. Churning out these books for the then-handsome sum of a thousand or twelve hundred dollars, he sometimes would complete dozens of pages a day. As with all his writing, he did not count the many hours he spent researching as "real writing." Research, which was primarily hours spent reading, scribbling or typing endless notes, or delving through miles of library shelves, was considered "fun." It didn't count toward his standards of productivity, which were measured only in the number of finished, clean pages he could complete in a day.

When Scott was writing, or felt that he was behind in his work, even the most tempting distractions were ignored. In poorer times, an invitation to a meal was usually accepted, accompanied by the bare minimum of time for socializing before he would return to his red IBM Selectric which sat on a paper-crammed desk. Usually the ring mark from a Coke can stained the papers, and a light dusting of cigarette ash clung to the spaces between the keys. Knee-high piles of research papers, books, rough drafts, letters and other ephemera marked narrow pathways leading to his desk, his small, overflowing altar, his bed, and other essentials. His apartment on Orange Avenue never fell short of being a fire or earthquake hazard. To specially honor a guest, or when his parents or landlord were likely to visit, he would strive to clean up, but the results were frequently invisible. During the periods he had a roommate, the disaster areas were more limited, but when he was living alone, the creative chaos spread everywhere.

Magical Household

After Scott's first books were published, many people asked his help as a collaborator on their own works. While Scott was usually willing to offer general advice, or to read something over if his work schedule and interest permitted, he was adamant about writing alone. This solitary creative life was to change with *The Magical Household*. Based on a suggestion from David Harrington that was too good to ignore, Scott decided to work on the book with David. Scott's concerns about collaborating soon eased. In his autobiographical material, Scott wrote:

> *In about 1980, David Harrington kept bugging me to write a book entitled* The Witches' Cottage. *In spite of his protests, I*

finally talked him into working with me on the project. This was a heavy research book. We worked and worked. I wrote and rewrote, incorporating David's suggestions. Among these were: don't put chapters on protection and purification in the front of the book; go through the house room by room, etc. Early drafts of this book were quite dull; the final mss. was pretty good. As soon as we'd finished TMH (in 1987), the year it was published, we started on our next collaboration—Spell Crafts. (TMH might have been my first occult book done on a computer.)[1]

David's contribution as a collaborator par excellence became quickly evident, and the constant contact between Scott and David relieved the isolation of the writing process. David exhaustively researched any magic pertaining to dwellings, writing up his notes, often sprinkled with humorous notes or drawings, and presented them to Scott, who pored over them and put the information they contained into his own inimitable style. Scott describes the writing of *The Magical Household* in its Preface:

We started on New Year's Eve. In the following months, while I worked at what was to become Cunningham's Encyclopedia of Magical Herbs, *we scribbled ideas, impressions and rituals on paper. Long, rainy afternoons spent at the downtown San Diego public library reading up on ancient house customs merged with nights when we ransacked our personal libraries to fill in the gaps in our knowledge.*

Over the next two years, we finally put together a book of sorts. It wasn't what either of us had envisioned, so I continued to rewrite, edit, and expand the information, with David providing witty comments and erudite criticism on each draft.

Scott was especially enchanted with the illustrations Llewellyn provided for the book. David Harrington acquired the original artwork of the cover created by Robin Wood. The interior illustrations were equally lovely. Designed to be reproduced in black and white, Scott felt that Martin Cannon's paintings caught the essence of the soul behind *The Magical Household*. In the future, Scott urged Llewellyn to have these artists do the artwork for his books.

David did not pull punches working with Scott; if he thought Scott was going off in a poor direction, he didn't hesitate to tell him so. Years later, Scott would comment that David had excellent instincts on what would make a section or chapter work, and Scott relied even more on this skill when they wrote *Spell Crafts*.

Scott's Own Magical Household

Scott not only wrote about magic—he lived a magical life. His apartments, (though untidy, in spite of his suggestion that witches' houses must be clean and orderly) were wonderlands filled with magical objects, some made by his hand, others collected from his publicity tours and trips to Hawai'i. He was an unabashed collector, and he would acquire many objects of a similar type. A favored collection of cauldrons, large and small, metal or even plastic, numbered in the dozens.

One of Scott's favorite incenses was Copal, which he began using many years before it became a popular "New Age" fragrance. For a time, at least one bookstore in San Diego relied on Scott for their supply, which he personally purchased in Mexico. After David took him to Tijuana for the first time, Scott made regular pilgrimages across the border, especially relishing the "Day of the Dead" images, which he would bring home and share with his friends. He was particularly fond of little skulls, which he would sometimes conceal in his hand and suddenly "flash" at the unwary. This affection for the little skulls went hand in hand with his enjoyment of "ugly" witch figures, which often garnered criticism from witches who preferred beautiful images.

Scott saw these skulls and witches as representatives of crucial aspects of the gods and goddesses—their aspects as death deities, deities of change, rest, and rebirth. People who were uncomfortable with these playful images, he found, were often even more uncomfortable with the realities these images represented. The crone and laughing skull found a place with him, alongside the bright and beautiful images of the gods and goddesses. As the grandson of farmers who still lived on the land, the cycles of life and death were well understood by him. To Scott, the crone was a symbol of great antiquity and power, and he was unafraid of this aspect. He also had many representations of the Goddess in her younger and more beautiful forms, and these shared shelf and wall space along with the crone.

Nor was the God forgotten. Scott himself liked to collect figurines of the Hawai'ian gods, and he also collected kapas (printed bark-cloth fabric hangings). He used these Hawai'ian mementoes to decorate his house. He also collected glass fishing floats in all colors and sizes that he called "witch balls" and used them in his spells.

United in Scott's personal space, the different cultures and approaches somehow achieved a harmony. At the same time, he tried to respect the uniqueness of each deity image and the culture that created the image. He did not care for the mixing of cultures within a system, protesting, for example, the use of the Eastern meditation syllable "Aum" to begin a Western European witches' rite.

Halloween Hauntings

When fall came and the decor in the seasonal aisles at the drugstore turned to black and orange, Scott was delighted. Fall was his favorite season. He enjoyed the leaves turning, the orange pumpkins in roadside fields, the crisp air. He was glad to see the heat of summer fade and "jacket weather" begin.

In San Diego, there was an established tradition of grand witches' celebrations at this time of year. Key among these were the massive Hallows parties hosted by Marilee, with a hundred or more participants, party games, hearty Hallows stew, and many small and large rites and rituals led by Marilee throughout the evening. Scott, while generally avoiding crowded celebrations, usually would make an appearance, occasionally offering to do divinations by dripping wax into water and interpreting the resulting images.

David recalls having the dubious honor of allowing Scott to invade his home for a different kind of celebration: "One year Scott decided he wanted an additional celebration, and here the little boy who had recreated Disneyland in his backyard resurfaced. Scott wanted to try his hand at creating his own Halloween celebration built around a haunted house theme. Since his apartment was crowded, he asked if he could use my home to stage this event. I worked the 3:00–11:00 P.M. shift so this left him all afternoon and evening to set up this tableau. I expected that I would return home to find a few black and orange crepe streamers and some punch. I was in for a rude awakening.

"A couple of days before the high holy day, the day of the party, Scott's old Toyota chugged to my door. My mouth hung open because the little car was crammed full of bundles of various sizes and one huge box that was mysteriously emitting smoke-like vapors. With trepidation I handed him the key to my house and left for work, wondering what I had let myself in for.

"We had agreed that I would call him before coming home from work so that he would be 'ready,' whatever that meant. As I neared home, the house was entirely dark and silent as a tomb. I gave the agreed-upon knock on the door and a scream rent the night air. The door was suddenly opened by unseen hands and there stood my large iron cauldron with smoke billowing out and rolling down my front steps.

"As my eyes adjusted to the darkness there stood Scott with a finger to his lips requesting silence. He didn't have to motion—I was stunned. Nothing in my house was recognizable. Great spider webs draped the walls and corners, bats with glowing eyes hung from the rafters, and eerie organ music emitted from nowhere. He led me through the house and opened the bathroom door. Even though I knew it was all make-believe, the sight of two grinning skeletons lying in a tub of blood, raising glowing champagne glasses, was disconcerting.

"Back in the dining room, he had arranged a 'dumb supper' for the dead with glow-in-the-dark clay food he had carefully shaped by hand. Meat, vegetables, even a dessert graced the plates, served to yet more skeletons. And for us—the living, there was a huge witch-shaped cake with hot apple cider.

"This became a tradition for us, and each year his displays grew more elaborate. As for me, I would still be finding bits of glow-in-the-dark clay or fake spider webs well past Yule."

The Political Scott

Scott was continually active as a letter-writer on bills and issues that he felt warranted special attention by his elected representatives. He voted regularly, and during his last illness, made certain he made it to the polls to vote for Clinton. He made a dark joke that, for the first time, a candidate he was backing might actually win, but he might not be alive to see him take office or benefit from any changes. Scott was also convinced that politics in general needed more female energy, and he was inclined to be a bit sexist in voting for virtually any female candidate. He argued this point over one election[2] where a husband had been convicted and imprisoned due to business practices. Scott didn't believe that her husband's legal problems were a consideration; the fact that she was a woman was the overriding factor in his support.

Scott recycled cans, plastic, and newspapers long before these practices became well-known, fashionable, or convenient. He regarded his recycling as an act of magic, and commented that he couldn't see how someone could call themselves a pagan and not be active in recycling and other efforts to heal the earth. His small kitchen was filled with garbage bags for various recyclables, which he would pack into his car and drive to the appropriate recyclers.

Cautious about generating publicity in the San Diego area, Scott refused any local television or radio appearances. He did accept out-of-town and national television appearances and radio interviews. He particularly enjoyed appearing on the "Sally Jessy Raphael" show with Selena Fox, founder of the Circle Sanctuary and newsletter, and Ray Buckland. He was aware of the dangers, physically and psychologically, that public discussion about his witchcraft could create.

In early October of 1984, at the "Wicca—An Answer to Changing Times" conference sponsored by The Circle of Metamorphosis at the Hanalei Hotel in San Diego, Scott and I [deTraci] had vendor tables. Gavin and Yvonne Frost were speakers and were also conducting initiation rites. Scott was selling copies of *Magical Herbalism* and inscribing them for the purchasers. I was selling used books on magical subjects, as were several other vendors. Suddenly, a slip of paper peeping out between the pages of a book caught my eye. In one of the metaphysical books was a fundamentalist religious tract that had not been there moments before. Just as the vendors were beginning to realize something odd was going on, we heard a commotion outside. On the steps, about thirty picketers were noisily protesting the fact that a "witches' conference" was being held at the Hanalei. The leader was a well-known San Diego fundamentalist preacher.

Someone from the conference locked the doors from the inside, and we stared out through the glass at the angry faces. Here, in San Diego, we were facing an anti-witchcraft mob. And we knew it could easily escalate into violence.

Rumors were beginning to surface that this preacher was behind various bombings of family-planning clinics in San Diego, a crime for which he was later imprisoned. It was obvious from the tone of the leaflets and picket signs that these people did not regard our lives or religious freedom very highly. They called us Satanists, informed us we were condemned to hellfire, and accused us of various ghastly practices. In the bright San Diego sunshine, where the picketers were wearing summery shorts and tops, we were chilled by the reminder that hatred and religious oppression lurk everywhere, and need very little encouragement to surface. Similar scenes must have greeted earlier witch hunt victims. The only differences were that we lived in a society where we made the "hunt" unnecessary with trusting openness, and that the local authorities might assist us instead of helping our oppressors.

Eventually the San Diego police and Hanalei officials managed to disperse the picketers. The incident left us shaken and angry. Scott was understanding when he heard of problems that other Wiccans suffered for their faith, and he believed that one's faith did not need to be revealed to everyone. He valued his own privacy, and did not believe that he had to sacrifice his solitude to further the public acceptance of any part of his life. Discretion, he knew, could save a life or a reputation. This was reflected in an article that he wrote for the "San Diegan Pagan":

The Public Pagan
A public Pagan isn't one who wears a flashing pentagram to work, to play, to the grocery store.

A public Pagan isn't one who casually says, "Yeah, I worship the Goddess," whenever the subject pops up.

A public Pagan isn't one who performs rituals in parks, dressed in flowing black robes, brandishing knives over flaming cauldrons.

A public Pagan isn't one who confronts Fundamentalist Christians, trying to tear apart their beliefs.

These are excellent ways to become an ex-Pagan, an ex-human being, an ex-incarnated soul. However . . .

A public Pagan is one who wears a smile in the face of our sometimes overwhelmingly monotheistic society.

A public Pagan is one who casually thinks, "Yeah, I worship the Goddess," whenever the subject pops up.

A public Pagan is one who reveres the trees, the seashores, the sky and the waters.

A public Pagan is one who tries to see the thrust behind all religions, regardless of creed.

A public Pagan is one who recycles plastic, glass, paper and aluminum.

A public Pagan is one who contributes something, no matter how small an amount, to ecological organizations.

A public Pagan is one who lets deeds speak for themselves.

Similarly, he expressed the goals of a natural magician in an article published in *Llewellyn's 1990 Magickal Almanac:*

To walk in harmony with nature, never taking without giving.

To understand that magic is an alliance between humans and the Earth for the betterment of all.

To use magic as an instrument of loving change, not hateful destruction.

To see the spiritual in the physical and to understand that neither is higher nor more perfect than the other.

To wisely use natural energies only when in genuine need, not for greed.

To know that nothing is impossible if we will work beyond personal limitations.

To work magic for others only with their permission.

To celebrate magic as a union with the energies that gave us our physical forms.

To improve ourselves, our friends and our world for the greater good of all.

Scott was also vehement on the subject of chain letters, which he regarded as a form of black magic. On at least one occasion, he discovered which friend had sent him "luck" in the form of a chain letter, and immediately sent off a furious letter detailing his anger at a negative attempt to manipulate him. The unwary person who had sent on the letter got a lesson in magic as well as a lesson in Scott's ability to conjure up righteous anger.

His strong feelings on this prompted him to write an article on the subject, for *The Rose & Quill*,[3] a magical journal published in San Diego by Judith Wise and Scot Rhoads. He writes:

> *A year ago it seemed I was receiving a chain letter nearly every month. After I'd wadded up the first two or three, I began doing a short ritual—ripping the letter into small pieces and burning it in my cauldron.*
>
> *However they're worded, whatever "good" intentions the person who sent it on to you may have had, all chain letters are tools of negative magic, and those who perpetuate them by sending five or ten or twenty copies to friends are guilty of furthering negativity.*
>
> *Harsh words? Not at all. Look closely at any chain letter. Typically they wish you "good luck" and money and may even include the word God or Jesus. They relate stories of the wonderful things that happened to others who passed on the chain—and the tragedies of those who broke it . . .*
>
> *Most chain letters are also subtly demeaning to women. Don't believe me? Read one closely sometime . . .*
>
> *The purpose for this article? Its aim is to halt the spread of chain letters among our community. The next time you receive a chain letter, burn it. Destroy it. Obliterate this proof of the ignorance of others; crush the chain beneath your feet. . . Chain letters are just that—chains. Shackles ready to hold us back, but the only power they have to bless or curse us is that which we give them . . .*
>
> *If you think that I'm crazy for writing about this topic, think about it for a minute: Every chain letter is a veiled psychic attack.*

Just as Scott could find positive energy in a tiny leaf or flower, he was equally vigilant in discovering the ways we can unwittingly let negative energy gain a foothold in our lives.

The Romantic Scott

Scott was a great romantic, but regarded himself as unlucky in love. After a couple of early heartbreaks, he avoided romance while idealizing it as a goal he would never achieve. He concentrated on loving the deities, loving abstract concepts, and pouring himself into his work. He provided a sympathetic ear for friends who regaled him with their stories of love gone bad. These were enough to reinforce his desire to stay separate. Yet he believed in the transforming power of love and knew that this was the base of the most potent magic. He wrote:

> *Anyone who [has] been in love needn't be told of the incredible inner transformations that occur in this state. True, lasting love creates permanent changes within the love and the beloved. Loving another person and caring for them is an act of energy transference.*
>
> *If positive change through energy transference is the essence of magic, then love can rightly be considered to be an aspect of magic . . . Practicing love-motivated magic enhances the quality of our lives. It makes us stronger, healthier, more secure individuals without crushing others along the way. It also changes our attitude—"enemies," illness, defeat, and rejection are actually everyday challenges, not opportunities to vent hatred at ourselves . . . Love is always more powerful than hate. Love is creative, hate is destructive. Magic is a tool of love, guided by a simple doctrine: harm none.*

But though his life was destined to be a solitary one, it was not to be a lonely one. As a writer, he would reach thousands.

Magical Aromatherapy

Rosemary sighs on a hot summer day
The fragrance of jasmine sings on the breeze
I inhale the perfumes of nature
while the lemon balm seeks out the bees.

—from one of Scott's early journals

The use of essential oils and aromatherapy gained popularity with the New Age community in the late 1980s. Essential oils are the distillations of fragrant plants, containing the complex essence of each. Vibrant and powerful, these natural essences put synthetic scents to shame. As a natural magician, Scott loved essential oils and had used them for a long time, obtaining many of them from his friend Marilee Bigelow. It was no surprise when he was approached by Llewellyn to do a book on the subject.

> *In 1988, Carl came to me with the idea of writing another mass-market book. Somehow or another, we decided that it should be about the magical uses of perfumes. I quickly realized that I had never mentioned aromatherapy in any of my books. Thus, Magical Aromatherapy was born. This was a quite costly book to produce. I spent hundreds and hundreds of dollars buying genuine essential oils and travelling around the country to meet with aromatherapy experts. Still, I enjoyed the final book.*

As part of his extensive exploration of aromatherapy, Scott attended conferences and purchased oils for his own experiments. He had a natural "nose" for scents and was a reliable "test" to determine if an oil was truly pure, as advertised, or if it had been cut, and, if so, with what substance. Good oils were a great pleasure to him, and he shared this love of essential oils with Marilee who had extensively studied essential oils and distilled some herself and sold others through her Starfire Herb Company. Both Marilee and Scott would pass around cotton balls anointed with a single precious drop of an unusual or high-quality oil, just as others might hold a wine tasting or serve exotic hors d'ouevres. At restaurants, Scott would take the lemon from a glass of ice tea or the orange rind decorating a plate and squeeze the rind over his lighter. The tiny sparks flying up, he pointed out, showed the volatility of the essential oils in citrus skins.

The first scent of a true essential oil is a life-changing experience, and many people discovered the magic of scents through Scott. Scott was never satisfied with synthetic recreations after he had experienced the true nature of the plants he adored through their special essences. One indulgence was what he termed a "rich man's bath," which he only permitted himself rarely. He would fill the tub with hot water, and add a lavish sprinkling of essential oils, particularly the five-dollars-a-drop rose, and then soak in the scented waters for hours. Other favored scents included neroli, jasmine and plumeria, and especially the fragrance of sandalwood. He had a collection of sandalwood ranging from large carved figurines, raw chunks, small beads, fans, and powdered incense.

Searching for obscure information, Scott corresponded with Robert Tisserand, one of the world's experts on essential oils and aromatherapy. Tisserand was an early advocate of the use of essential oils, publishing a number of scholarly and popular books on the subject. Scott recognized him as a master in the field of aromatherapy, and was honored when Tisserand agreed to write the foreword to *Magical Aromatherapy*.

Scott's books on herbs and his forthcoming *Magical Aromatherapy* prompted Maureen Buerhle to invite him to speak at the 1988 International Herb Growers and Marketers Association, where he lectured on *Magical Aromatherapy* and *Ritual Uses of Herbs*. He met with many aromatherapists and attended their lectures, taking his usual extensive, illegible notes.

Sometime in 1988-89, Scott prepared a speech on magical aromatherapy for the 1989 conference of the International Herb Growers and Marketers Association. Scott was obviously altering his style to suit a more scientific audience:

> As part of my studies into the physiological and psychological effects of genuine essential oils on human beings, I've investigated the lesser-known effects of naturally aromatic plant materials. I've drawn upon personal experimentation and 3,000 years of records regarding these subtle effects to create a "new" form of aromatherapy.

Traditional aromatherapy's aims are to heal the body and psyche and to create alternative states of consciousness (such as peace and euphoria). Magical aromatherapy has far greater aims. This practice unites the individual's consciousness and bioelectrical energy to manifest specific, needed changes that cannot be accomplished by any other method. In short, it is a form of magic.

"Magic," as used here, refers to processes which haven't as yet been investigated or explained to the satisfaction of the greater scientific establishment. Magic is the projection of subtle energies to produce needed results.

In practice, magic utilizes the naturally inherent energies contained within specific objects (such as plants and minerals). Fragrant plant materials or products produced from them release some of these energies in the form of odors. Magical aromatherapy, then, consists of inhaling an odor and of consciously welcoming its energies into your being.

Visualization (the practice of forming mental images) is a common tool in magic of all types. In magical aromatherapy, better results are obtained by visualizing the needed change. Suppose I wished to increase the success of my business. I'd sprinkle a few drops of basil essential oil onto a handkerchief, clear my conscious mind and form a mental image of my business as a thriving, cash-engendering concern.

While visualizing I'd inhale the scent of basil and welcome its specific, subtle energies into my being. Because the conscious mind has a direct effect on the body, my visualization, combined with the scent of basil, redirects my bioelectrical energy toward creating and maintaining a successful business.

And so, a "ritual" of this sort may indeed propel me into putting more time into my business, with a greater return for my increased efforts. This may be enough, or I may decide to move this energy (basil+bioelectrical) out of my body into the world at large.

This is once again achieved through visualization. Inhaling the basil, I visualize this energy streaming from me in all direc-

tions, perhaps as a greenish mist. It moves into the atmosphere and attracts more business.

This example encapsulates the theory and practice of magical aromatherapy. The energies contained within naturally aromatic plant materials, combined with those of the human body and the mind, produce a needed change.

What are the aims of magical aromatherapy? Often, satisfying the basic needs of life: promoting our ability to give and to receive love (rose, jasmine). Protecting against physical danger (black pepper). Increasing prosperity and business success (basil, bergamot mint). Maintaining physical health (carnation).

Additionally, magical aromatherapy can be utilized to induce meditative states (sandalwood, frankincense), to enhance psychic awareness (celery seed, cinnamon), to increase our awareness of the spiritual (cedar) and a host of other positive, necessary changes.

As is readily evident from the above lists, magical aromatherapy utilizes fresh and dried plant materials as well as essential oils. This is a striking deviation from traditional aromatherapy. Where essential oils are unobtainable (lily of the valley, apple blossom and plumeria, to list just three), the fragrant plant materials are used to create these internal and external changes.

Magical aromatherapy and traditional aromatherapy merge at some points. Both are used to induce peace, increase physical energy, promote sleep and to sharpen the conscious mind. Generally speaking, the magical effects of essential oils are linked, in some way, to the better-known physiological effects.

Just as with traditional aromatherapy, only genuine essential oils or the plant materials themselves will effect the change; synthetic "essential oils" are of no use in either form of this ancient practice.

Additionally, the strength of essential oils has to be respected. Negative physiological effects (the least of which is severe headache) may occur if they're inhaled for extended periods of time.

Magical aromatherapy won't create miracles. Remember—magic is a natural process, a projection of subtle energies to produce needed results.

Through simple, easy rituals calling for nothing but our minds and the scent itself, we can forge our futures by imagining and inhaling the precious fragrances of herbs, flowers, and fruits.

Cooking up The Magic In Food

After *Magical Aromatherapy*, Scott's next effort was *The Magic In Food*. His autobiography notes:

> *I began keeping notes regarding the magical properties of food in 1973. I'm not joking. 1973! I finally began heavily researching this subject in 1989 and eventually wrote the manuscript, which was completed in 1990. My working title was* Food Magic, *though I didn't like it. Many conferences with the folks at Llewellyn didn't produce a better title. Still, I finally dubbed this book* The Magic of Food. *Llewellyn thought better of this and determined that* The Magic In Food *was somehow more evocative of the book's focus. I worked closely with the photographer who produced the exquisite photos for the book, lending her some of the props that were used. I still think it's a wonderful book, but the cover doesn't draw the correct readers.*

The Magic In Food probably has the least number of copies in print of any of Scott's books. At one point, Llewellyn discussed adding a more extensive recipe section to the book, or perhaps bringing out a companion volume. Scott began work on a selection of recipes for this proposed project. He pored over family recipes, traditional treats from different cultures, and also researched other magical meals that had been described in journals and books.[4]

However, Scott's own high standards kept him from proceeding with this addition to *The Magic In Food*. He was adamant that every recipe be pre-tested by at least two cooks using different kitchens, and the sheer logistics of supervising the double-testing of a hundred or so recipes daunted him. Several of his friends volunteered to test a recipe or two, but were understandably reluctant to undertake ten or twenty recipe tests.

The Magic In Food still has not found its audience. Scott could not understand why this book did not sell as well as his others. Ironically, *The Magic In Food* contains more personal insights than many of Scott's other books. The subject of food is so neutral and universal that he felt he could discuss his own attitudes and experiences without unduly influencing or offending anyone.

1. David and Scott worked on *Spell Crafts* intermittently over the next several years. The completed manuscript went to Llewellyn late in 1992, and was published in September, 1993, five months after Scott's death.
2. The 1992 election of Susan Golding as mayor of San Diego.
3. This magazine was later retitled *New Moon Rising*.
4. A new 400-page revised edition of *The Magic In Food* was published in January, 1996. Retitled as *The Magic of Food* (Scott's original title), it has a new cover and an expanded recipe section. The color photo section was dropped. Twenty-seven familiar and favorite recipes from Scott's notes were included in this edition. More than half of the first printing of 5,000 were sold within a month.

Chapter Eleven

Out of the
Broom Closet

Schism in the craft means freedom.
—Scott Cunningham, circa 1973

OR A LONG TIME, SCOTT WAS RETICENT ABOUT WRITING ABOUT THE Craft and his involvement in it. Part of this hesitation was for reasons of personal privacy, but he was also concerned that by emphasizing Wicca as his religion, some readers would feel that his writing on natural magic required that they formally adopt Wicca as their faith. He did not wish to require such a commitment from anyone.

In 1987, Rosemary Guiley was compiling her book, *The Encyclopedia of Witches and Witchcraft* and wrote to Scott asking if he would like to be included. His response to her reveals some of his feelings on writing about the craft:

> *Until recently I've avoided writing about Wicca. However, Llewellyn recently published [1988] a short pamphlet I penned entitled* The Truth About Witchcraft, *though my name didn't appear on the project (this was the case of most of their "truth*

about" books.)[1] *The response was so favorable they talked me into writing a 200-page version of it which will include my byline. Llewellyn is also readying for publication my next book for them,* Wicca: A Guide for the Solitary Practictioner. *Along these lines, since I've begun producing and appearing in video tapes, one entitled* What is Wicca?[2] *is in the works.*

Even though my magical books have been written from a Wicca viewpoint I've never allowed myself to limit my audience with constant references to it. However, with these new books I am "coming out of the closet" as it were.

In the same letter he included some biographical details so that Rosemary could form questions to ask him:

—Has participated in various covens but has now settled into comfortable solitary practice.

—Is skeptical regarding occult occurrences without personal investigation.

—I view Wicca as a modern religion—no history dating back to Paleolithic times, please—that has much to offer the world.

—I see religion as reverence for humanly-constructed personifications of universal, timeless energies. Magic is the movement of these energies from physical, manifested forms (ourselves, plants, herbs, and etc.) The two are complementary and, indeed, can merge to create magical religions, such as Wicca.

—I think the time has come to strip Wicca of its quasi-historical trappings, of its mythological links with Atlantis, Druidism and etc. and to present it to the public as a modern religion sprung from primeval concepts which utilized both ancient and modern symbols.

Indeed, there's no evidence that the origins of Wicca as we know it today, in all its variety, date back to earlier than 1900 —and that's being generous. Perhaps the earliest date that Wicca can claim for its origins are the mid-1940s when Gerald Gardner began working on what was to become Wicca, along with the help of Doreen Valiente which was so adequately documented in two of Stewart and Janet Farrar's latest books.

> However, the "antiquity" of a religion has no bearing on its ability to achieve the one goal of any faith—to promote and facilitate contacts between Deity (however envisaged) and humans.

Many readers have expressed curiosity about the cover pictures of both the pamphlet and the book versions of *The Truth About Witchcraft*. Some readers have wondered if Scott's friends or family were portrayed. Actually, both of these books use cover images from photo libraries, and neither book cover has any personal connection with Scott or Llewellyn Publications staff.

The writing of *Wicca: A Guide for the Solitary Practitioner* was a long process. Its roots were in the *American Traditionalist Book of Shadows*, a collection of information which Scott had put together, based on his workings with Dorothy, his independent magical work, and his study of existing materials on witchcraft. He had assembled this system for his own use, and practiced it for many years. He "traded initiations" in this system with Judith Wise, who had in turn initiated him into the Myjestic system. He had also put together an "herbal grimoire," a book of shadows based firmly on the magical use of herbs. Most of the material in the *Standing Stones Book of Shadows* which makes up the majority of *Wicca: A Guide for the Solitary Practitioner* was derived from the *American Traditionalist Book of Shadows* and training materials. Scott enhanced this material with his herbal grimoire. Scott details some of the process in another autobiographical fragment:

> At one point, in perhaps 1985 or 86, I told Buck[3] that I was working on a book concerning Wicca. He said, "So am I. What's your approach?" [he asked.] I answered, "Wicca for the solitary practitioner." I'm not sure if that was the origin of the title; the book had been called everything from The Smoking Cauldron to etc. etc. etc.
>
> I was worried, while writing it, that the book wouldn't reach as wide an audience as others on the subject, since I absolutely refused to include the explosive word "Witch" in the title. My fears were unfounded.

Wicca: A Guide for the Solitary Practitioner found a wide readership from the start. But Scott need not have worried about any lack of pyrotechnic power.

The Smoking Cauldron Explodes

With the publishing of *Wicca: A Guide for the Solitary Practitioner*, Scott found himself at the center of raging controversy. His book provided a way for anyone to become a practitioner of Wicca, regardless of coven training or affiliation. Some witches found it highly offensive that individuals could practice Wicca separate from a coven, doubted that Scott had been initiated at all, and harshly derided the book. Most of the criticism came from actively teaching covens or groups with a strict hierarchy. What Scott proposed—and provided—was a guide to what they perceived as spiritual anarchy. Orthodox Wicca, like most "organized" religions, now demanded a coven structure. Here was one of the pagan community's most beloved spokespersons saying that all of that was unnecessary—though not necessarily undesirable—for spiritual development.

Scott finally found it necessary to respond to the accusations that he wasn't initiated or had been thrown out of a coven or, generally, despite all of the books that many of the same individuals had highly praised, didn't know what he was talking about. The following material he intended to include in the book *Living Wicca*, but it was removed prior to publication, probably because he did not want to distract from the contents of that book.

Is He or Isn't He?

The most controversial chapter in this book's predecessor [Wicca: A Guide for the Solitary Practiioner, 1988] discussed initiation. Many took umbrage with the simple idea presented within this chapter: initiation isn't always a process that one human being performs on another. Some seemed to read this chapter as if I were stating that initiation is never necessary. And many (both privately and publicly) assumed that my words indicated that I'd never been initiated.

Though I've had many teachers, and have been initiated into several traditions over the years, I purposefully withheld writing about such matters in Wicca precisely because it was a book for solitary Wiccans: those who didn't have the luxury of a teacher. Telling wonderful tales concerning my early training and initiations would have accomplished nothing in that forum. To be blunt, I didn't want to thrust my training in the faces of those who couldn't receive it themselves.

However, for the record, I'll here publicly state something of my magical training. I do keep my vows of secrecy, and save for a rather suggestive passage in one of my books (which was brought to my attention by one of my High Priestesses), I've never printed anything that was given to me in confidence. Therefore, some information I must keep to myself . . . [4]

In 1980 I decided that I wished to broaden my training. Having worked in only one system for nearly a decade, I felt it was time. (Dorothy had moved to New York.) After a false start (complete with initiation) into a rather peculiar "ancient" system, I began learning two new ones simultaneously. Though this proved to be somewhat difficult, the two people who were training me had been High Priestess and High Priest and, though separated by hundreds of miles, were still in harmony. I learned much.

On May 25, 1981, I was initiated into the Reorganized Traditional Gwyddonic Order of the Wicca. A three degree system is in use in this tradition, and I received my 1st and 2nd degree simultaneously. (Why not? I wasn't going to argue the point with my teacher.)

On July 6, 1981 (aren't records wonderful?) I was initiated to 3rd degree in the ROTGOOTW, after passing rather strenuous magical tests. On the same date, I also received initiation into the APGW [Ancient Pictish Gaelic Way], a still hidden family tradition.

And finally, on November 11, 1981, after much study, I was initiated into a fourth tradition.

So, yes, I have received initiation, and I don't really mind if others don't "recognize" them. I've also initiated others into Wicca and, from all accounts, these initiations have been successful.

I've had many wonderful teachers: Dorothy, who first opened my eyes, introduced me to the Goddess, explained the circle and the tools, and taught me magic; G.,[5] who showed me much and then, unavoidably, closed the door; M.,[6] who generously shared his wisdom and friends and taught me his tradition; and finally J.,[7] whose love for Wicca is only outshined by her love for everyone and everything.

Many others who haven't formally taught me have contributed much to my growth as a Wiccan. These include Marilee, whom I met in 1973 through Dorothy, and who was once a fellow covener; David Harrington, fellow author and true natural magician; John and Elaine, who walk a similar path; and that now nameless Methodist minister who, quite surprisingly, taught me how to see auras, the fine art of meditation and the basics of yoga—a long, long time ago.

Conventional religion never spoke to me. When I "fell into" Wicca without even trying, I knew that I'd come home. Yes, I've had teachers. Yes, I've been trained. Yes, I've been initiated by fellow Wiccans within circles of light. And yes, I'm now telling you all these things—not out of pride or vanity, but to clear the record . . . to answer unasked questions . . . and, hopefully, to give you some confidence that I know whereof I write.

Knowing that I have, indeed, learned from those who know, have literally sat at my teachers' feet, and have received initiation will possibly lend more power to my words, if only in your mind.

Books are usually thought of as second best to a real, physically present teacher. But for thousands of persons, books (mine and those by others) are the only teachers available to them.

I've always tried to share my good fortune through my books. I hope that I've achieved some small measure of this.

Although the controversy eventually died down, many still resented Scott's demystification of Wicca. But his readers welcomed *Wicca*, and Scott began to plan a sequel where he would discuss more of the underlying philosophy of Wicca.

·❧·

1. While this is true for most of Llewellyn's *Truth Abouts*, Scott's name did appear on the front cover of this booklet. It also appears on the reformatted and redesigned version produced in 1994.
2. Unfortunately, this project never succeeded in getting beyond the drawing-board stage.
3. Raymond Buckland, who was working on *The Complete Book of Witchcraft*.
4. Here Scott describes his study with Dorothy. This material is included in Chapter 2, "Into the Circle."
5. This is not the Ginny Therion previously indicated by the initial "G" in Scott's writing.
6. Mel Fuller.
7. Judith Wise-Rhoads.

Chapter Twelve

A Scare in Salem

N THE SPRING OF 1990, WITH HIS BOOKS REACHING MORE READERS than ever before, Scott embarked on a grueling publicity tour that took him to many cities in the Midwest and on the East Coast. His days were a frenzy of lectures, booksignings, and workshops. He began having headaches, which he at first assumed were stress-induced migraines, though he had never suffered migraines before. He called friends who suffered from migraines, asking advice. Various remedies were suggested to him, but it didn't seem logical that he would suddenly be getting migraines. He saw a doctor in one town, a chiropractor in another, but no one paid too much attention to his "migraines." We all grew more and more concerned about Scott, but he seemed to be doing everything he could for himself.

Perhaps there is still something in the town of Salem that is hostile to witches. After Scott's arrival in Salem to teach a class, his mysterious headache intensified and left him semi-conscious. He was rushed to the hospital by his hosts, who had no idea how to get in touch with Scott's family. Finally a call to Llewellyn reached Nancy Mostad, the acquisitions editor, who contacted deTraci. Scott, the actor, would have appreciated the high drama of the situation. As it happened, deTraci was working on a project at one of the Disney Studios soundstages and was called to the stage phone for an emergency message. For once, production challenges took a distant second in importance. Calls to Scott's parents' house were unsuccessful, but finally Scott's brother, Greg, was reached through his employer. He then contacted Scott's parents.

In the meantime, without insurance and unable to speak for himself, Scott was considered indigent and treated as a charity case. By a lucky coincidence, deTraci's then boss, Dr. Barry Sandrew, had worked with physicians at that hospital. He contacted a friend who was a staff neurologist there who immediately looked in on Scott. By this point, Scott's father, Chet Cunningham, had been contacted and he immediately flew back to Boston to be with Scott who was suffering from cryptococcal meningitis.

News was still scanty, but within a few days, Scott was able to talk on the phone. Chet flew back to California to help his wife Rosie, who was battling multiple sclerosis.

Scott, alone in Boston, now had one ardent request: "Something to read—anything to read!" There was no such thing as a hospital library cart. Even when gravely ill, his urge to read and research was overwhelming. We sent him fifteen pounds of books and magazines immediately. When he left the hospital in Boston, he gave the books to other reading-deprived patients.

After several weeks in the hospital, when Scott was well enough for the long flight back to California, he was immediately transferred to UCSD [University of California San Diego] Medical Center. In the same hospital where he had successfully conquered lymphatic cancer almost a decade before, he now fought cryptococcal meningitis complicated by opportunistic infections.

Several "Medical Funds" were set up for Scott, and many people made donations to help offset his medical expenses. Scott was deeply touched that so many people cared about him, and embarrassed by the benevolent attention now lavished on him. In most cases complete addresses on the donors were not forwarded to him, but Scott wrote letters of thanks to many, even including a "Rite for Protection" which he sent as a gift to those who had contributed.

Scott's initial recovery took weeks, but he stabilized and appeared improved, though easily tired. Massive doses of daily medication held the disease in an uneasy truce.

A New Year Begins

Scott began 1991 with guarded optimism. His first major magical act of the year was a prosperity spell (cooking cabbage with silver). On January 5, he began work in earnest on his Hawai'i book. Hazel Cunningham, his grandmother, was in town and he visited her at his parents' house several times. She showed him how to make folded paper boxes and asked him what sort of teddy bear he would like her to make for him. The Gulf War erupted, troubling him. To Scott, war was a foolish waste of human energy and lives, a tragedy regardless of which side was "right."

The long drought for southern California was broken in 1991 and Scott recorded each rainfall with joy. One day, he wrote "How I wish I could wrap myself in a rainy night to sleep while droplets melt into my face." He collected rainwater to use later in spells. To invoke rain, he drew a rune on a piece of parchment and left it out until the symbol was washed away by rain.

On January 26, he happily noted a visit to the as-yet-unopened *E.T.* adventure at Universal Studios. Marilee Bigelow was working on the creation of the ride, and he loved his VIP opportunity she made possible for him to experience the ride before it was open to the public.

Between notes of visits with friends, he also noted doctor appointments and medical test results. He kept up a brisk pace of booksignings and even occasional classes.

Hawai'i beckoned to him even more now that he had finally begun work on his *Hawai'ian Magic* manuscript. On February 5, he and David Harrington traveled to the islands, visiting his favorite sites and doing more research. When they returned February 16, Scott was stunned by news that Grandma Cunningham, whom he had seen only weeks before, was dead. His parents went to Oregon to gather her things, and brought back some teddy bears she had made. Scott selected one in memory of the promise she had made to make him one.[1]

Four days after he heard his grandmother had died, Scott's life was jolted by the murder of his landlord during a robbery next door to his apartment building. George Watson, in addition to running the building, was also the proprietor of the "Vacuums and Guns" store on Orange Avenue next to the apartment building. He was surprised by three young men seeking additional weaponry. He shot and killed one of his attackers and wounded another, but was wounded himself and died a few hours later. Though Scott had not been a close friend of his landlord, he had seen the man daily for almost twelve years.

Scott was interviewed by reporters hungry to get a human-interest reaction for the *San Diego Union-Tribune*. Scott knew then that it was time to leave the increasingly dangerous neighborhood, and he immediately began to look for a new place to live. He chose a modern two-bedroom, two-bath apartment near Lake Murray.

There was another reason he was willing to leave behind the small apartment where he had written dozens of books. As his health declined, he became more and more aware that his bedroom paralleled an electrical transformer box mounted on a utility pole only five or six feet away from his apartment wall. Though he was skeptical regarding claims that EMF radiation was damaging, he wondered if this device could have contributed to his health problems.

By comparison to the apartment on Orange Avenue, which overlooked a busy corner with a gas station and a 7-11 market, the Lake Murray apartment seemed like another country. Instead of endless traffic droning outside, his new neighbors complained that the sound of the small water-fall on his patio was keeping them awake. He set out his Hawai'ian plants, jasmines, ginger, and ti plant, and turned off his waterfall early each night. Inside, Scott set up his iron bedstead and covered it with a handmade quilt from Grandma Cunningham. His new office, pristinely neat for a day or two, soon resembled the usual creative chaos, but at least he was no longer sharing a room with his bed and altar. With all this extra space, Scott even tried to keep books and papers out of the living room. He didn't succeed for long, but at last many of his cherished Hawai'ian arti-facts now were displayed on his walls and in his shelves where he could enjoy them daily. He settled in to work, interrupted only by endless medical appointments.

The Sequel to Earth Power

After the continued success of *Earth Power*, Scott recognized that his readers were hungry for a sequel. He embarked on the writing of "Earth Power II," later titled *Earth, Air, Fire & Water*. He wrote of its creation for the *New Times*:[2]

> *When I was fifteen years old, I was handed a visa of sorts. This "visa" consisted of an open invitation to explore the byways of human thought and practice that have become known as magic . . .*
>
> *I soon learned of the Elements. Earth, Air, Fire and Water were potent sources of energy upon which magicians have always called. I began keeping lists of Elemental correspondences in my bound spellbooks, carefully recording this information by candlelight with a dip pen and a bottle of black ink.*
>
> *I also explored the Elements to determine their magical qualities. Swimming in the sea or pools brought a greater understanding of Water's loving and psychic energy. Building and lighting bonfires got me in touch with Fire's transformative properties (which I later applied during candle magic). Raising herbs and hiking in the mountains connected me with the Earth's fertility (soon utilized in money magic), and I learned to call the winds by the garden gate (which was later useful for spells involving travel).*
>
> *In my studies, I travelled throughout time and space to uncover the secrets of folk magic. By comparing and compiling those mysteries with those I had been taught and had experienced, I formed a system of natural magic built along ancient lines.*
>
> *Each day brought new discoveries and I spent many nights putting this knowledge into practice. My father, who is a writer, urged me to record some of this lore in book form. I wrote Magical Herbalism between 1976–79, then sent it to Llewellyn with the hope that it would be published.*
>
> *By the time it was released in the spring of 1982, I was busy writing on other forms of folk magic: the Elements, knots, mirrors, the sea, stones, images and trees. This was the magic*

that I had learned and had practiced for so many years. In 1983, Llewellyn published this information in Earth Power. *I was twenty-seven.*

This book's great popularity surprised me, though perhaps it shouldn't have, for most other texts of the day had been filled with hate spells, garbled (and unworkable) rituals and noisome ingredients. Earth Power, *with its gentle message of magic as a tool of love, seemed to speak to a new generation eager to rediscover the old ways.*

After the publication of Earth Power, *I wrote many other books on a variety of magical topics and even created a video tape.* Earth Power *continued to sell, and I received letters from around the world regarding this book. Many of their writers asked me to produce another work concerning this way of magic.*

I began collecting notes toward this end in the late 1980s. Then, in April of 1990, I decided that it was finally time to start work on a continuation of Earth Power.

I threw myself into this task. Several times while writing it I thought of a fabulous ritual to include—only to remember that it had [already] appeared in Earth Power.

So I struck out into rarely explored territory. Much of this book details the uses of unusual tools of magic (such as stars, sand, magnets, clay, snow, wells and ice) as well as new looks at stones, candles, mirrors and the sea. I also included evocative preparatory chants, a basic introduction to magic and two ecological rituals.

But this didn't seem to be enough, so I wrote an additional chapter (the first of its kind) outlining, in explicit detail, a simple method of creating spells for a variety of purposes. I completed the book on November 1, 1991. It is now available.

Earth, Air, Fire & Water *continues the magic begun in* Earth Power. *Though it's a simple guide to this art, I wrote it with the hope that this book's words would provide inspiration and useful tools to those who seek to improve their lives.*

True natural magic is a process of inner transformation; one in which we join our energies with those of the Elements to create positive change. In this age of great uncertainty and doubt, magic can be a powerfully effective ally.

Earth, Air, Fire & Water *awaits those who feel the call of the green earth; who hear the wind's whispers; feel the flickering flames and drink from rippling waters. It's based on the premise that all things contain energy, and that this energy can be used to create powerful, positive changes.*

Magic comes to life only in the hands of its practitioners. May your magic live with Earth, Air, Fire & Water.

Once again, Scott's truer feelings about the creation of a book are revealed in his autobiography:

In 1991, after leaving the hospital, I thought I should go back to work. I began Living Wicca *but, realizing that religious books are more difficult to write, I set this aside and began writing* Earth, Air, Fire & Water. *The work went fairly easily. This was a sequel to* Earth Power, *though I knew that I could never capture the same spirit evident in that book's pages. It was released in October, 1991. It sold out the first printing of 10,000 copies in three months. . . .*

Finally, I truly began working on Living Wicca *in late 1991, and finished the first draft on Wednesday, January 8, 1992.*

Writing *Living Wicca* was a challenge for Scott. It was, first of all, a more spiritually oriented sequel to his popular *Wicca.* At the same time, he knew he had to respond to the many criticisms levelled at "Wicca" by traditionally oriented, hierarchical covens and their leaders. Finally, he knew that the book was likely to be the last work he did in this life, on the subject of his personal religion. It was the final roadmap that he could draw for his readers, the last chance he would have to guide footsteps along the path he had helped to carve from the bewildering wilderness of remnants of the ancient mysteries. His health was unreliable, and he had recently known pain, fear, and the portents of his own mortality. Yet he could dedicate a chapter to "Prayers and Rites of Thanks and Offerings," and created "A Solitary Ritual of Thanks" which includes this prayer to the God and Goddess:

Lady of the Moon, of the stars and the Earth;
Lord of the Sun, of the forests and the hills;
I perform a ritual of thanks.
My love shines like the flame;
My love floats like the petals
Upon You.

Lady of the Waters, of flowers and the sea;
Lord of the Air, of horns and of fire;
I perform a ritual of thanks.
My love shines like the flame;
My love floats like the petals
Upon You.

Lady of the Caves, of cats and snakes;
Lord of the Plains, of falcons and stags;
I perform a ritual of thanks.
My love shines like the flame;
My love floats like the petals
Upon You.

1. This stuffed bear later accompanied him during his many hospital stays, and he would unashamedly fall asleep clutching it.
2. "Earth, Air, Fire & Water: The Birth of The Book" under the section "Natural Magic" *New Times* January/February 1992.
3. Scott's diary notes that he began work on the Hawai'i book on January 5, 1991.

Part V

Falling Leaves

1992

Chapter Thirteen

A Year
of Words

A
FTER FINISHING THE FIRST DRAFT OF LIVING WICCA, SCOTT ONLY
allowed himself an overnight break before plunging into
the final manuscript for Spell Craft.[1]

With David's help, Scott expanded the scope of the book, including
dozens of projects to adorn and enhance magical households and magical
lives. With Scott's usual thoroughness, every project in the book was carefully tested and the instructions revised repeatedly.

In 1992, Elaine Gill of Crossing Press contacted Scott Cunningham.
She wondered if he would be interested in doing a book for them, as they
were planning to expand their metaphysical line. As a matter of routine,
she offered Scott a substantial advance. With mounting medical bills, and
the constant battle to pay self-employment taxes, Scott agreed to do a
book for Crossing. It was not an easy decision. Through his years of
working with Llewellyn, Scott never tried to use his name or sales record

to receive an advance, and it was hard for him to contact Carl Wesch
and tell him that was a factor in his decision to write for Crossing. Car
course was well aware that Scott wrote fiction books for other publishe
but this was the first time that Scott would write for another metaphysic
publisher. Scott had a contractual agreement with Llewellyn to offer then
the right of first refusal on his next manuscript and he took this very seriously. Scott felt that now he had fulfilled his obligations on existing book
contracts.

Understanding Scott's predicament, regretting that Scott had not
simply told Llewellyn that he needed to receive advances, Carl did not
block Scott's working with Crossing. Scott asked Carl if there were any
subjects that he would not be interested in for Llewellyn, and Carl
suggested a couple of subjects. One of these, *Sacred Sleep*, was written
rapidly in the late spring of 1992, and completed in seven or eight weeks.
Scott did not spare himself, throwing himself into research and working
long hours, often neglecting to eat while he was in the frenzy of writing.

A Brush with "Channelling"

For the first time, during the writing of *Sacred Sleep*, Scott felt that certain
information was being "given" to him. He laughed about it. "I've never
been able to stand people who claim all their work is channelled. And
now it's happening to me!" A pattern for an invocation to Isis, he felt, came
too readily to his mind.[2] One afternoon, while lying down for a brief but
well-deserved nap, he spread his arms above his head, opening his body
to the Gods. Immediately he felt that this position was one that had been
used in the ancient dream temples, and he included it as a posture for the
temple sleep.

Dreamtime

As might be expected while writing a book on dreams, Scott dreamed
constantly of *Sacred Sleep*.

> **March 20, 1992**—*Dreamed of Pan, messenger deities, deities
> appearing in a dream.*

March 21, 1992—*Everybody (in the dream) was into dream incubation. I decided to try it, and was scared before I tried it. Motifs of public nudity (swimming pool).*

April 3, 1992—*Saw great illos [illustrations] of deities approach during divine sleep.*

Drinking purified water can make dreams (Divine) clearer.

Saw a book—Chinese one, romances and Babylonian dream interpretation. I skimmed thru contents . . . though great and in English, a bit confusing.

The book's price was $100 and was spelled in English URU100UR.

Scott included his own interpretation of this dream in Sacred Sleep:

> *. . . I realized that this was a divine dream. A Goddess (probably Nisaba, the Sumerian Goddess of writing and wisdom) was informing me that the book on which I was laboring lacked structure and contained too much information. The letters that I saw on the inside front cover twice (or perhaps, thrice) spelled the word Ur (an ancient Sumerian city-state). The high price tag was indicative of this dream's great importance, and the fact that it was written in pencil I easily equated with the stylus used for writing cuneiform in ancient Sumer.*

Scott's ongoing worries about serving his readers' needs also surfaced in his dreams of this time:

> **March 25, 1992**—*Dennis Hayes of Crossing Press said, "you put footnotes here and then, later, take them out because they're so much trouble."*
>
> *"I write to serve the readers," I said.*
>
> *"No way," he replied.*
>
> *I wake at 5:52. Many other dreams lost, the above was the last.*

On the night of March 28, 1992, one year before his death, he dreamed of Isis:

> *I won some kind of contest on which I appeared on a pre-taped*
> *segment of a TV show. The contest (I believe I answered a ques-*
> *tion) had something to do with Isis. deTraci was thrilled. Then,*
> *when watching TV with DT, I realized I was missing "my" show.*
> *Panic.*

Later in the evening, he dreamed of "checking his balance" at an ATM.

> *$10 came out, the screen said "Free," and out pops a stiff, two*
> *foot long paper thing. It was a ticket to Greece.*

His concern over writing for Crossing Press also emerged in this dream:

> *Elaine said, "From now on, I want all reviews to be printed in*
> *their entirety. No blurbs, no snippets.[3] Circle will print them all."*
> *"I agree! Why lots of reviews are pages long and some*
> *commentaries are nearly books themselves."*
> *Carl: "And it was also probably in part, in answer to their*
> *letter cautioning me that you wouldn't be exclusively writing for*
> *Llewellyn any more."*
> *Dreams of being back in (H . . .), that old sleepy town, and*
> *having to fulfill my obligation."*

Coping

Shortly after *Sacred Sleep* was finished, Scott's vision deteriorated. He had worried for some time about this possibility, but instead of pacing himself, he pushed himself even harder, determined to write as much as possible in the shortest amount of time. His concerns were both creative and financial: he wanted to finish his most valued books, particularly his Hawaiian Magic book, and he also wanted to ensure that he would have enough money to survive if he were incapacitated by permanent blindness. With his usual dedication to meeting his current commitments, he frequently set aside work on his beloved Hawai'ian magic book in order to meet other book deadlines. He completed a scholarly version of the book, and, with the knowledge of Carl Weschcke, submitted it to at least one general trade publisher, trying one more time for the wide-market release he craved:

> *. . . I turned my sights on writing my book of ancient a religion and magic. I finished the first draft in 1991 and set it aside. Harper San Francisco turned it down in February, 1992. I was pleased.*

Despite his desire to be accepted by the academic world with this book, he preferred that it would ultimately go out under the Llewellyn imprint, as so many of his books had before.

Although Scott knew that his prognosis for long-term survival was not good, he especially feared a long period of blindness. Later, he began to feel as if he could adjust and discussed purchasing a recently available electronic reading machine, that would digitally scan any book and read it aloud. Although these machines were expensive, it seemed to him to be a way he might be able to continue researching even if his dread of blindness became justified.

The Writing of Divination

While continuing work on his books for Llewellyn, Scott completed another book, *Divination,* for Crossing. Although he was still active during the research and writing for this book, by the time the final proofs were sent to him, Scott's health was declining. Elaine Gill recalls that Scott simply could not expand several segments as proposed, particularly with his continued commitment to Llewellyn books and his pet project—the Hawai'ian magic book. The book went to press as he submitted it.

Writing and More Writing

Scott details his push to complete as many books as possible during his final productive year:

> *Finally, I truly began working on* Living Wicca *in late 1991, and finished the first draft on Wednesday, January 8, 1992.*
> *On Thursday, January 9, 1992, I began working on finishing up my chapters for* Spell Craft *and had several discussions with*

David regarding his contributions. The book is nearly finished.
We've been working on this book since 1987. It's been through
many manifestations (just like Magical Household*). In 1990*
Spell Crafts *was going to have an Elemental theme: crafts*
related to Earth, Air, Fire and Water. David wisely told me that
this was too limiting. It was.

One day in February of 1992, I was talking with Nancy
Mostad on the phone. I had to make more money,[4] so I asked
her if she wanted me to do another Truth About *book, this one*
on herb magic. She was delighted. I wrote it that weekend and
sent it to her on Tuesday. It was thirty five pages and it took me
about twenty four hours to write—a far shorter period of time
than the difficult Witchcraft[5] *book had taken.[6]*

As of 1992, Scott had solid plans for several books. Because of his
limited strength, deciding on which to concentrate was difficult. He was
absolutely committed to finishing *Living Wicca*, believing that it would
serve as a testament and summation of many of his beliefs. He had long
researched a book on Babylonian and Sumerian magic, knowing that few
resources on those cultures existed for the magical practitioner, and had
begun writing this volume. However, the remaining intense research
required would take too much time and energy, and he suspected that his
vision would fail before he could finish gathering information.

He also made the decision to set aside the *Animal Companionary* which
he and David Harrington had been working on for several years. Although
over a hundred entries in this encyclopedic work were already completed,
Scott stopped work on this project. He never was much of an animal lover.
His experiences with pets were limited, and most were forced on him by
well-meaning friends. When he was occasionally called upon to feed his
parents' dogs when they vacationed, he described the pets in such grue-
some terms that his friends believed that he was feeding the Hounds of the
Baskervilles instead of a couple of reasonably well-mannered cocker
spaniels. An Aesop fable that Scott "retold" for *Llewellyn's 1993 Magickal
Almanac* inadvertently sums up his feelings on animal companions:

A Sorceress: A Fable from Aesop

Night had stilled the whole world, silencing the tongues of every creature. Trees swayed as they drowsed above sleeping bushes. The forest was hushed.

A Sorceress, a rare woman versed in the arts of fearful magic, entered the gloomy forest. She made a large circle, set up a tripod and burned fragrant vervain as she intoned ancient incantations.

Her dreadful words resounded through the air, awakening every creature, plant and tree for miles around. The Sorceress blew her mystic words on the wind, disturbing cattle and people in far distant places. The countryside shivered.

Her impassioned incantation even drew the moon itself into the wood to assist in her magical quest. In the eerie light, spirits of the long dead appeared before the Sorceress in shadowy forms, demanding to know why they had been awakened from their long sleep.

"Tell me," she said, her face lightened by the triangular flames of the smouldering vervain. "Tell me where I can find what I have lost: my favorite little dog!"

"Impudent creature!" the spirits shouted in unison. "Must the order of nature be reversed and the sleep of every creature be disturbed for the sake of your little dog?"

Moral: Don't waste great powers on trivial matters.

Few animal lovers would agree that a lost pet is trivial. Scott's indifference to pets was often challenged; several of his friends, including his co-author on the *Animal Companionary*, possessed considerable menageries. Although Scott was not particularly attracted to animals, they enjoyed Scott. Even ill-trained dogs would obey him when he spoke in a firm tone of command, known as his "dog voice."

Though Scott was now at the point of setting aside projects rather than beginning new ones, he did consider creating the "magical cookbook" that Llewellyn had hoped he would write. In June, 1992, when his strength was good, he wrote the table of contents, introduction, and dozens of recipes for "Cunningham's Magical Cookbook." Unfortunately, he did not continue on this playful manuscript which includes such culinary delights as "The Drunken Pumpkin," a fish dish called "Mermaid's Love," and a recipe to ensure the diner's prosperity, known as "Money Soup."[7]

Other projects at this time were also lighthearted. Scott had always wanted to create a board game similar to the ones he had enjoyed as a kid. He created his "Flying Witch Game" for entertainment. Scott designed a maze-like playing board and made a detailed mock-up of the game box. David Harrington created miniature velveteen-clad witches on brooms for the players' markers. The rules were simple, but it was not an easy game to win. Players rolled dice to see how far they would "fly," landing on marked spaces, and drew cards that would grant the witches a magical helping hand or curse them back to the game start in a flash. Though he never attempted to market this game, it became a popular pastime among his friends.

Yuletide Greetings

Scott's Yuletide letter for 1992 gives no hint of his illness, and shows that his sarcastic wit was still intact:

> **Happy Winter!**
>
> *As the days grow cold and storms blanket snow over lots of cities that are far away from me, I can only think of my home in California and say:*
>
> *Heck, you'd never catch me moving to a place where you wake up and find that your dog's frozen, your house is doing its impression of an ice cube, and the heater's moved!*
>
> *Spring and summer, of course, bring me new thoughts: Heck, you'd never catch me moving to a place by a river that floods every year, or that's smack dab in the middle of Tornadoville, or that enjoys languid days of 105-degree weather and 99% humidity sprinkled with insects the size of tanks.*
>
> *Fall prompts thoughts of: Well, it's 80 degrees, sunny, and all the tourists who don't realize that this is when we have perfect weather have gone back to their ice-damaged, sun-burned homes to count the dead insects stacked up on their porches.*

Winter, of course, usually follows fall (though Congress may have a thing to say about this—after they vote themselves a raise). And unfortunately, even here in California, we share many of the same winter ills that the rest of the U.S. faces.

I'm referring, of course, to the holiday(s) season. the government's delusion that everyone in the U.S. of A. follows the same religion has caused big problems for a lot of folks, including Televangelists who apparently believe that "Dollars Drive out Demons" is a pithy and deeply spiritual message. (But I'm getting off the track.)

The great diversity of religion in America today is proof that we'll never, ever share the same beliefs—or the same taxis to religious services. Still, some confused persons try to merge different religions: a Christian man may decide to thrust a UL approved illuminated angel figure on top of a purely Pagan symbol of the Sun God's rebirth. Which religion is being honored here? Does the guy himself know? How does the angel feel about being rammed onto an itchy stick?

So many religious holidays are clustered in winter (among others—Yule, Hanukkah, Kwanzaa, Christmas, Macy's Day, After Christmas Sales Day, and lots of others that I won't even attempt to spell) that it's difficult to greet others with seasonal wishes. Anything other than "Happy Winter" may be politically incorrect (hence, this letter's title) and could lead to anything from lawsuits and sneers to thirty minute theological tirades delivered at high volume while waiting in line at the post office to send Yule packages to your beloved Witch friends.

Such difficulties are easily avoided (see below), but the underlying problem can only be solved through greater understanding (in time, even most yahoos might begin to grasp the concept that religious diversity isn't a "liberal" plot).

For those of you who don't happen to belong to "conventional" religions, I have a few words of advice that may get us all through this trying time with the least amount of tension:

If a red-nosed, bell-ringing person says "God bless you" after you put a dollar in the kettle, don't ask "Which one?"

A cheery greeting of "Merry Christmas" should not prompt a response of "You're Mary? I'm Scott" or, even worse, "Why do you presume that I acknowledge your religion's main event?"

When someone sets up a Santa figure on her or his front yard, don't become confused and say, "So—You worship an obese, grizzled man in a red suit on December 25th?"

Don't compare nativity scenes to picturesque, rural Mexican villages that you've visited; this may cause great offense.

Don't even think of the possible mythological entanglements of apparent reindeer worship.

And if, indeed, a friend of yours cruelly jabs a UL illuminated angel figure onto a purely Pagan symbol with no associations with the new religion, don't forget yourself and say, "Ah, Joe; they didn't have blondes in the Holy Land."

No. We must be strong. We must persevere. We must accept that there will always be persons who worship in far different ways and who'll never believe that most of their celebratory accoutrements were stolen from our religion. If we hold our tongues, we can survive this season and might even enjoy it.

No, Hermione—Santa Claus has nothing to do with Christmas, Hanukkah, Yule, Kwanzaa, Macy's Day or the After Christmas Sales Day. In fact, Santa's main role is to separate adoring parents from their money in exchange for festive photos of Santa and their kid(s) taken by young women in green stockings.

(The jolly, almost-non-religious Santa has nothing to do with Happy Winter, or with anything else mentioned in this letter. However, I didn't wish to appear to be cheap and not fill up this entire second page, so I padded it right here.)

"Happy Winter," then, expresses far more than glee that the trees all look dead and that it seems that the sun will never, ever ever come out again. This simple, cheery phrase actually contains deep spiritual thoughts (which can, and will, be understood by our parents, employers and neighbors in many ways, most of which will be wrong).

However, it's of the utmost importance to utilize this phrase as often as we can, if only to spread further confusion concerning this blessedly confusing time of year.

I'm almost out of room, and must close this Yuletide—er, Wintertide letter. Please remember these things:

—Respect all religious paths, even those that haven't been celebrating at this time of year for nearly as long as we have

—Try to sense the mystical connection between all religions, even if most of their representatives remind you of why you're not one of them.

—Finally, say "Happy Winter" often and loud, and perhaps someday, you'll touch a soul who'll look at you with trembling eyes and say, after careful thought, "Huh?"

Have a Happy Winter!

A Winter's Night Feast

December 15, 1992. Braving twenty-degree weather, Scott Cunningham arrived in St Paul, Minnesota, for Carl and Sandra Weschcke's annual Yule party for Llewellyn Worldwide. Nancy Mostad, Llewellyn's Acquisitions Editor and his friend, picked him up and they drove over winding roads through snow-covered fields illuminated by the bright, white moon above. They arrived at the sprawling Weschcke manor which was aglow on this special night. Scott was greeted warmly at the party that, this year, was essentially dedicated to him.

Scott was among the most widely read, and perhaps the single most widely trusted, of writers on Witchcraft and the occult. His books— creative, poetic, intensely ethical—were each eagerly awaited by the Wiccan community. Teachers of wildly varying disciplines and traditions recommend his works to their students. In the past year he had finished seven books. Once he used to wonder if he could ever make a living from his magical writing, and admired the authors who could. He was now the envied one, the standard.

During the evening, he was presented with a small, finely made booklet. A dark ribbon and rosette adorned one corner; the paper cover was handmade, reminiscent of the old stippled endpapers in antique volumes. In it were his books, one title to a page, with the worldwide sales figures for each. The tally of his books was in the hundreds of thousands.

There he was, in wintertime Minnesota, barely out of a hospital bed, to say goodbye. Though tenaciously fighting his illnesses, and still writing, everyone was aware that this would probably be the last time he visited. He greeted his many friends, and, as usual, he joked.

The Private Sale

After returning from Minnesota, Scott prepared to move back with his parents. Everyone who knew Scott was aware that this was not a prospect he relished. He designed a "Private Sale" to allow his friends to "purchase" mementos of him and avoid a maudlin dividing-up of his possessions.

Scott Cunningham's Private Sale
Friday, January 29, 1993

Hi. I thought I'd bore you with a short note to explain what will occur this evening and why it's happening in the first place.

As you probably know by now, I'm moving out of this over-priced apartment and moving in with my under-priced parents. This returns me to the location of my very first Wiccan and magical rituals—some of which I wish to forget, some of which scared the daylights out of me, and others that greatly enhanced my magical development.

Since I'm moving and will no longer enjoy the comforts of my massive, messy apartment, I find that the time has come to part with some of the books and magical objects that I've acquired during the past twenty years. I simply no longer have the room. I'm referring to this evening as a "private'" sale because the general public wouldn't have the slightest clue as to the uses and symbolism of much that is displayed here (i.e., they wouldn't move at a garage sale).

I wish to make a few things quite clear: this isn't a money-making event. Everything is underpriced (save for some of the books). I decided not to put price tags on anything for two reasons: first, price may vary depending on the amount of desired items; second, I'm extremely lazy. When looking around,

remember that I'm very cheap—it won't cost as much as you're
probably thinking.

I've rambled on for too long. Many (sensible) persons won't
even read this far, so I'll sign off for now.

> *Walk in Balance,*
> *Bright Blessings,*
> *Flags, Flax, Fodder,*
> *Bless and Blessed Be*

The "sale" wasn't a solemn distribution of goods, it was just an indoor garage sale. He sold and signed copies of his own books. It was probably the last time that he signed such a quantity of books. For many who attended, it was the final time to embrace their dear friend.

It was a blessing that the sale was held on a day when his energy level was high. He was active and talkative, playing host and directing people to the vegetable trays and cheerfully writing up "receipts" that never totalled as much as expected. Smiling, laughing, he said a goodnight to his guests, pretending that it was not a final farewell.

1. Scott refers to this book as *Spell Craft*. The title was ultimately changed to *Spell Crafts*.
2. Scott and I (deTraci) discovered that we had put identical patterns for designing ritual invocations into books we were working on separately. Both invocations were to Isis, different only in the actual titles and attributes. We both felt this was a divine "nod" to our work.
3. Probably *Circle Network News*, the prominent pagan paper.
4. Scott's financial problems were accelerating with the progress of his illness. Even with the relatively liberal MediCal, the state of California program which assists uninsured patients with life-threatening diseases, his co-payments were running thousands of dollars each month. Although he could have deferred much or all of these payments, Scott felt an ethical obligation to pay as much of his ongoing expenses as possible as they were incurred.
5. *The Truth About Witchcraft*
6. Scott's notes omit his efforts for two other Crossing Press books, which he was also working on at this time.
7. These recipes and many more of Scott's favorites were included in a new revised edition of *The Magic In Food*, re-released in January 1996 as *The Magic of Food*.

Chapter Fourteen

Returning

If you would be a magician, honor the Earth. Honor life. Love. Know that magic is the birthright of every human being, and wisely use it.

This book of magic is ending. Yours, however, is continuing. May it be a book of joy.

—Scott Cunningham
Afterword to *Earth, Air, Fire & Water*

AFTER SCOTT'S "GARAGE SALE," HE AND HIS FATHER PACKED UP the furniture and thousands of books, moving it all into the converted garage of his parents' home. Scott's old room had been converted to expand Chet's office long ago, so he took up residence in his sister Christine's former room.

Shortly after returning to live in his parents' home, Scott was readmitted to the University of California San Diego Medical Center. He told his friends to skip visiting him, and often kept his returns to the hospital a secret. If a day or two passed without a return call from messages left on his answering machine, those close to him learned that a call to the switchboard at UCSD would provide his room number.

But these final days were productive ones, as Chet Cunningham writes: "The last book he wrote has not yet[1] been published by Llewellyn. He struggled those last few months to get it done. We set up his computer and his laser printer so he could work on it, and he did as much as he could each day. He had wanted it to be a definitive study on the Hawai'ian religions, a scholarly work with many footnotes to substantiate what he said, and a huge bibliography. One day he told me that he had decided he couldn't finish the larger scope of the work. He scaled it down and for three days went through the 200-page manuscript on the computer, removing the footnote designations.

"At last it was finished and he printed out the copy and I boxed it up and sent it off to Nancy Mostad at Llewellyn. He smiled and gave a little sigh. It was the last book Scott worked on."

The spinal meningitis had returned in full force, and it was suspected that the lymphoma he had successfully battled in 1984 was taking advantage of his condition to return. In February, he underwent surgery to relieve an infection threatening his brain. He fell into a coma and was in intensive care for several days. To stabilize him, the harsh drugs to prevent blindness were discontinued and the last of his eyesight faded away. He rallied a little and, after a brief stay in a convalescent hospital, returned home. We knew it could not be long, but hope is a hard thing to let go.

The quiet, faith-filled strength of both Chet and Rosie was a comfort to friends of Scott who had hoped to comfort them. Chet once responded to a polite comment by a concerned friend of Scott's that "This must be very hard on you," with the almost sharp words "It's hard on my son, not on me."

On Sunday morning, March 28, 1993, in the house where he had woven his first magics, Scott did not wake up. The complex of AIDS-related[2] diseases could no longer be combated. At about 3:00 that afternoon, without regaining consciousness, he shed his tired body and passed from this world.

Weaving the Spiral

Scott rarely spoke about his belief in reincarnation, believing that this life was the one given to us to live now, not other lives long past. In a 1981 article for *The Shadow's Edge*, written under the pen name, Halcyon, Scott shared his feelings on the subject.

Reincarnation is one of Wicca's most valuable lessons. The knowledge that this life is not our only one, that when our physical body dies we do not cease to exist but are reborn in another body, answers many questions, but raises a few others.

Why? Why are we reincarnated? To learn the many lessons of life. And why are we to learn these lessons? To perfect ourselves. This is the whole reason why we're here on earth—to achieve the perfection of the soul.

This usually takes many lifetimes. We don't know how many—some traditions say seven or nine, others many more. This is usually up to the individual soul.

The soul is sexless, ageless, possessed of the divine spark of the Gods, non-physical, eternal. Each manifestation of this intelligence (i.e., each body) is not identical with the previous one; if this was so, the soul would stagnate. The sex, race, place of origin, economic class and every other individuality of the soul is determined, before birth, with the counsel of the gods. This is important; we decide what our lives will be before we come here; there is no God to curse or mysterious forces of "fate" which we can throw the responsibility upon.

Our actions in our previous lives also affect the following ones. Karma (for every action there is a reaction) also influences our lives, but since we incur the karma, we must be ultimately responsible for this as well.

Karma is not a system of rewards and punishments. It is meant to help the soul towards "right action." Thusly, if you do evil, evil will be returned to you; good will bring you good; and this aids in perfection of the soul.

When the body dies, the soul leaves it and journeys to the Land of Faerie, the Land of the Young, the Shining Land; all names for the Summerland. Here the soul is refreshed and lessons are reviewed with the God and Goddess before embarking upon another incarnation. This place is neither in "heaven" or the "underworld;" it simply is, existing in vibrations higher, less dense than ours. Most Wiccan traditions describe it *as a land of eternal summer, with grassy fields and sweet, flowing rivers; the earth before the advent of man.*

After the proper time, the soul is reincarnated and life begins again all over.

Wicca does not teach that we ever incarnate in the bodies of insects or animals; however, it is easy to contact the lower souls residing in these incarnations. What happens after the final incarnation? After rising upon the spiral of life and death and rebirth, those souls who have attained perfection break away forever from the spiral and reside with the Gods. They are known as the Mighty Ones, the Old Ones, the Watchtowers, and are invoked to watch and give power to our meetings.

So fear not death, seeker; it is the door to birth, and as you rise and fall upon this plane of existence, know that death is but the beginning of another life.

Although Scott recognized that remembering past lives could be of interest, he was generally opposed to past-life regressions. In *The Encyclopedia of Crystal, Gem, and Metal Magic*, he provided a past life regression rite using fossils.

I have mixed feelings regarding past-life regression, and I hesitated to include this ritual—simple as it is—in this book. This is an area fraught with self-delusion. Still, if you have an interest in these matters, it's far better to attempt a glimpse backward yourself, rather than trusting another to do it.

In his final book on Wicca, *Living Wicca*, Scott writes:

Wiccans as a group don't ritualize mourning. Death is a doorway through which souls pass to re-enter the realm of the Goddess. Bodies are simply suits that we wear and use until they wear out, or until we have no need for further lessons and opportunities in this lifetime. Bodies should be taken care of, but their deaths (the soul never dies) aren't, traditionally speaking, times for ritualized sorrow. How can it be, in a religion that embraces reincarnation; that sees bodily death as but one of many such transitions that the human soul will experience?

Naturally, Wiccans grieve, and many have small rites to mark the transition of a loved one. Few of these rites have been printed. You may write your own if you feel the need.

Many did.

1. *Hawai'ian Magic* was published in 1995.
2. Scott might be criticized for "concealing" the true nature of his illness. He had no personal shame about it, but he was anxious to shield his friends and, particularly, his mother, from worrying about him. He also had no desire to be treated as a perpetual invalid. He had had his fill of that type of treatment during his treatment for the potentially fatal lymphoma in the early 1980s.

   He also needed the release of talking with his friends about things other than illness. Frequently, he was at the hospital for appointments, tests, and even brief stays of a few days, which he did not mention. Everyone who knew the exact nature of his illness naturally discussed it with him. He was flooded with unwanted information on this or that new treatment, new drugs, herbal cures, and so on. He wanted his work and his life to be what was important, not his ailment. In these aspects, Scott was decidedly non-political, except to defend his own right to privacy.

   From the day that he told me (deTraci) exactly what was going on, our conversations changed. I was one who knew, and knowing how many hours we spent discussing this or that detail of his disease, I think we would have enjoyed each other more in those last months if we had kept up the facade of innocence. What finally prompted him to discuss it with me was the fact that rumors were leaking out into the magical community. Suddenly I was getting phone calls from people I scarcely knew, asking me in veiled terms how Scott was. I talked to him about this, still keeping up the pretense, and he told me to tell anyone who asked about his condition to ask him about it instead. Then one night in June of 1992, he called and abruptly said: "We have to talk about some bad things now." I don't know what prompted this sudden call. In a few minutes, everything that I had kept tamed beneath the surface was now conscious, horrible knowledge.

Part VI

Root and Growth

1993 and beyond

Chapter Fifteen

Farewells

ON MARCH 31, THREE DAYS AFTER SCOTT'S PASSING, A WAKE WAS HELD for him at deTraci's house. Childhood beliefs about death rose up in full force: not the religious guidelines, but the tradition that the soul lingered by the body for three days before departing. Word passed through the grapevine in San Diego and elsewhere. Marilee Bigelow flew in from Northern California; Don Kraig arrived from Los Angeles; others came from Arizona. Carl Weschcke, President of Llewellyn Publications, and Nancy Mostad, Llewellyn's Acquisitions Manager and the one who had worked most closely with Scott at Llewellyn, sent their respects. Carl wrote:

> *Perhaps you would care to read this Wednesday evening for me. How does one put into words feelings that manifest as tears? I wrote this shortly after Sandra called to tell me that "we've lost Scott." Strangely, I dreamt that Scott died a week ago Sunday,*

and then the next night I dreamt that I was healing him. Instead, this day I'm saying something to his friends that means a lot to me.

When Scott flew out here just before Yule, we all felt tremendously honored that he wanted to be with us. He will be with us for as long as we remember him—and I know that I will remember him all the rest of my life. Scott is a very good person.

Three years ago, at the Las Vegas ABA, Scott Cunningham told me that he was going to die. He wanted me to know because he felt that responsibility as an author. He then had published ten books with us and was our best selling author. Aside from friendship, Scott wanted me to know that we could no longer count on him for a steady stream of best sellers.

Scott will be remembered by many people for many reasons. I will remember him as a friend, a brother, a partner. I know I will continue to love him as a friend, and will continue to be grateful to him for his friendship and for his shared visions, and for the help his books gave to Llewellyn not only as best sellers but as messages to a readership for whom the phrase "New Age" really means "builders of a New World."

But I will also always remember Scott as an author. He was professional and devoted to his Craft. Every book went through many drafts, and was compounded from thousands of reference notes he'd been making for years. And the final draft was always completely re-typed (before he had a computer) before being sent to us. Never did Scott produce any thing that wasn't first rate in his eyes. Nor did he ever include information that he hadn't checked for accuracy, and for value and safety. He was sensitive to his readership, and felt that he had to know that none could be harmed by what he wrote. He learned his Writing Craft from his father and it was a matter of real pride and joy that he felt his father's respect for his work even though they did not share the same interests.

We published his first "occult" book, Magical Herbalism, in May 1982 after the manuscript had been in my hands for several years. We first met the next year in San Diego (when I also first met Don Kraig, then his roommate), and then he made many trips to St. Paul, and to most ABA conventions. We spent a lot of time together talking and planning books. We have three Cunningham books yet to publish: Living Wicca *(June 1993),* Spellcraft *(September 1993, written with David Harrington), and* Traditional Hawai'ian Religion and Magic *(June 1994). Both the Wicca book and that on Hawai'ian magic were a long time in the writing—with many trips around the country and to Hawai'i for research—and represent Scott's final message, and his love for Wicca and Hawai'i.*

Scott: You will be missed by many of us, but many tens of thousands of readers have benefited by your work and will continue to read your message for a long time to come.

Love and Blessings,
Carl Llewellyn Weschcke
March 29, 1993

Nancy Mostad, who had worked closely with Scott on most of the books he did for Llewellyn, wrote about her time with Scott:

I am proud to have been one of Scott's friends and to be able to share with him in the work he loved so much—writing for our people, the magical community. We had some awkward moments as our relationship first began. Carl Weschcke had told me what an important author Scott was and thus put me in even greater awe of him. I remember the first time I spoke with him and how he hooted with laughter when I called him "Mr. Cunningham."

"That's my dad," he said.

As we worked together, we grew together as friends. One of our favorite pastimes was to make up some pretty uproarious jokes about various characters in the magical community. How many times, I wonder, were those magical ears burning. Laughter has a power all its own and I believe those little jokes helped keep Scott with us long enough for him to finish Living Wicca, Spell Crafts, *and, most significantly,* Traditional Hawai'ian Religion and Magic,[1] *which Scott considered his*

most important work. As unknowing victims of our revelry, you
helped him in his work, in his struggle, in his departure.

   I loved Scott Cunningham and I told him so. And I still do.
He will forever be in my heart. The last time I spoke with him,
he gave me a great gift. His last words were:

   "I love you, too."

   "May the Mother in Her Eternal Grace embrace us and
carry us through this time of shared sorrow."

The wake was not limited to the pagan community; Scott's parents, Chet and Rosie Cunningham, attended, along with members of the book-selling community in San Diego who had found Scott such a welcome customer and fellow book-lover.

Respecting Scott's aversion to public rituals, no formal circle was held, though the group did gather together to hear the reading of the messages from Llewellyn. Each took a few of Scott's treasured tourmaline beads as a memento. He had collected these over a long period. (An amusing moment Scott would have appreciated came when one of the mourners, distracted, took a tourmaline bead from the tray and ate it. We assured the mourner, with a pun that Scott might have made, that all would come out all right in the end.) A massive jumble of herbs, found in the bottom of one of his herb cabinets, were gathered into a cauldron and scattered into the garden.

Marilee Bigelow arrived bringing additional sorrowful news: Ruth Phillips, the teacher and creator of the APGW, whom Scott loved and admired, died three days before Scott, on Thursday, March 25.[2] The loss of both Ruth (who was a magical teacher of Marilee's, and who had also spiritually "adopted" Marilee into the Bigelow clan as her successor), and of Scott, her dearest friend and past Priest, was a double blow for Marilee.

It was a night of magic as so many people who knew and loved Scott put personal differences aside to honor him. Scott was alive again in every conversation and reflected in every tear.

A few days later, another public ritual was organized by a pagan group in San Diego. This rite was attended by fifty or sixty people, many of whom were Scott's readers who had never met him or heard him speak, but still needed to mourn his passing. In the open, grassy space in Palm

Canyon at Presidio Park individual after individual approached the center of the circle, lit a candle, and said a few words about the impact Scott had on his or her life. The circle closed with "Corn and Grain:"

Corn and Grain
Corn and Grain
All that falls shall rise again

Hoof and Horn
Hoof and Horn
All that dies shall be reborn

We all come from the Goddess
And to her we shall return
Like a drop of rain
Flowing to the ocean.

Many other groups and circles held private remembrances of Scott. It is impossible to know how many times Scott was remembered and blessed on his way, but across the nation, it must have numbered in the dozens with hundreds of persons participating.

Almost immediately reports came filtering back—a dream of Scott, visions, a sense of his presence. Scott, who took a very no-nonsense attitude about death and survival, apparently appeared to many. David and I wondered over some of the reports, honestly envying those that had known Scott briefly or not at all and yet who seemed to be receiving the proof of his survival that we lacked. We were skeptical until the (drum roll please) "Dream of the Russian Hat."

I had an odd dream one night of having pursued a blue cat, catching it and trying to return it to its owner. While looking for the house address indicated on its tag, I came across an Italianate villa where an old man was dying. I offered him some comfort on what was a very pleasant transition. In the house, in a party-type atmosphere, I ran into Scott. He gave me some papers supposedly containing information I was looking for for his biography, information I found only after the dream. I talked to him and to others at the party, but then it was time for him to go to bed and I went to give him a massage as I had done at the hospital. He was now wearing a Russian hat, black fur, and I looked at him in surprise. I said, "I like your hat," and he was very pleased that I noticed it, saying that he was glad I recognized it for what it was. Then I helped him to bed, told him that I loved him, and the dream ended or drifted into something else.

In the morning I pored over this dream, trying to find meaning, especially the part about the hat. I wrote it all down and tried alternate meanings on it. It was a Russian hat, Russian sounded like rushing, was he in a hurry to get to another plane? Or was time of the essence in some other way? It could be a Cossack hat, Cossack was like cassock, priests wear cassocks, could this connect with Scott as a priest of the Wiccan religion? and so on.

When David Harrington visited, I mentioned the dream to him, somewhat apologetically, since here again we just had an ambiguous mess and no real detail or recognizable messages. As soon as I began to tell the dream, David grew quiet, listening. Then I mentioned the hat. I'll never forget his words.

"But you didn't know about the Russian hat, did you?"

I could hardly get out the words, sensing that here, in this silly hat dream, was the confirmation we both wanted so badly.

"No. What hat? What do you mean, the Russian hat?" I sounded almost angry as David told me the story.

Scott and David and a mutual friend had a running joke about a Russian costume which their friend tried to foist off on Scott every Halloween. Sometimes Scott would put on the hat and play around with it at other times. But the Russian hat was a private joke that I had no memory of ever hearing about before. It had all taken place some years before I met Scott. As far as I knew, the hat was never in Scott's possession during the time I knew him.

The esoteric symbolism of the Russian hat turned out to be that it was a Russian hat, and the reason Scott was so pleased in the dream that I noticed it was because he knew that by giving this image to me, which could only be verified by David, we would know that he really was okay. And still wearing crazy hats.

"Great Scott!"

After the *New Times* (March 1993) announced Scott's passing, many book-stores and metaphysical centers set up what amounted to "shrines," usually consisting of a photo of Scott, a display of his books, and a burning candle. These were stumbled over unexpectedly by his friends. Karen Lowe, visiting several bookstores in Los Angeles, found shrines at two of them. Her friendship with Scott made her an object of special interest, an attention she found discomfiting and unexpected. This sort of devotion Scott would have found amusing and undeserved, though he might have understood the need expressed in the creation of these tributes.

Another commemoration of Scott's passing took place the following October. Six or seven years before, Scott and I (deTraci) had discovered that the Cafe del Rey Moro[3] in Balboa Park offered a concoction called a "Witches Brew" as their October "Drink of the Month." This light-hearted drink consisted of light rum, dark rum, orange curacao, triple sec and grenadine served up in a tulip glass.[4] On our way to see *Behold Hawai'i*, an Imax film being shown at the Space Theatre, we were substantially delayed when we stopped on a whim to test out the potency of this Witches' Brew. Scott generally did not indulge in alcohol, since even a glass of wine would go immediately to his head. But Witches' Brews were an indulgence. October visits to the Cafe del Rey Moro bar became an annual custom.

There is a tradition of holding a "dumb supper," where a place is set and a meal served for the spirit of one who has passed. That October, the staff of the Cafe were surprised by the number of people who had an invisible friend with them for whom they ordered visible Witches' Brews. Many glasses were raised to toast the spirit of a man we knew as Scott Cunningham.

1. Traditional Hawaiian Religion and Magic was published under the title of *Hawaiian Religion and Magic*.
2. At the same time, it seemed that Ruth and Scott would be well placed to continue their friendship in the other world. During one of my visits to Scott's bedside I woke him from sleep. We talked perfectly normally for some time, and then he mentioned,

out of thin air, that "Ruthie came to visit me." Both, it turned out, were on the edge of transition: Ruth passed over just three days before Scott.

3. Unfortunately, this delightful spot was closed and torn down in 1995.

4. Scott's valiant attempt to recreate this elusive recipe has been recorded in *The Magic of Food*, the new, revised edition of the *Magic In Food*, Llewellyn Publications, 1995.

Did the Magic Fail?

CONFRONTING SCOTT'S DEATH HAS BEEN DIFFICULT FOR ALL WHO knew him, as well as his many readers who may not be able to understand how he could be taken from us so harshly. We all struggle with the "unfairness" of death, and these struggles seem to take on special meaning when they involve someone so spiritually active.

Scott firmly believed that whatever occurs to us, we allow to happen and give permission for its occurrence. While this is an opinion some of us may not share, nevertheless it was his. In 1992, just months before his death and when his health was severely declining, he wrote in his "Ask Scott" column:

> . . . You wish to be healed? Do a healing spell—but also listen to doctors, take the correct medication, and really, truly want and need to be healed. Too many of us enjoy the luxury of illness: days off from work and other responsibilities, being the center of attention, basking

in the concern and care of loved ones. If you're sick and wish to continue being sick, no spell or drug will cure you. Even doctors agree with this. However, if you need and wish to be healed, you will be.

There is also the belief among some philosophies that if a spiritually evolved individual chooses a difficult manner of death, he or she takes on a special measure of the suffering and reduces the pain of those who follow. In this sense, these persons become "Divine Sacrifices" whose power helps to eradicate the cause of the suffering. Seen in this light, the idea that someone might choose to die in a painful way becomes more understandable. The idea of a priest of the Goddess being called upon to die in the faith was not alien to Scott, as he indicates in this poem:

> *One dreamless, windswept night I woke*
> *To whispers from the Moon.*
> *From far behind the clouds she spoke,*
> *in mystery and rune:*
>
> *I had a Priest in ages past*
> *Who walked beyond the wall*
> *Who aided me when spells were cast,*
> *and cried the sacred call.*
>
> *I loved my Priest from far above,*
> *He loved me from below,*
> *We dared to consummate our love*
> *Beside the fire's glow.*
>
> *Reflected by the starry shore*
> *A shining golden dart*
> *Of sunlight pierced the clouds and tore*
> *My lover's trembling heart.*

He loved the Goddess. She called him to Her once, but relented and allowed him—and us—another decade of his life on earth. Although Scott was outwardly successful and apparently content, emotionally he had never made the human romantic connection that he desired in his heart. After a bad romance, he had sworn off any real attempt to become emotionally involved again. The pain he had felt then was searing enough that giving up the pursuit of love felt less painful than ever beginning over again. The complexities of sexuality in the eighties and nineties contributed to his hesitancy, but he was repeatedly emphatic that he would never pursue romance again. Scott was an intensely romantic being who systematically denied himself any romantic opportunities, throwing all of his energies into his work, yet never getting quite far enough ahead of his bills to fully enjoy the benefits his success brought him. While he loved his friends and the time spent with them, he was aware that romantic union eluded him. He was compassionate in listening to the romantic woes of his companions, but was also critical of his friends allowing themselves to indulge in hopeless romances.

This, of course, applies only to human love. Perpetually dissatisfied in his human relationships, and determined, even before his diagnosis, that he must live an asexual existence like some Goddess-priests of old, Scott could look forward to a lifetime of work, work, and more work, interrupted occasionally by visits with his friends who, often as not, would ask his advice on the romantic subjects he had rejected. He would be swept away in films and books of romantic fantasy, then turn to his computer and force that energy into one book after another. Outwardly content with his life, he would rarely admit to any inner dissatisfaction. He had made his bargain with the Goddess, and would stick to it with typical Cunningham resolve. He was Her priest, and would accept, with a grace that rarely failed him, the golden dart when it pierced his heart at last.

No, the magic did not fail. The cycles of nature that Scott always reverenced turned and caught him up in their spinning.

Scott believed in reincarnation and the cycles of returning. If he has any choice in the matter, we may be wise to look for him among the native peoples of Hawai'i, particularly if some young writer twenty or thirty years from now becomes a warm chronicler of the island culture.

> *E pani i kou mau maka a hiamoe me ka maikai—*
> *Close your eyes and sleep well.*

—from Frank Pelekai,
native of Maui, now in San Diego,
given to David Harrington "For the Memory of Scott"
May 5, 1993

The Witch Alone

Beyond the town, beneath the Moon,
Beside the standing stone,
There lives a woman, fair of faith,
We call the Witch Alone

She sings to Sun and Moon and Stars
And gathers herbs and weeds,
with which she fashions ancient charms
and other magic deeds.

She worships not at altars built
By hands of mortal men,
But in the misty, magic glade
Beyond the farthest glen.

What need has she of flashing swords,
Of crystals glowing bright,
Of censers and of colored cords
That grace the Wiccan rite?
Her tools are fashioned from the earth,
And wind and fire and rain;
Her rites are dances, wild and free
That call the Gods amain.

When spring and summer pass to fall,
And twilight fills her eyes,
She'll lie upon the browning grass
And smile as she dies.

For though she leaves her mortal shell
Of flesh and blood and bone,
She knows she does not die, but lives
On as the Witch Alone.

—Scott Cunningham, circa 1973

Appendix 1

Friends and Readers

Remember

SCOTT'S READERSHIP WAS WIDE AND VARIED, BRINGING TOGETHER seekers of many regions, nationalities, and races. He received fan mail from all over the world, and as news of his death spread, many of his readers spontaneously wrote to Llewellyn to express their grief. Later, we requested additional letters from readers including their memories of Scott. As news of Scott's passing spread, Llewellyn ran a request in the *New Times* for readers to send their remembrances of Scott. Many also sent their condolences to his parents, Chet and Rosie Cunningham. When it came time to write the biography, we also made a similar request. Because of space restrictions, we have selected the letters most representative of the hundreds received, and we thank everyone who chose to remember Scott in this way. What is included here is a small fraction of the material we received.

Dorothy (Morgan) Jones, Scott's first magical teacher, writes of their time of study and magic:

"I met Scott in high school. We were in so many classes together and found we had a lot of common interests, so it wasn't long before we became close friends. We were even in the same dance class and became partners—we danced together every day—we even lied about our ages and got into discos to dance on the weekends.

"It was also our luck to live out in the hills in San Diego. When we weren't dancing, we were hiking or swimming or laying about in the secluded canyons. We had a lot of time to talk when we were out in the hills and it was a time in our lives when religion and philosophy were very important, especially since we'd started to question the beliefs of our Christian parents. At the same time, the pull of nature was strong.

"Soon, we were gathering herbs and plants on our walks, discussing the cosmic order of things and dancing naked around wooded pools, just like good pagans. We didn't know that's what we were until one of those supermarket check out books about the occult got into our hands.

"Then the serious reading and research began. We were overjoyed to finally have a clear path. We studied, we worked, we celebrated. There was a beautiful secluded beach where we would camp all night for moon rituals. Greeting the dawn at the ocean's edge was a favorite time for us."

Scott's influence on the magical community is well-known, but there is another group that Scott went out of his way to guide and help: new writers. Several people have written mentioning their contact with Scott and his no-nonsense, inspirational effect on their literary lives. John Dellea writes:

"I never actually met Scott. I called him up when I was first trying to get a book of interviews off the ground. He asked me what I was about, and where I was coming from with regard to perspective. He offered some valuable tips to a total unknown who was in way over his head.

"I missed him on a number of occasions, ranging from here in Denver a few years ago, to Salem, back when he first got sick. When I had the chance to do the first travel on my own project, I went to the East Coast instead of the West. I continue to kick myself over the fact that I did not have the chance to meet such a great man in person.

"The couple of times we talked on the phone, he told me about writing as he saw it, a magical practice. He told me that his best day of writing produced eighty-two pages of clean copy, and we both talked a bit about that magic circle that you put up when you write. He talked to me straight, and had no high and mighty ego trips to flaunt. He was an honest man who cared deeply about the people in the pagan movement and his loved ones. In the course of telling me about writing, he referred to his father, for whom he obviously had a great deal of respect. We talked about publishers, and the photo on the cover of *The Truth About Witchcraft Today*, and I sent him the copy of *Entrepreneurial Woman* magazine that may still be among his papers.

"Look, I'm having a hard time writing this letter. I talked to him on the phone a few times, and he came off as a good, honest, caring guy. He did a lot of good with his writing, and in spite of whatever he may have had to suffer through in his life, he was kind to me, who he didn't know from Adam. I think that says about as much about him as anything ever could."

Scott always was encouraging to new writers. Ashleen O'Gaea thanked him for his encouragement, which resulted in the publication of her first book, *The Family Wicca Book*.

"His confidence in me was one of those splendid gifts life sometimes gives us." she wrote. Another writer, Laural Jones, had just had her first article published when she attended a book signing for Scott. As he signed her book, he recognized her name from the article. She was thrilled at the recognition, and said, "Maybe someday I'll write a book, too, if I ever get my hands on a word processor." Unknowingly, Laural had stumbled into an area where Scott had very strong opinions. He took any complaint regarding equipment as nothing more than an excuse not to write. His eyes twinkled as he commented, in all (apparent) innocence, "Gee, I wonder how Shakespeare, Homer, Bacon and all the others managed to cope?" They both laughed, but Laural took the joking correction to heart. "I've been writing ever since!"

One writer, Rhea Bartha, apologized for sending in several handwritten pages of material. Scott would have applauded her for writing no matter what.

"Scott's passing affected me so very deeply . . . I look forward to his last few works with reverence. He opened the door for me and I fervently pray you will keep all his works available to the public for years to come. My first introduction to Scott Cunningham was through his book, *The Truth About Witchcraft Today*. I have always been attracted to this religion and sporadically from adolescence I've 'picked up the broom' and read what little I could find. Twelve years ago, after the death of my last parent, I started the search for some type of comfort in various religions. Each of the several religious dogmas I studied left too many unanswered questions, were too restrictive and had no common sense or intelligence about them. So once again I turned to Wicca. I came across Scott's books and the door was thrown open wide.

"Here was a book that was so simple and beautiful I wanted to shout from the rooftops—"People! Listen! This is Great!" I devoured everything I could find of Scott's. Slowly the local Wiccan world opened up to me. I located a coven. Two New Age book stores opened locally and that alone was something to see in a smaller city in the Bible Belt. All of this has happened in the last four years.

"Each of Scott's books was like a discussion with a trusted friend. Everything confirmed what I felt in an honest and intelligent manner. My lifetime interests in animals, art, and nature were increased a thousand fold. However, where I tried to force new things I was disappointed. I could read tarot cards but no matter how I tried to scry a mirror or crystal ball—no matter how long I looked at hot fireplace coals or incense smoke I saw nothing.

"I came to the realization that even the best Witch can't do everything and through Scott's many works I was able to accept this. Relax and do what you do best. My world was opening up and Scott would show me the path for years to come. Then this Summer, at one of the aforementioned bookstores, I found a copy of *Circle Network News*, which the store would be carrying. As I perused the issue that evening I came across the announcements and read Scott's name. Surely not my Scott, I thought. Maybe it was another Wiccan author who had passed over. He was so young, so many more books to write, doors to open, and information to teach. Surely not my Scott!

"That night I held a special ritual for him. Even though he had passed away three months before, even though it wasn't the proper phase of the moon or day of the week I held my humble ritual. The only 'pagan' ingredient I had was one of my special candles. The ritual, though brief, left me feeling blessed that I could say good-bye in my own way to this special friend.

"The next morning I stood outside waiting for my ride to work. 'Scott,' I said aloud, 'You are a part of all this now. The birds flying overhead, the sun and moon above, the leaves on the trees and the wind blowing through the grass!'

"Suddenly I had the most wonderful feeling. It was like a big hearty hug. I knew it was the presence of Scott!!

"Since that day I have slowly improved in my psychic abilities, my meditative studies, and my understanding of life. I have been blessed with Scott's writings. The tone of my religious life has been set."

A common theme through many letters portrays Scott as swinging open the doors to knowledge and faith:

"He opened the doors wide open to let the beauty in nature and in life itself shine through. I owe my happiness in Wicca to Scott. My views of life have deepened and as a result (I) have put a lot more back into it."

Another reader notes:

"(Scott) . . . helped to fill a large void in my life which has changed my total Being for ever. And though our paths did not cross in the physical sense, surely they must have in spirit, as Scott seemed to know exactly what I needed to learn, and, by paper and pen, he opened many doors for me and showed me the way."

One reader opened her house to Scott for one of his visits to Hawai'i:

"What I remember most about that stay was Scott's ritual rising to meet the sun everyday, regardless of how late he had been up with the Tutus (grandmothers) recording their stories. He was a congenial and easy houseguest. Our parting dinner was "pun"ctuated with "punny" remarks and easy conversation. Scott did leave me with one admonishment in selecting a magical name—to select one that was not being over used. I thought I had, but sign me . . . Selene."

One letter was written simply:

"Dear Scott . . . I'm a 41 year old sailor in the US Navy and I live onboard my ship. My wife and children live a thousand miles away. I am a solitary Wiccan by choice and even though I live inside a machine my spirit walks in the North. This is what you have given me: the ability to see the Goddess everywhere and have faith.

"I thank you for what you have done for me and the joy you gave me. Farewell, my friend I never got to meet in this lifetime."

One reader credited Scott with her recovery from drugs:

"I grieve to hear of Scott Cunningham's passing. His books pulled me out of a three-year addiction to crack cocaine. I substituted a constructive addiction (Wicca) for my destructive addiction, and I will always be indebted to Mr. Cunningham for bringing me back to life."

Reawakenings touched other readers in different ways:

"(Scott) helped me to reawaken that child in me who adores nature, fantasy, and wonderment of life. For years it was within, but dormant, from the lack of support and understanding of others. I used to try to shut that door in fear of ridicule. With Scott's books . . . I've been having so much fun! The child within me is very happy!"

Catherine Penn sums up the feelings of many readers:

"I have never met Scott but his books helped me down my pagan path so much . . . I am still in a state of shock . . . I am so sorry he is gone, but he really isn't, as I can feel his presence very strongly."

Scott's "presence" has been reported by many. Scott himself was a great skeptic regarding communication between the living and the dead. He believed it occurred, but was rare. Diana Haronis, who had met Scott at classes at the Mystic Moon in San Diego, writes:

"I was mixing up some magickal oils, and I found that I was out of one of the ingredients that I needed. Suddenly I felt that Scott was there. (I've always been able to feel spirits). So, I asked him what would be a good substitute to use for the missing ingredient. I closed my eyes and let my hand glide slowly over the numerous little bottles until I felt which one he was directing me to. It wasn't one I would have thought to pick, so I said, 'Really, Scott?,' and I looked it up in his *Encyclopedia of Magickal Herbs*. Sure enough, it was the perfect choice for what I was working on. I wrote to my friend Judith Wise-Rhoads, who owns the Mystic Moon in San Diego, and told her of my experience. I hadn't talked to her in a long time, but I really felt he wanted her to know. She said it was the confirmation she had been waiting for! She had received a message in meditation that Scott would be working with his guides on the other side for a couple of months, and then he would begin coming through to work with people who shared his interests. She had been waiting for a sign that he was around before she would try to communicate with him!"

Diana also wrote a poem for Scott, which we reprint here by her permission:

For Scott

I met a man with laughing eyes,
A man both innocent and wise,
He seemed to walk between the worlds,
A faery soul in earthly guise.

He'd stroll along a moonlit beach,
And hear the ocean's rhythmic prayer;
And in a forest deep with ferns,
He'd see the spirits hiding there.

He told us many wondrous tales,
Of magic plants and sacred brooks.
And brought to us a mystic realm,
Within the pages of his books.

He dwells now on a fairer shore,
More joyous than the earth contains,
But for each life his spirit touched,
A spark of magic still remains.

Vinny Gaglione, the owner of Spellbound (bookstore) in New Jersey, remembers an evening with Scott. Scott had been instrumental in helping Vinny get his store going, generously offering to teach classes and generally offering a guiding hand. Vinny stated bluntly:

"Scott Cunningham is the reason my store is successful."

Recently, he opened a West Coast store, again on Scott's recommendation.

"One night Scott and I and some friends were eating some pizza at the shop. I was harassing Scott about doing some scrying. Scott finally got fed up, and began scrying in someone's beer foam. Then he told me to eat half my pizza and he scryed from the cheese on the piece that was left. He was incredibly accurate. Wherever Scott was, whatever the situation, he could make magic real. He hated being called out to prove himself, but when he needed to, he did."

Vinny remembers calling Scott for some advice on a certain spell he needed to do. Scott didn't know the answer, and gave Vinny the number of his friend Ray Marlborough. Scott was never afraid to say "I don't know." Instead, he would admit it when something fell outside his knowledge, and do everything he could to provide access to someone who did know the answer.

On another occasion, Scott and Vinny battled over a candle spell. Scott had originally given the spell to Vinny. Vinny made a couple of changes, and told Scott he was going to include it in a book he was writing. Scott said that he was writing a book (*Earth, Air, Fire & Water*) and that he'd get it into print first. For months, Scott would call up and tease Vinny: "Have you got the book written yet?" Vinnie would say no and Scott would renew the threat that he'd make it into print with the candle spell first. On the day that *EAFW* was accepted, Scott triumphantly called Vinnie. This is the story behind Scott's mention of Vinnie in the Acknowledgements: "Vinny Gaglione, for allowing me to steal back a candle ritual that he'd lifted from me."

Scot Rhoads of the Mystic Moon in Lemon Grove, and editor of the journal *New Moon Rising*, writes:

"When someone close to me dies, I am not crushed. I don't mourn Scott Cunningham—I'm sure he's doing great! I mourn our loss. We are the ones who have to continue knowing that in this life we will not be able to enjoy any more of his tangible input. But we only miss it because Scott has made such an outstanding contribution to our lives in the first place. When we look at what we have, there is reason to rejoice. And yet, it seems to be my nature to mourn what I did not get. I think of all the books he could have written, all the funny phone conversations we could have had . . . The most optimistic belief in reincarnation will not eliminate my sense of loss—but it helps.

"I try to focus on what Scott has gained, in life and in death, and I try to focus on the many good things that he has left behind for us. In that spirit, we are reprinting the articles he had generously donated to our magazine to help us to get started. I often remember a conversation when his health had forced him to focus exclusively on the books that he wanted to finish before his death; he mentioned that he felt guilt for not being able to do any more free articles for us. This more than anything reminds me of his dedication and generosity. We are certainly richer for having had him as a friend and we are all richer for the legacy of his wonderful books. Thank you, Scott!"

Judith Wise-Rhoads shared some of her memories of Scott in an article for *New Moon Rising*:

"One of the great perks that go with running a bookstore is meeting wonderful people like Scott who become friends for life. It was in 1977–78 when I opened my first bookstore (Ye Olde Enchantment Shoppe in San Diego) with a partner who later left.

"Scott taught his first class at the Shoppe—actually, we taught it together. It was like a vaudeville act. We had a lesson plan with part lecture and part questions and answers. Somehow I ended up on Scott's lap then he was on my lap. It was hilarious and great fun but totally unpredictable—it just happened! The best times seems to just evolve. His classes were always fun as well as very informative.

"There were about five of us in the Shoppe one night at closing time, just shooting the breeze and drinking coffee. Nobody wanted to go home yet. Scott was the one who thought up Strip Tarot and we all just made it up as we went along. (It was innocent!)

"Scott was concerned about his wonderful parents, whom he loved dearly. His last six months to a year, he talked about not wanting to be a burden on them. He took care of himself independently as long as he could. His very sweet mother, an invalid, and his father (also a writer and where Scott got his ability) did a great job of raising a courageous, talented and sensitive individual with a unique sense of humor.

"Since one's sense of humor comes from one's High Self, Scott's spiritual side was clearly well developed. He was so funny, always joking, and yet so human . . . Those of us who knew him appreciated how funny and endearing Scott was."

One reader, Gene Lockwood, wrote to Llewellyn and described Scott's generosity with his time:

"I was really taken back by the news of Scott's passing. I had spoken to him in March of 1992. In January of 1992 I had written to Scott to ask his advice on where I could purchase Gum Mastic. At the time I could not locate a source. At the beginning of March Scott called to give me a few sources. I was very surprised that he should call me least of all. I have read most of Scott's books but I never got a real sense of who Scott was until we spoke on the phone. I was real surprised when he asked for my opinion on what should be included in his forthcoming book and what topics I thought would be good for a future book. Scott explained to me that he was working very hard and just finished his current book. He had so many ideas and didn't know which way to go first. As I spoke to Scott I felt he was the person I viewed in his video and more important, I felt as if Scott and I had been friends for a long time. We spoke for about an hour on the phone. Now I can understand why Scott was trying to accomplish so much in so little time."

Lorna McGaw writes:

"I had known Scott only slightly for a couple of years before I learned what a caring person he could be. I had run into him several times at the Renaissance Faire and the Herb Shop and Hallows parties, but never really knew him. There came a day when I had someone leave me whom I cared for deeply and I was very upset and unhappy. As it was, I was going into a shop near Scott's apartment and ran into him in the parking lot. He said hello to me and then, in a very concerned way asked me how I was. Something broke loose in me and I told him that someone I cared for had left me. Scott at once took me in his arms and held me in a very soothing way and insisted on coming with me to the store. I began to feel less wounded, as though I were healing already. He radiated warmth and caring for me, yet he hardly knew me at all. I never forgot this. Later, I got to know him much better and he fell in love with my rum cake that I made for winter solstice. He asked that a rum cake be my gift to him every year and so it was, always on the same red plate, which he would return to me for next year's cake. He said he ate it all himself and never gave any away. He liked

Scott, age four, and his older brother Greg, age six, in Michigan, prior to the move to California in 1960. Although the piano pictured here is a toy one, it wasn't long before Scott was studying piano in earnest, at one time planning a career in music.

Five-year-old Scott on a pony in front of his house, 1961. A local entrepreneur brought ponies through the suburban streets of San Diego, offering photos to parents.

Six-year-old Scott with one of the family dogs in California, 1962. His parents later bred and raised cocker spaniels.

Scott on a visit to the San Diego Zoo posing with a statue of Mbongo, 1963. The lush tropical foliage and exotic plants fascinated Scott, who, as a boy, dreamed of discovering lost cities overgrown by jungle.

A Halloween poster that Scott created in second grade. Halloween was always Scott's favorite celebration. He loved to create lavish and spooky decorations for the occasion.

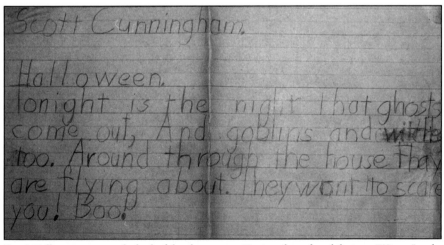

Scott Cunningham.

Halloween.
Tonight is the night that ghosts come out, And goblins and wittle too. Around through the house thay are flying about. They want to scare you! Boo!

Scott's Halloween poem on the back of the above poster. He strongly preferred the term "Wiccan" and had trouble using and spelling the word "Witches," even at an early age.

Thirteen-year-old Scott in a posed shot jacking up the family Ford Falcon station wagon. In reality, Scott had little patience with anything mechanical. These photos were set up by his father, who needed illustrations for articles he was writing on car maintenance. Circa 1969.

Scott posing for a photo illustration of one of his father's articles.

Junior High Yearbook photo of Scott, 1970.

Scott's parents, Chester Grant and Rose Marie Cunningham, affectionately known to all as "Chet" and "Rosie," in 1978.

Scott and his mother, Rosie, in 1987.

Scott's younger sister Christine and their grandmother, Hazel Cunningham, 1988.

Scott in a happy family gathering, 1990. Left to right, nephew Matthew, mother Rosie, brother Greg, and Scott. His brother Greg finally coaxed Scott into buying a modern computer system to replace the 64K dinosaur that kept eating his files.

Scott in the back yard of his parents' home, posing with his father's prized apple-banana tree, 1986. His father introduced him to the love of tropical plants.

Carl Weschcke, president of Llewellyn Publications, and Scott, 1983, San Diego, California.

The back of the former Cunningham family cabin on Mount Laguna, Cleveland National Forest, San Diego County, Caifornia. The octagonal cabin was home base for many of Scott's early explorations in the magic of nature.

Scott and deTraci arranging a set for Herb Magic, 1987. *They created and produced this video, with support from Llewellyn Publications.*

Scott demonstrating an herb on the set of Herb Magic, 1987.

Pentagram herb display, on the set of Herb Magic, 1987.

Scott on the set of Herb Magic, 1987. *Scott wrote the script and insisted on using cue cards to ensure that everything was taped as scripted, which gave a stilted feel to some scenes.*

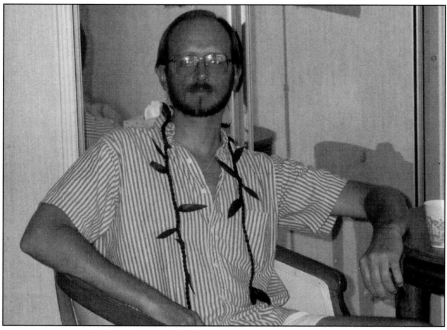

Scott wearing a lei of ti leaves during one of his many trips to Hawai'i, circa 1987.

The Plumeria was Scott's favorite Hawai'ian flower.

Relaxed and happy, Scott in Hawai'i, 1980s. His first visit in 1984 was a life-changing experience. He returned several times in the 1980s and early 1990s.

Scott at the Polynesian Cultural Center in Oahu, wearing a headband he wove from a native plant, 1991.

A leaf from the Ki plant bundled for offering as a blessing.

Scott wearing a fish hook necklace (Makau), his favorite amulet.

The Goddess Pele claims a modern roadway with Her molten lava.

Scott on the Big Island in Hawai'i at the Pu'ukohola Heiau. These stone temples of the ancient Hawaiians fascinated Scott. This temple is located about an hour's drive north of Kailua-Kona and was built in the late 1700s by Kamehameha I on the advice of a Kahuna to magically assist his unification of the islands.

Scott on the Big Island, Hawai'i, in front of Kilauea steam vent, calling up the Goddess Pele. The power, myth, and magic of Pele was an important part of Scott's fascination with Hawai'i.

Scott at the Llewellyn booth at the American Booksellers Association Convention in the late 1980s.

Ruth Phillips with her friend and colleague, the famed Witch—Sybil Leek.

Scott with David Harrington in Hawai'i on the island of Oahu at the Polynesian Cultural Center, 1991.

Scott at a booksigning, circa 1991.

Scott at the West Coast Round Table, a literary event where he was an invited speaker. Ambassador Hotel, Los Angeles, California, 1987.

"The Flying Witch" board game Scott created and often played with his friends. He was well aware of the sacred origins of most games, and considered the "Flying Witch" stereotype to actually be a manifestation of the Crone aspect of the Mother Goddess. His rules were strict and he was a cutthroat opponent.

A few of the dozens of mass-market novels Scott wrote to support his magical writing, covering the spectrum from Westerns, romances and TV-show novelizations to science fiction.

Some of the foreign language translations of Scott's magical books.

Scott's magical books and videos that are published by Llewellyn.

to eat it while writing at his computer on his books, and so the circle of rum cake continued for many years until he was gone."

Ray and Tara Buckland wrote to the *New Times*:

"When we moved to San Diego in 1984, we were delighted to find that Scott Cunningham also lived there. We had each admired the other's writings for some time and we quickly became good friends.

"Scott had an excellent knowledge of herbs, as attested to by his several books and excellent video on the subject, and generously shared that knowledge with Tara, who had a similar interest.

"Scott and Ray would sometimes find themselves both booked to do workshops at the same pagan or Wiccan gathering, perhaps halfway across the country. And we would frequently bump into one another at local pagan and Wiccan celebrations.

"With the making of Ray's Witchcraft video, Scott was invaluable as an unofficial helper; cheering everyone on and making an outrageous home video of "The Making of . . .", including many of the worst outtakes!

"He was a multifarious writer, inspired no doubt by his prolific writer father, Chet. In our last conversation with Scott he was complaining about the fact that he was working on two or three different books and didn't know which one to try to finish first.

"Those who were acquainted with Scott were well aware of his biting, satirical sense of humor but only those close to him knew that he was a deeply loving, caring and loyal person who would do anything for friend in need. He could be generous to a fault.

"His writings are extremely popular and will continue to be so for many years to come. A fitting tribute, we feel, to a man who dedicated himself to helping others and who will be sorely missed both by those who knew him well and by those who only came in contact with him through his books."

Don Kraig wrote an article for the Llewellyn *New Times* issue dedicated to Scott.

"Scott and I fell into our friendship by chance . . . I went into an occult shop in San Diego and there happened to be an ad posted on the wall.

Someone was seeking a roommate. I called and viewed the apartment. That was my first meeting with Scott Cunningham. I looked at the room which was for rent, measured it to make sure that I could fit all I wanted into it, and gave Scott the money for the room.

"Thus began my five years of sharing a two-bedroom apartment in San Diego with Scott. During that time we never had even one argument. I think that was simply because we put up with each other's foibles. We were both very good at making jokes. This included insulting each other and attending each other's lectures and making rude remarks from the back. Neither of us took offense because we both knew that we respected each other deeply.

"One of the reasons I respected Scott so much is that he thoroughly researched everything he wrote about. I remember one time that he wanted to write about corn dollies. These are designs made by knitting pieces of straw into patterns. Rather than simply copying from another book, he purchased some straw and learned the technique for himself. Unfortunately, the straw he began with came from nearby Tijuana, Mexico, and much of his early experimentation did not work due to the poor quality of the material. He left it out for a few days and one morning, when I opened the door to my room, I was confronted with hundreds of tiny moths which had hatched from eggs in the straw! For days I was slapping at them and pushing them out of my way.

"I owe Scott a great deal. It was through Scott that I first became affiliated with Llewellyn.

"Scott and I were on parallel mystical paths, but they were not the same. Even so, we had many similarities in beliefs. Both of us detested the tricksters and rip-offs who used the occult to separate people from their possessions. We also both disliked the wars-of-words going on between groups and individuals who were honest, but who had differences of opinion. It seems that some groups or individuals may say that everyone is entitled to his or her path, but in actuality, refuse to let others go where they may. In this time of various groups trying to denounce occultism in any form, we need to stand together. It is my hope that besides the continuing presence of the information he shared in his books, people following mystical paths will begin to allow others to do as they will as long as it harms none. This would be a fine epitaph for Scott Cunningham.

"Scott was my friend, my roommate, my teacher, my advisor, and as much the butt of my jokes as I was of his. When I heard that he passed over on my birthday, I knew that he must have chosen that day on purpose, just to make sure that on one day out of the year I would remember him.

"He needn't have worried. I'll never forget him."

Jana Branch, then-editor of the Llewellyn *New Worlds of Mind and Spirit*, wrote in the May/June 1993 issue:

"The news of Scott Cunningham's untimely passing has been hard for everyone at Llewellyn. He came from California for Llewellyn's company holiday party, and we were buoyed by his warm presence, good spirits and rather wicked sense of humor. Our phone lines have been filled with sad, shocked voices asking what happened . . . what happened?

"Is it synchronicity that just now Scott's latest book, *Living Wicca*, should be released? He talks about the Wiccan Mysteries, how you can't define them, put them in words, that you can only live by them...and die with them.

"One body is gone, but his other body—his written word—is still alive and well. I just hope that Scott had some inkling about how many people were affected by his work and his life. For my money, it doesn't really matter what you say about a person after he's gone. But it does matter how you live. And if his memory and words can help you make that difficult day-by-day journey in a truer light, then his legacy is secure."

Marilee Bigelow supplied her memories of Scott for the Church of the Eternal Source newsletter and several aromatherapy publications:

" ... Scott left an important legacy for us all. He preserved and recorded oral traditions which might otherwise have been lost. He strived to get what he considered "valuable information" out to the public, and he pushed himself (sometimes to excess) to make his deadlines and keep his commitments.

" ... We spent many late nights doing research in my library, discussing herbs, oils, and magic. Our exchange of information, and knowledge, coupled with our mutual quest for the best purity and quality of products, made us ideal travelling companions, and we visited innumerable botanical gardens in our journeys. In addition to our other links, he was my High Priest in three of the magical traditions we were initiated into, so performing magical rituals was also an integral part of our precious relationship.

" ... Scott has a special place in my heart, and our friendship which has spanned more than twenty years has been, and is, very dear to me. I am so deeply grateful for the time I was able to spend with him, and treasured our visits (especially this past year when I could see his health was declining). I loved Scotty and cared about him, and feel pain at his passing. He was a Joy to my heart and I will always regard him as a beloved comrade and the finest of persons.

" ... In his aromatherapy book he informs me that the 'spring bloomer,' the Hyacinth flower (Hyacinthus orientalis) is the essential oil I need for halting and overcoming my all-consuming grief. He writes that if one inhales the fragrance, which is ruled by Venus, it will bring love and peaceful sleep. I hope he's right."

Scott Cunningham—A Remembrance

Chet Cunningham, in addition to providing us with thousands of pages of material from Scott's writings and access to family photographs, also provided the following reminiscence of Scott:

"Millions of memories come crowding back, flooding me with joy and surprise and sadness and wonder as I think back over the quick thirty six years that I knew Scott Cunningham. It's an awesome responsibility, raising a brand new human being into childhood and watch and try to guide a little and make suggestions as that small one grows and develops and becomes an adult. It's a responsibility that staggers me now that I think back to when I had it.

"Scott was a little more of a loner than our other two children. I had learned a few things about child rearing from the mistakes made on our firstborn, but I insisted that Scott should be in Cub Scouts when he was nine. Wolf badge, the first step along the way.

"Scott wore the uniform, went to the meetings, but wasn't overly enthusiastic about it. Then the day came for him to pass his first Wolf badge/rank test. The night before I cautioned him that he would be asked some questions about the Cub Scout oath and law and some of the guiding principles. I suggested that he might want to study the Wolf book so he would be ready.

"The next day before we went to the Cub Scout meeting I asked him some of the questions. He didn't summarize or paraphrase. He gave back to me exactly what the book said, word for word. He had memorized the pages in the book I had suggested he read. That should have told me a lot more about Scott than I realized at the time.

"When Scott took on a project, it was full throttle, gung ho, Nellie-bar-the-door.

"I remember early 'shows' he put on, usually magic shows when he was eight to ten. The magic was minimal, he never had any of the magic kits or stock items, but he enjoyed doing it. As he got a little older he graduated to other kind of 'shows' most of them with flashing colored lights. We spent a lot of time putting sockets on boards and running drop cords to the wall outlet then flashing them on and off. I still have a drawer with some of those colored bulbs in them from twenty five years ago.

"In Junior High school, Scott hated physical education class. This was because he was not good at sports, throwing, batting, catching, kicking. What most of us are not good at, we don't like to do and don't do, but in junior high everyone did P.E.

"Scott and I skipped the trauma of Little League baseball. There was no small fry football or soccer in those good old days. I'd learned that some boys like baseball and some don't. My oldest drove the point home when he was in a group of young players who would be assigned to a minor or a major league baseball team. When the coach asked our older boy which team he'd rather be on, he told them neither one. It was a quick end to the baseball season for my oldest boy, but I learned the lesson.

"Piano lessons came along. Scott threw his energies into the keyboard. He practiced, practiced, and practiced. He progressed through one teacher and we found another one, a man well versed in classical piano, but also a showman who played regularly in local night clubs and bars around San Diego.

"Scott soared. He loved the various types of music his teacher could play. Scott was good. After two years, his new teacher suggested that he move on to a teacher who would be better for him and who could give him solid advanced techniques in the classics. I began to wonder if Scott would become a concert pianist. The new teacher was on the staff at San Diego State University, and Scott was still in high school. I drove him to lessons and waited for him. As I remember, the lessons were $20 each. That was a lot of cash in those days, but this teacher was one of the best in San Diego.

"Somewhere along the line the bloom came off the piano. Other interests became more important for Scott and the lessons dwindled down to nothing.

"I've heard that music and mathematics are the best foundation training for clear thinking and creativity. I'm not sure that's right, but from somewhere Scott developed the ability to research a project. He had an abiding love affair with Hawai'i and the last book he wrote was about the religions of the islands.

"The researching diligence formed early in Scott's writing career. He knew little about trucks, but he wrote articles and columns for me about trucks in industry, big ones, diesels and over-the-road and construction rigs. He also took over my column called 'Your Car,' a ghosted column written for local auto dealers to run in their newspapers as a paid advertisement. He wrote this ad weekly for five or six years, always researching carefully everything he said.

"When he did the book on *Magical Aromatheraphy,* he again did massive amounts of research. In his library, we found boxes and boxes of books, papers, and journals on the subject that he had used in his quest.

"It's easy to say good things about a man not here to defend himself. We know that Scott was held in high esteem by thousands of his readers around this country and overseas. We received hundreds of cards and letters from his friends and readers all over and Scott's Mother and I wish to thank all of you for your kind words. We have a feeling that Scott's fifteen [magical] books will live on and on and that hundreds of thousands of people will read and benefit from them. We wish he had been with us for another thirty six years, but we are thankful that his short span here was productive and satisfying for him, and we cherish those thoughts as we mourn our loss.

"Thank you again and may your path be straight and level, may you have a kind word for everyone you meet as you walk along life's pathways into the glory of the eventual setting sun."

A Note on the Writing of This Book

David Harrington and I (deTraci Regula) were strangers prior to writing this book. Thrown together by Llewellyn to do this project, we shared our friendship with Scott and little else. In ten years, we had met only twice. David was convinced I disliked him and I, unaware of this, thought David was indifferent to me. With suspicion on both sides, we reluctantly met and began to go through the masses of Scott's papers. During our early meetings we were trying to hide our sorrow. We didn't communicate much as we found bits and pieces that reminded us of our friendship with Scott. Some of the fragments we found meant nothing to one of us but everything to the other. We went through a mountain of tissues as we read and sorted and cried.

Gradually, David discovered that I didn't even remember something he'd said to me years ago. I learned that writing Scott's biography was the last thing he wanted to do. We began to see the qualities—maybe "quirks" is a better word—which Scott had enjoyed in each of us. We love books and bookstores, bad jokes and word puns, pets, and "collectible" toys (which we don't collect—we play with them).

One day, David decided we should go to Hagstone Cove, one of the spots which Scott and he had discovered. I had never been there—Scott didn't mix his friends or activities, except on rare occasions. Restaurants, stores, and other places would usually only be visited with the person who had discovered the spot.

It was a gray day as we drove west toward Point Loma, a long, high peninsula which encloses the western side of San Diego Bay. The sloping sides are filled with large older houses, but the top and distant western slope are all part of a military reservation. The public is allowed limited access to the historic Point Loma Lighthouse and the large military cemetery. We drove past the gatehouse and passed the field of white crosses. It was a quiet day, and the military atmosphere reminded me of Scott's belief that he had served in World War II and died then. With few changes, Fort Rosecrans, with its cement gun emplacements facing the Pacific, could still be in the 1940s. We passed the last of the military buildings and turned onto a steep road leading down the ocean side of the point. Here, the territory changed and the grassy downs felt like the coastline of the Eastern seaboard. A New England-style lighthouse, built to replace the old Spanish-style one, now a museum, enhanced this effect. David parked the truck and we got out, walking down a path, avoiding the throngs of tourists and schoolchildren. The cliffs were steep and the ocean spread out like a silvery blue blanket, woven with small ripples. The rises of the waves yet to break slowly rolled toward the coast. Perhaps, I thought, these same waves had brushed the beaches of Scott's beloved Hawai'i.

I followed along behind David, not sure where we were going. We took a turn on the path, and began to descend. Suddenly, there was Hagstone Cove, a protected castle-like cove facing south, avoiding the force of the waves. The high walls of the cove carved from the cliff protected a small beach made of millions of marble-sized, jewel-like pebbles. Miraculously, considering the nearby crowds, we were absolutely alone in the cove. David had brought a *ki* leaf which he had harvested from one of his plants. He knelt to select stones from the cove, added a piece of lava he had brought with him from Hawai'i, and wrapped the leaf around the offerings. Then he stood and cast the bound blessing out into the waters of the cove. It splashed beyond the edge of the incoming waves. All was sea-silent for a moment, the whish of the waters, a distant cry of a seabird, the breeze gently caressing the sandstone cliffs.

Then the crowds descended on the cove, shattering the silence. We moved back through the strangers who had materialized around us. As we climbed up the path together, we were beginning to realize Scott's final gift. He left us his words, our shared memories of him, and now, our new friendship.

—deTraci Regula

◦

HERE IS THE COMPLETE TEXT OF SCOTT CUNNINGHAM'S BOOKLET, *A Formula Book of Magical Incenses and Oils,* self-published while *Magical Herbalism* was still in preparation for publication.

(Interior Cover)

(Page One—Table of Contents)

Introduction

There is no mystical secret about preparing incenses and oils for use in magic; the secret is simply that it isn't that difficult!

For centuries, however, reliable, complete incense and oil formulae haven't been available to the general public.

This small booklet, then, has been written to fill some of this need. Most of the ingredients are easily obtainable at occult or herb shops, or even at a grocery store, and the procedures for making oils and incenses are simple.

So this book explains the "what" (the ingredients) and the "how" (their preparation). But when should they be used? Whenever the need exists, use these oils and incenses. You'll know if you're looking for a love, or if a friend is sick, or if you'll be performing a full moon ritual. Feel free to use these recipes anytime you sense the need.

I hope it needs not be said that magic that attempts to harm, manipulate or control others always ends in self-destruction—it isn't worth the heavy penalty that awaits.

Use these recipes with care and love, for the good of all. Blessed be!

Preparation of formulae you will notice that for several of the recipes in this booklet no amounts are given; this is traditional, but don't let it scare you off.

Use your intuition when mixing incenses; add as much of each ingredient as you believe is required.

For oils, use your nose—the scent is important.

Tools

You'll need a large ceramic bowl in which to mix the incenses, and a glass bottle or jar to mix the oils.

An eyedropper is a great help in mixing oils, as you can add them one drop at a time to ensure the proper amounts.

Mixing Incenses

Add each ingredient to the bowl. When you are satisfied by the amount (or have followed those specified, if any) gently run your fingers through the incense mixture slowly, concentrating on the work the incense is to do. If it is a love incense, concentrate on love, for instance.

After a few moments remove your hands. The incense should be well mixed and vibrating with energy and magical power. Pour it into a bottle, label it, and keep until needed.

Mixing Oils

Add each oil to the clean glass bottle, constantly sniffing to see if the scent seems right, when it is, gently swirl the contents of the jar around (thinking of your magical goal). Pour into a smaller bottle, hold it in your hands, think of your magical intent, and then label it and keep it until needed.

Using Oils and Incenses

The incenses discussed in this book must be burned on charcoal blocks, which are available at any occult store or religious supply house. Simply light the charcoal block, set it in a censer or a dish filled with sand, and pour the incense onto it.

Oils should be either rubbed onto an object, like a candle, or on your own body.

Incenses

Altar Incense
Frankincense
Cinnamon
Myrrh

> Equal parts. Burn to cleanse the altar.

Circle Incense
Frankincense
Myrrh
Benzoin
Rose Petals
Cinnamon
Vervain
Rosemary
Sandalwood
Bay Laurel

> Equal parts. Use for general magical rites, rites of worship, or when no other incense is called for or available.

Divination Incense
Cloves
Chicory
Cinquefoil

> Equal parts. Use when employing any form of tool for divination—tarot cards, the crystal ball, the rune sticks, and so on.

Full Moon Incense
Sandalwood
Frankincense
Rose Oil

> Equal parts sandalwood and frankincense, three drops rose oil. Burn on the full moon when performing other rituals or spells, or during meditation on the full moon.

Healing Incense
Cloves Nutmeg
Lemon Balm
Poppy Seed
Cedar
Honeysuckle Oil — three drops
Almond Oil — three drops

> Burn during healing rituals

House Consecration Incense
Dill Frankincense
Wood Betony
Sandalwood
Dragon's Blood
Rose Geranium Oil
Myrrh

> Burn when moving into a new home to cleanse it, or when you feel the need in your present address.

Venus Incense
Lavendar*
Dragon's Blood
Myrtle
Rose Buds
Orris Root—ground
Musk Oil— one drop
Patchouly

> Burn to attract love, preferably on a friday night. Burn frequently in the bedroom.

> * Editor's Note: Scott preferred this uncommon alternate spelling for "lavender," and only reluctantly changed it for his published works. For this self-published project, he used the "lavendar" spelling he favored, and we've retained it here.

Offertory Incense
Rose Petals
Vervain
Cinnamon
Myrrh
Frankincense

> Burn while honoring the goddesses and gods, or as an offering in thanks for a spell that has worked. This can be used in place of "altar incense."

Prosperity Incense
Cloves
Nutmeg Cinnamon
Citron Peel
Anise

> Burn for wealth and prosperity.

Protection Incense
  Frankincense
  Wood Betony
  Dragon's Blood

  Rosemary can be burned alone, if that is all that is available.
  Use when you feel it is needed.

Purification Incense
  Sandalwood Powder
  Cinnamon Oil

  Mix together so that the oil moistens the powder; burn when you
  feel negative vibrations in your house or office.

Study Incense
  Mastic or Benzoin
  Cinnamon

  Burn to strengthen the mind during study, or to develop your
  powers of concentration. Also use this incense to gain knowledge in
  any form, and in any manner—channelling, clairvoyance, and so
  on. Since this works on the conscious mind, though, and not
  directly on the subconscious, this is not best suited to psychic work.

Sun Incense
  Sandalwood
  Clove
  Orange Blossoms
  Orris Root

  Burn for honors, riches, and spells involving jobs, promotions, or
  employers.

Uncrossing Incense
Dragon's Blood
Frankincense
Rosemary

> For banishing evil, curses, hexes.

Love Incense
Venus
Rose Buds
Red Sandalwood (santal)
Benzoin
Patchouly

> For love rituals.

Oils

Altar Oil
Frankincense
Myrrh
Vervain
Lavendar
Sandalwood

> Use to bless and purify your altar.

Anointing Oil
Olive Oil— one cup
Myrrh— one teaspoon
Cinnamon— 1/2 teaspoon

> Add herbs to olive oil. Seal in a tight jar. Let sit 30 days. Strain and use for anointing candles, or when other oils are not available or suitable.

Far Sight Oil
    Acacia
    Cassia
    Anise
       Wear to aid in seeing your past lives.

Healing Oil
    Sandalwood
    Carnation
    Rosemary
       Blend the essences and anoint for healing.

Nymph Oil
    Ambergris
    Gardenia
    Jasmine
    Tuberose (or Rose)
    Violet
       Mix and wear on self. For women only. To attract men.

Satyr Oil
    Musk
    Patchouly
    Civet
    Ambergris
    Cinnamon
       Mix and wear on self. For men only. To attract women.

Prophetic Dream Oil
    Olive Oil— 1/2 cup
    Cinnamon— one pinch
    Nutmeg— one pinch
    Anise— one teaspoon

        Heat until warm but not hot, apply to forehead and temples before sleep.

Other Formulae

Protection Sprinkling Powder
    Plain salt
    Dragon's Blood—powdered

        Mix together and sprinkle to banish negativity and evil from your home or place of business.

Holy Water
    Spring water
    Plain salt

        Sprinkle salt on to water, saying the following:

                Banish evil and negativity!
                This is my will, so mote it be!

        Use for consecrating objects, purifying homes.

Ritual Herb Bath Mixture
    Rosemary
    Fennel
    Mint
    Lavendar

        Mix, tie up in cheesecloth squares and add to the bath for purification before ritual.

The Writings of
Scott Cunningham

Articles—Magical

Scott wrote extensively for many magical publications, some of which vanished after a few issues, others which have endured for years. He rarely turned down a request for an article by a magazine struggling to establish itself. We have listed every article that we are aware that Scott wrote, or of which he kept a copy, but this list probably omits many others. If any editor or reader is aware of an article that is not included here, please let us know and we will try to add it in a subsequent printing.

Articles Prepared for Publication:
    "Hawai'ian Magic Today"[1]

The Georgian Newsletter
    "Mandrake" Article for Jan. 1980 Issue
    "Atlantis & The Wicca" after April 1980[2]

New Moon Rising:[3] *Journal of Magick and Wicca* (Previously *The Rose and Quill*),Vol. 1, No. 1
    "A Stone Banishing Ritual," Vol. 1, No. 2
    "Wiccan and Magical Games," Vol. 1, No. 3

"Seeing the Goddess in Your Home," Vol. 1, No. 4

"Chain Letters," Vol. 2, No. 1

"Pagan Bibliophiles," Vol. 2, No. 2

"The 'Solitary' Path," Vol. 2, No. 3

"Why I'm Not a Witch," Vol. 2, No. 4

"The Magic of Chocolate," Vol. 2, No. 5

"The "Ugly" Witch Figure as the Crone Aspect of the Goddess,"
     Vol. 2, No. 6

"Should I Do It While I'm Sick?," Vol. 3, No. 1

"Two Wiccan Rites," Vol. 3, No. 2

"Teaching the Magical Arts," Vol. 3 No. 3

"Belief and Magic," Vol. 3, No. 4

"Chants," Vol. 3, No. 5

"The Wiccan Spirit," Vol. 3, No. 6

"Three Magical Waters," Vol. 4, No. 1

"Love and Magic," Vol. 4, No. 2

"Circle Stories," Vol. 4, No. 3

"A Solitary Talk"

"The San Diegan Pagan"

San Diegan Pagan, Vol. 4, No. 3 Autumn 1989 C.E.
     "The Public Pagan"

The Shadow's Edge
Most of these articles were written under the pseudonym Halcyon. In later articles, the articles appear under the name Scott Cunningham. The "Green Magic" articles usually omitted any topic title. We have indicated the subject matter in parentheses.

Summer Fest Issue Vol. 1, No. 1 6980
     Green Magic—(Striga Asiatica)
          (Probable – Halcyon is listed on production staff,
          but none of the articles is attributed to any author)
Cornucopia and Autumn Equinox Issue, Vol. 1, No. 2
     Green Magic—Wormwood
          (Probable – Halcyon is listed on production staff,
          but none of the articles is attributed to any author)

Summer Fest Issue, Vol. 2, No. 1
    Green Magic—(Seven Herbs Most Commonly Used in La Vecchia)
    Coven Crack-Ups by Liana and Halcyon
Winter Solstice Vol. 2, No. 2
    Green Magic—(Vervain)
Lupercus-Spring Equinox April 6981 Vol. 2, No. 3
    Green Magic—(Angelica and Selentrope)
    Crossroads—Reincarnation
Tana's Day May 6981 Vol. 2, No. 4
    Green Magic—(Bay Laurel)
Tana's Day May 6982 Vol. 3, No. 3
    Green Magic—(The Apple)
    Magical Properties of the Bell
Shadow Fest October 6982 Vol. 3, No. 1
    Green Magic—(Attunement and Enchantment)
Lupercus February 6982 Vol. 3, No. 2
    Green Magic—(Ritual Incenses)
Cornucopia August 6982 Vol. 3, No. 4
    Green Magic—(Broom)
Lupercus February 6983 Vol. 4, No. 2
    Green Magic—(Elder)
Shadow Fest October 6983 Vol. 4, No. 1
    Green Magic—(Oak)
    Crossroads—The Standing Stones Tradition
Spring/Summer 6983 Vol. 4, No. 3
    Sybil Leek—An Appreciation
    Green Magic—Purifying the Home with Herbs
        (Mentions next issue, Purifying the Body)
Shadow Fest October 6984 Vol. 5, No. 1
        Green Magic—Purifying Ourselves

Sign of the Pentagram (date not known).
    "Is There an American Witchcraft?"[4]

Aromatherapy Publications
Magical Aromatherapy: The Ritual Inhalation of Essential Oils, 1989

The Magi, June 1991
    Interview with Scott Cunningham

Llewellyn: New Worlds of Mind and Spirit
This magazine was originally called The Llewellyn New Times. Please note: Scott's books were often promoted in *New Worlds.* We have omitted listing articles which were primarily ads for his books.
January–February 1990, No. 901
    "Scent Magic—An Interview with Scott Cunningham"
        by Steve Deger
May–June 1990, No. 903
    "A Desperate Plea for Scott Cunningham"
    Mention is also made of a benefit concert held for Scott
March–April 1991, No. 912
    Cover photo of Scott
    Article, not written by Scott, on "The Magic in Food"
    Listing of Books and Photo
    "An Open Letter from Scott Cunningham"
May–June 1991, No. 913
    "Ask Scott"—first appearance of his column.
January–February 1992, No. 921
    "Earth, Air, Fire & Water: The Birth of a Book"
    "Ask Scott"
March–April 1992, No. 922
    "Ask Scott"
May–June 1993, No. 933
    "Living Wicca"—Excerpt
    Obituary
July–August 1993, No. 934
    "Remembering Scott Cunningham"
February–March 1994, No. 941
    "Spell Crafts"—Review (not written by Scott or David)

Llewellyn's 1990 Magical Almanac
"Dressing with Power"
"Goals of a Natural Magician"
"Magic in Hawai'i"
"The Wild Time"
"Excerpt of Yule Lore From 'Wicca'"

Llewellyn's 1991 Magickal Almanac
"The Magical Teacher"
"Magical Technology"
"The Magical Pantry"
"A Snow Spell"
"Spells"

Llewellyn's 1992 Magickal Almanac
"A Primer in Natural Magic and Spells and Rituals"
"The Yule Tree"
"Magical Secrecy"
"The Magic of Shells "
"Treasured Sources"

Llewellyn's 1993 Magical Almanac, Editor, Contributor
"The Sorceress: A Fable From Aesop"
"Birthdates of Famous Persons Somehow Connected with Witchcraft"
"Chain Letters: Mailed Curses"
"Magical Container Gardening"
"The Magic of May Dew"
"Ancient Egyptian Incenses"
"An Ancient Mesopotamian Exorcism"
"Fingernails and Magic"
"Zodiacal Signs and Their Ruling Deities"
"Hecate"
"Magical Household Hints"
"The Man in the Moon?"
"Astrological Poem" (Quote)
"Birds of the Deities"

"Almanac Introduction"
"Gathering Magical Plants"
"Sabbats and Full Moons for 1993"
"Ancient Greek Oracles"
"An Old Divination"
"Ancient Egyptian Spell to Cure a Dog Bite"
"Magical Words: A Short Glossary"
"Hawai'ian Power"
"Ancient Herbal Spells"

Llewellyn's 1985 Astrological Guide to California
"On the Beach"

Second Annual Edition *National New Age Yellow Pages,* compiled by Marcia Gervase Ingenito. Highgate House, Publishers
"Love in Your Spice Cabinet," 1988

Circles, Groves and Sanctuaries by Pauline and Dan Campanelli
"Midsummer"

Sacred Sites, Ed. by Frank Joseph. Llewellyn Publications, St Paul, 1992
"Hawai'i"
"Halema'uma'u: Pele's Home At Kilauea"
"The 'Wizard Stones' Of Waikiki (O'ahu)"

Books—Magical

A Formula Book of Magical Incenses and Oils. A "Pixie Publishing" Production, 1982 (Self-Published)
Magical Herbalism, 1982
Earth Power, 1983
Cunningham's Encyclopedia of Magical Herbs, 1985
The Magic of Incense, Oils, and Brews, 1986 (Original Edition)
The Magical Household (with David Harrington), 1987
Herb Magic (Videotape), 1987
The Truth About Witchcraft, 1987

The Truth About Witchcraft Today, 1988
Wicca: A Guide for the Solitary Practitioner, 1988
The Complete Book of Incense, Oils, and Brews, 1989 (Revised and
    expanded version of *The Magic of Incense, Oils, and Brews*)
The Magic in Food, 1991
The Truth About Herb Magic, 1992
Sacred Sleep (Crossing Press),1992
The Art of Divination (Crossing Press), 1993
Living Wicca, 1993
Spell Crafts, 1993
Hawai'ian Religion and Magic, 1994
The Magic of Food, 1996 (Revised edition of *The Magic in Food*)

Translations Into Foreign Languages

Herb Magic Video. Translated into Japanese.
Magical Herbalism. Translated into Dutch and Japanese.
Earth Power. Translated into Japanese and Spanish.
Cunningham's Encyclopedia of Magical Herbs.
    Translated into Czech, French, Italian, and Slovenian.
Cunningham's Encyclopedia of Crystal, Gem, and Metal Magic.
    Translated into Greek, Italian, and Spanish.
Complete Book of Incense, Oil & Brews. Translated into Spanish.
Magical Aromatheraphy. Translated into Spanish.
The Magic in Food. Translated into German and Japanese.
Earth, Air, Fire, & Water. Translated into Spanish.
Hawai'ian Religion & Magic. Translated into German.

Partially Completed Manuscripts—Magical

The Oldest Spells: Sumerian and Babylonian Magic
The Animal Companionary (with David Harrington, to be completed by
    deTraci Regula and David Harrington)
Cunningham's Magical Cookbook (many recipes added to the *1996 The*
    Magic of Food)
India Tales (mentioned in his diary as he wrote it in 1992; no further
    details, no manuscript found).
A Glossary of Witchcraft[5]

Unpublished Short Works—Magic-Related

Papers[6]
The Green Knight—Man or God?, 1975
The Systems of Magic in a Wizard of Earthsea and the Last Unicorn, 1975
Divination, 1975
Witchcraft and Sorcery During the Middle Ages
Witchcraft Is Alive Today
Arthur
The Sexual Roots of Witchcraft
Hawai'ian Magic Today

Books of Shadows

The American Traditionalist Book of Shadows[7]
The American Traditionalist Training Guide
The Ancient Pictish Gaelic Way
    (Working from materials from Ruth Phillips)
An Herbal Grimoire (Much of this material has been included in Scott's
    herbal books and in *Wicca: A Guide For The Solitary Practitioner*.)

Novels[8]

Shadow of Love, Carousel Books, 1980
    Under the pen name Cathy Cunningham
The Cliffside Horrors, Carousel Books, 1980
After the Kill, Carousel Books, 1980
Cult of Terror, Carousel Books, 1980
Aztec Gold, Tower Books, 1981
The Mildewed Coffin, Carousel Books, 1981
Double Hazard, Carousel Books, 1981
Curse of Valkyrie House, Leisure, 1981
    Under the pen name Cathy Cunningham
Mafia Rock And Roll, Carousel Books, 1981
Death Resort, Carousel Books, 1981
Revenge at Gila Peaks, Carousel Books, 1982
Danger at Deadtrees, Carousel Books, 1982
Abducted!, Carousel Books, 1982

Operation: Death Ray, Carousel Books, 1982
The Deadly Art Game, sold but unpublished

Under the pen name of Dirk Fletcher for Leisure Westerns:
Spur #1: *High Plains Temptress*
Spur #11: *Nebraska Nymph*
Spur #12 *Gold Train Tramp*
Spur #13: *Red Rock Redhead*
Spur #23: *San Diego Sirens*
Spur #27: *Frisco Foxes*
Spur #28: *Kansas City Chorine*
Spur #29: *Plains Paramour*
Spur #30: *Boise Belle*
Spur #31: *Portland Pussycat*
Spur #32: *Miner's Moll*
Spur #33: *Louisiana Lass*
Spur #34: *Deadridge Doll*
Spur #35: *Wyoming Wildcat*
Some of these Spur titles have been recently reprinted in Double
Westerns published by Leisure.

For Blitz Books (football novels for juveniles)
On the Road
Guts and Glory

Knot's Landing TV Novelizations:
#4 *Misguided Hearts,* Pioneer Communications, 1986
#7 *Tell Me No Lies,* Pioneer Communications, 1986

Unpublished Short Fiction Titles:
A Lesson From Uriel (Fantasy)
Journey To Cilqren (Fantasy)
Til Death (Comedy/Tragedy Play)
Doorway To The Stars (Sci-Fi)
Davod (Fantasy)

Second Chance (Reincarnation)
Newly Revised Edition (Fantasy)
Death Box (Sci-Fi)
Murder In The Mobile Home Park
Untitled Coven Novel
Untitled Ancient Greece Reincarnation Story
Untitled Hawai'ian Murder Mystery

General Interest Articles

"Winterizing for Low Truck Downtime." *Canadian Forest Industries,*
    October 1976

"Winterizing Southern Truck Fleets." *Southern Motor Cargo,*
    October 1976

"1976 Concrete Products Tire Roundup." *Concrete Products,*
    December 1976

"Short-Load Operator Sees Long-Range Opportunity." *Concrete Products,*
    January 1977

"Be Wise: It's Time to Winterize." *Concrete Products,*
    September 1977

"R/M Outfit Grows by Thinking Small." *Concrete Products,*
    September 1977

"Lube Oils and Where They're at Today." *Canadian Forest Industries,*
    May 1978

"Winterized Trucks Spell Reliability." *Food Distributor's News,*
    September/October 1978

"Winterizing Your Trucks." *Canadian Forest Industries,*
    October 1978

"1979 Truck Roundup." *Concrete Products,*
    February 1979

"How to Lower the Cost of Your New Truck." *Canadian Forest Industries,*
    April 1979

"Clearing the Air About Air Filters." *Concrete Products,*
    July 1979

"How to Lower the Cost of Your New Truck." *Concrete Products,*
    July 1979

"Lube Oil Today." *Concrete Products*,
   1979
"Tru Bloc Takes on a New Look." *Concrete Products*,
   October 1979
"The Ins and Outs of Truck Air Filters." *Today's Transport*,
   December 1979–January 1980 (Translated, printed as
   *"Interiordades De Los Filtros De Aire De Camion" in Transporte
   Moderno,* Diciembre 1979, Enero 1980)
"Truck Survey: Lineup for 1980." *Dairy Field*,
   January 1980
"1980 Truck Roundup." *Concrete Products*,
   February 1980
"Truck Leasing: A Practical Look." *Modern Bulk Transporter*,
   February 1980

Columns

"Did You Hear...." humor/advertising column, ghost-written for
   Coronado Radio and Electric, appeared as paid weekly display ad in
   Coronado Journal, 1973-1975[9]
"All About Engines" practical truck engine upkeep column appeared in
   Water Equipment News, 1978 to December 1982
"Your Car" automobile upkeep/advertising column, ghost-written for
   various auto dealers, appearing as paid weekly display ad in
   newspapers across the country, 1980 to the present

❦

1. This article was found among his papers in presentation form. Since Scott would
   generally not refine a piece this carefully unless he was submitting it, we assume that
   this did see print. However, we have no indication where he submitted it.
2. Scott mentions writing this article "for the newsletter" in his diary entry of April 14,
   1980. We have not been able to find a copy of this article. It is possible it was written
   for a different newsletter, but since he was actively writing for the *Georgian Newsletter*
   at this time, we are tentatively attributing it to that publication.
3. There was an earlier publication by this name to which Scott may also have
   contributed articles. In the Hallows '82 issue of this publication, there is an interview
   "by Minerva" with a Wiccan under the name of Myrddin, which is a name Scott used

magically in the Celtic tradition. Some of the opinions expressed in this interview are similar to those held by Scott, but we have been unable to confirm if this interview was actually with Scott Cunningham.

4. Scott mentions this article in his diary entry for November 1, 1978. Presumably, it was published.

5. We've assigned this title to a collection of alphabetized short articles which do not appear to have been included in his published magical works.

   This manuscript eluded us until late in the writing of this biography. Scott was an early advocate of recycling and almost always reused his drafts or spare copies of fliers to write early versions of other manuscripts. What would appear on one side of the paper to be a "Spur" novel manuscript was, in some cases, an early draft of one of his magical books or notes for a magical article.

6. These papers were written by Scott for his college English classes.

7. Much of this material, adapted for the solitary by omitting coven practices, was included as "The Standing Stone Book of Shadows" in *Wicca: A Guide for the Solitary Practitioner.* This Book of Shadows was created by Scott and Dorothy Jones, working initially from materials in Dorothy's possession, and substantially expanded based on their own experiences. Scott notes that the name of the tradition was changed to "The Standing Stone Book of Shadows" to distinguish it from another "American Traditionalist" tradition which was unrelated to their practice.

8. In addition to these novels, Scott may also have "ghostwritten" others which were published under the names of their well-known authors. A letter dated June 28, 1981, mentions that "I just wrote a book for Pinnacle . . . It's ghost-written for Eddie Egan (*French Connection* cop) and they're going to be doing a big push on it. So I lucked out on that one." We've been unable to find any further mention of this book, or if, in fact, it ever was released.

9. Most of the material in this column consisted of largely recycled comedy from various sources, adapted for the needs of the article. However, Scott occasionally managed to inject a magical theme into his jokes: "There is no truth to the rumor that Gilliam Holroyd, the young witch in *Bell, Book, and Candle* gets so furious at her brother, Nicky, that she flies off the handle!" Broom handle, of course.

   "I hear a lot about Astrology. One time at a party a group was discussing it: One man said he was born under Aquarius, another a Libra, and another stated that he was born under a stop sign, in a taxi." Sad to say, these excerpts are pretty typical of the rest of the material, which is on file at the Coronado Public Library, in Coronado.

Scott Cunningham's Astrological Chart

SCOTT WAS NOT AN ACCOMPLISHED ASTROLOGER BUT HE RECOGNIZED THE POWER of a well-cast chart. He also believed that knowledge of another's chart could be used to work against them. For this reason, he rarely admitted his true birth date or time.

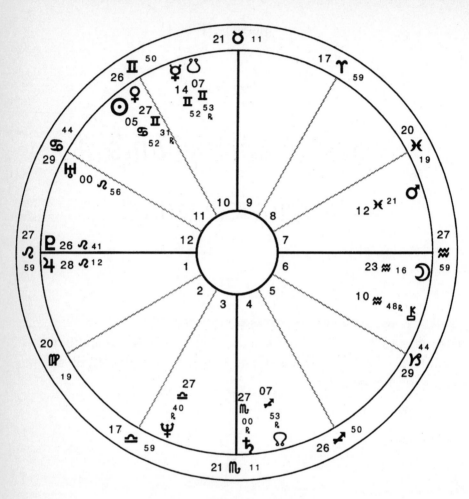

Scott Douglas Cunningham
June 27, 1956
9:25 A.M.
Royal Oak, Michigan

Longitude:	083W09'00	Latitude:	42N30'00

Moon:	23 17 Aquarius	Uranus:	00 56 Leo
Sun:	05 53 Cancer	Neptune:	27 41 Libra (retrograde)
Mercury:	14 53 Libra	Pluto:	26 42 Leo
Venus:	27 32 Libra (retrograde)	Node M.	06 38 Sagittarius
Mars:	12 22 Pisces	MC:	21 42 Taurus
Jupiter:	28 13 Leo	Ascendant:	28 23 Leo
Saturn:	27 01 Scorpio (retrograde)	Vertex	21 48 Capricorn

Notes for Scott's Natural Magic Workshop

Part 1:
Powers, Elements, Stones, Herbs

(Notes made by Scott for this Workshop)

Introductory

Your Own Mantra—Breathe, Relaxation

Definitions: Magic
    Magic is not Supernatural, but Natural
    Nature is all Powerful, a Powerhouse of Magic
    Magic is not Religious, but Powers behind it are at Heart of all
        Religions

Three Types of Power:
    Personal, Earth, Divine
    Aspects of each Type

Magical Morality

Personal Power:
    Two Types within, Projective and Receptive
    Two Types should be balanced
    Receptive and Projective Hands, explain

Ways to Contact Personal Power:
    Emotions, Thrilling Situations, Love, Muscular Contraction, Dance, Exercise, etc.

Ways to Contact Earth Power:
    Sit on Earth, Power Spots, Touching or Back against Trees, Feet in Water, Wind on High Hill, Lightning, Standing in the Rain, Static Electricity, Heat of Sun on Your Body or Feeling them on Rocks, etc.

Ways to Contact Divine Power: Mystical Experience, Trance, Religious Rituals, Opening the Body to be a Channel of this Power

Feeling Personal Power:
    Rub Hands, Tingle
    Form Sphere

What to do with this—Visualization, Simple Protective Rite
    For Home and Person. Explain Visualization

Pass out Herb Samples

Feeling Earth Power

Talk a bit about Divine Power—How we contact it through Ritual
    Elemental Magic

Earth

Our Home
    Foundation of all Elements
    Our daily lives revolve around this Element
    Making a Living, Eating, Gardening, Standing, Shopping, etc.

Suit of Pentacles
    Direction: North
    Season: Winter

Time of Day: Night
Color: Green
Magical Tool: Drum, Pentacle
Natural Symbol: Salt, Rock,Clay, Pottery, etc.
Age: Old Age
Types of Magic: Stone, Knot, Image, Herb
Types of Spells: Money, Fertility, Stability, Grounding, Employment,
    Business, etc.

Bury Something in the Earth, in a Pot, etc.

Air

Our Breath
    Intellectual Element
    Thought, Movement, Inspiration

The Conscious Mind
    At Work when we Think, Travel, Ponder, Theorize, Concentrate

Suit of Wants (Some Say Swords)
    Direction: East
    Season: Spring
    Time of Day: Dawn
    Color: Yellow
    Magical Tool: Wand, Censer
    Natural Symbols: Feather, Fragrant Flowers
    Age: Infancy
    Types of Magic: Visualization, Positive Thinking, Use of Incense,
        Divination, Dance
    Types of Spells: Travel, Improving Memory, Discovering Lost Items,
        Wisdom, Freedom

Toss Something into the Air From a High or Windy Place

Fire

Our Passion, Our Will.
    Contains the Essence of all Magic
    Change, Primal, Powerful, etc.
    Sexuality, Passion, Courage, Strength
    Destructive, But Creative (Explain)

Suit of Swords (Some Say Wands)
    Direction: South
    Season: Summer
    Time of Day: Noon
    Color: Red
    Magical Tools: Sword, Athame, Rattle
    Natural Symbols: Lava, Candle, Flame of any kind, Ash, Olivine, or
        any Volcanic Stone
    Age: Youth
    Types of Magic: Candle Burning
    Types of Spells: Banishing, Energy, Success, Sex, Healing or
        Destroying Disease and Negative Habits, Purification, Protection

Burn Something

Water

Our Love, Our Emotions
    Purification
    The Subconscious (Psychic) Mind
    Fluidity, etc.
    The Sea, Rivers, Lakes, etc.
        Psychics often Live Near Water, Lakes, Ocean

Suit of Cups
    Direction: West
    Season: Autumn
    Time of Day: Dusk
    Color: Blue
    Magical Tool: Cup, Cauldron, Bell, Sistrum
    Natural Symbols: Water, Quartz Crystal, Ice Snow, Shell

Age: Maturity
Type of Magic: Weather, Brews, Bathing, Purification
Types of Spells: Pleasure, Friendship, Marriage, Healing, Fertility, Happiness, Sleep, Dreaming, Psychism, Purification, Love

Place Something in Water

Places to Contact the Elements:

Earth: Caves, Mines, Valleys, etc.
Air: High Hills, Windy Places
Fire: Deserts, Hot Spots
Water: Sea, Rivers, Lakes, Springs

Elemental Meditations, Some Guidelines

Earth: Jewelled caves, burrows in the ground, holding a huge pentagram, burying yourself in green sand, walking in a salt mine

Air: Being blown by winds, having the winds picking you up into them, a leaf in a breeze, flying

Fire: The hottest desert you've ever imagined, being a flame, standing on an endless stretch of hot lava

Water: You are a drop of water that dissolves into the sea, plunging into the cool ocean, sitting under a cool waterfall with hands cupped

Elemental Spells

Earth: To be rid of something. Attune with the Element.
Take a bowl of sand, or earth, or salt. Sit before bowl and visualize or feel the desire or illness or whatever you wish to be free of. With your fingers pour the bad thing into the sand or salt. See it travelling out through your fingertips into the substance until it can take no more. Then, when the sand or salt is loaded with the bad thing and its causes, shake your hands off as if they were wet and immediately bury the sand or salt in the earth, or cover in a pot with fresh sand or salt or earth. It is done.

Air: To get something you need or desire: Attune with Element.
Take nine feathers of any color. Strongly visualize and state in words
your need while stroking the feathers. Do this with all fine feathers.
Then take them to a windy place and, while speaking or visualizing
your need, throw them to blast away in the wind. It is done.

Fire: To be rid of something: Attune with Element.
Take a charred stick or a piece of charcoal (or a charcoal pencil)
and write or draw an image of your bad habit, disease, etc. on a
piece of paper or a flat piece of bark or leaf. It must be something
that can be burned quickly. When the image is completed burn the
image in a hot fire or light in a red candle's flame and throw into
heatproof container. As it burns it is done.

Water: To draw something to you. Attune with the Element.
Go to a place where water abounds. Take with you four ice cubes,
or a large chunk of ice. Standing near the water hold the ice in
your hands while visualizing your need. Do this for as long as you
can, blocking out any signals of pain. When the ice is filled,
infused, empowered with your need throw it onto the surface of
the water. as the ice melts, it is done. (Can be performed in a
bathtub or bucket if necessary.)

Break?

Stone Magic

10 Basic Stones—
   Use polished and tumbled
   Ways to cleanse—Sunlight (for a day), salt water
      Hold in running water, ocean etc.

Authors' Note: These notes are dry compared to the witty, warm presenta-
tions that Scott created from this framework. We've included it here in the
hope it will jog some memories in those who attended his classes.

❧

Index

Stay in Touch. . .

Llewellyn publishes hundreds of books on your favorite subjects

On the following pages you will find listed some books now available on related subjects. Your local bookstore stocks most of these and will stock new Llewellyn titles as they become available. We urge your patronage.

Order by Phone

Call toll-free within the U.S. and Canada, **1–800–THE MOON**.
In Minnesota call **(612) 291–1970**.
We accept Visa, MasterCard, and American Express.

Order by Mail

Send the full price of your order (MN residents add 7% sales tax) in U.S. funds to:

> **Llewellyn Worldwide**
> **P.O. Box 64383, Dept. K559-2**
> **St. Paul, MN 55164–0383, U.S.A.**

Postage and Handling

- ◆ $4.00 for orders $15.00 and under
- ◆ $5.00 for orders over $15.00
- ◆ No charge for orders over $100.00

We ship UPS in the continental United States. We cannot ship to P.O. boxes. Orders shipped to Alaska, Hawaii, Canada, Mexico, and Puerto Rico will be sent first-class mail.

International orders: Airmail—add freight equal to price of each book to the total price of order, plus $5.00 for each non-book item (audiotapes, etc.). Surface mail—Add $1.00 per item.

Allow 4–6 weeks delivery on all orders. Postage and handling rates subject to change.

Group Discounts

We offer a 20% quantity discount to group leaders or agents. You must order a minimum of 5 copies of the same book to get our special quantity price.

THE MAGICAL HOUSEHOLD
Empower Your Home with Love, Protection, Health and Happiness
Scott Cunningham and David Harrington

Whether your home is a small apartment or a palatial mansion, you want it to be something special. Now it can be with *The Magical Household*. Learn how to make your home more than just a place to live. Turn it into a place of security, life, fun, and magic. Here you will not find the complex magic of the ceremonial magician. Rather, you will learn simple, quick, and effective magical spells that use nothing more than common items in your house: furniture, windows, doors, carpet, pets, etc. You will learn to take advantage of the intrinsic power and energy that is already in your home, waiting to be tapped. You will learn to make magic a part of your life. The result is a home that is safeguarded from harm and a place which will bring you happiness, health, and more.

0-87542-124-5, 208 pp., 5¼ x 8, illus., softcover $9.95

SPELL CRAFTS
Creating Magical Objects
Scott Cunningham & David Harrington

Since early times, crafts have been intimately linked with spirituality. When a woman carefully shaped a water jar from the clay she'd gathered from a river bank, she was performing a spiritual practice. When crafts were used to create objects intended for ritual or that symbolized the Divine, the connection between the craftsperson and divinity grew more intense. Today, handcrafts can still be more than a pastime—they can be rites of power and honor; a religious ritual. After all, hands were our first magical tools.

Spell Crafts is a modern guide to creating physical objects for the attainment of specific magical goals. It is far different from magic books that explain how to use purchased magical tools. You will learn how to fashion spell brooms, weave wheat, dip candles, sculpt clay, mix herbs, bead sacred symbols, and much more, for a variety of purposes. Whatever your craft, you will experience the natural process of moving energy from within yourself (or within natural objects) to create positive change.

0-87542-185-7, 224 pp., 5¼ x 8, illus., photos $10.00

MYSTERIES OF ISIS
Her Worship & Magick
de Traci Regula

For 6,000 years, Isis has been worshiped as a powerful yet benevolent goddess who loves and cares for those who call on Her. Here, for the first time, Her secrets and mysteries are revealed in an easy-to-understand form so you can bring the power of this great and glorious goddess into your life.

Mysteries of Isis is filled with practical information on the modern practice of Isis' worship. Other books about Isis treat Her as an entirely Egyptian goddess, but this book reveals that she is a universal goddess with many faces, who has been present in all places and in all times. Simple yet effective rituals and exercises will show you how to forge your unique personal alliance with Isis: prepare for initiation into Her four key mysteries, divine the future using the Sacred Scarabs, perform purification and healing rites, celebrate Her holy days, travel to your own inner temple, cast love spells, create your own tools and amulets, and much more. Take Isis as your personal goddess and your worship and connection with the divine will be immeasurably enriched.

1-56178-560-6, 320 pp., 7 x 10, illus., softcover $19.95

To order, call 1–800–THE MOON
Prices subject to change without notice